The Polity Reader in
Cultural Theory

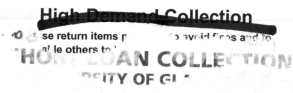

The Polity Reader
in
Cultural Theory

Polity Press

306
POL

Copyright © this collection and introductory material Polity Press, 1994.

First published in 1994 by Polity Press in association with Blackwell Publishers

Editorial office:
Polity Press
65 Bridge Street
Cambridge CB2 1UR, UK

Marketing and production:
Blackwell Publishers
108 Cowley Road
Oxford OX4 1JF, UK

ISBN 0 7456 1207 5
ISBN 0 7456 1208 3 (pbk)

British Library Cataloguing-in-Publication Data

A CIP catalogue record for this book is available from the British Library.

Typeset in 10 on 12 pt Times
by Graphicraft Typesetters Ltd, Hong Kong
Printed in Great Britain by Hartnolls Ltd, Bodmin, Cornwall

This book is printed on acid-free paper.

Contents

The extracts in this volume are taken from the following Polity Press books:

Zygmunt Bauman, *Modernity and Ambivalence* (1991)

Robert Bocock and Kenneth Thompson, *Social and Cultural Forms of Modernity* (1992)

Frances Bonner et al., *Imagining Women* (1992)

Pierre Bourdieu, *The Field of Cultural Production* (1993)

Peter Bürger, *The Decline of Modernism* (1992)

Mary Ann Caws, *The Art of Interference* (1989)

Peter Collier and Judy Davies, *Modernism and the European Unconscious* (1990)

Anne Cranny-Francis, *Feminist Fiction* (1990)

Joanne Finkelstein, *Dining Out* (1989)

Simon Frith, *Music for Pleasure* (1988)

Christine Geraghty, *Women and Soap Opera* (1991)

Jürgen Habermas, *The Structural Transformation of the Public Sphere* (1989)

Stuart Hall, David Held and Tony McGrew, *Modernity and its Futures* (1992)

John Hargreaves, *Sport, Power and Culture* (1986)

W.F. Haug, *Critique of Commodity Aesthetics* (1986)

Bob Hodge and David Tripp, *Children and Television* (1986)

Robert Hodge and Gunther Kress, *Social Semiotics* (1988)

Douglas Kellner, *Critical Theory, Marxism and Modernity* (1989)

Scott Lash and John Urry, *The End of Organized Capitalism* (1987)

Jean-François Lyotard, *The Inhuman* (1988)

Graham McCann, *Marilyn Monroe* (1988)

Michael Moriarty, *Roland Barthes* (1991)

G.J. Mulgan, *Communication and Control* (1991)

Roy Porter, *Myths of the English* (1992)

Mark Poster, *Jean Baudrillard* (1988)

Mark Poster, *The Mode of Information* (1990)

John Shepherd, *Music as Social Text* (1991)

John B. Thompson, *Ideology and Modern Culture* (1990)

Janet Wolff, *Feminine Sentences* (1990)

Acknowledgements

All the selections in this book are taken from works published by Polity Press. The choice of articles, Introduction, and descriptive material at the opening of the sections were the result of a collaborative editorial enterprise. The following individuals were involved: Anthony Giddens, David Held, Don Hubert, Steve Loyal, Debbie Seymour and John Thompson.

We would like to thank the authors and, for sources that originally appeared in other languages, the publishers for permission to reprint extracts as follows: 1, John Thompson; 2, Robert Hodge and Gunther Kress; 3, Elsevier Science Publishers B.V.; 4, Suhrkamp Verlag; 5, Kellner; 6, Suhrkamp Verlag; 7, John Thompson; 8, G.J. Mulgan; 9, Johns Hopkins University Press; 10, Stuart Hall; 11, Johns Hopkins University Press; 12, Scott Lash and John Urry; 13, Suhrkamp Verlag; 14, John Hargreaves; 15, Bob Hodge and David Tripp; 16, Robert Bocock and Kenneth Thompson; 17, Christine Geraghty; 18, Anne Cranny-Francis; 19, Janet Wolff; 20, Graham McCann; 21, Malcolm Bowie; 22, John Shepherd; 23, Simon Frith; 24, The Open University; 25, The *New York Review of Books*; 26, Mary Ann Caws; 27, Michael Moriarty; 28, Joanne Finkelstein; 29, Editions Galilée; 30, Zygmunt Bauman.

Every effort has been made to trace all copyright holders, but if any have been inadvertently overlooked, the publishers will be pleased to make the necessary arrangement at the first opportunity.

Introduction

Once regarded as a rather marginal, even eccentric, preoccupation, the field of cultural studies has now moved into the centre of the social sciences and humanities. The domain of cultural studies covers the social processes involved in the production, transmission and reception of symbolic or cultural forms. Neither 'culture' nor 'ideology' is particularly easy to define. The concept of 'culture' has a long history in social science prior to the emergence of a distinct domain of cultural studies. Some early thinkers made 'culture' the basis of all forms of inquiry into human social life and institutions. Thus Wilhelm Dilthey, the German historian and social thinker, distinguished between what he called the 'human' or 'cultural' sciences and the sciences of nature. What is 'human' is distinguished from the non-human in so far as it is 'cultural'. The objects of study of the human sciences are cultural ideas and cultural systems; the human sciences thus share very little in common with the sciences of nature.

Such a position, however, whatever its virtues, defines culture in such a broad sense as to make it almost meaningless. Attempts to formulate the notion of culture in a more restricted way came first of all from within the area of anthropology. Here culture has usually referred to the 'way of life' of a given group of people. Anthropology was seen as the comparative study of 'cultures': the habits, customs and also the material technology employed within different societies. 'Culture' is still today often used in this wide anthropological sense in the social sciences. We might contrast this usage with 'culture' as it is usually thought of in ordinary language – a much narrower conception. Here culture means education and taste. A 'cultured' person is someone who is able to appreciate the 'finer things of life', such as literature, poetry or art.

Culture is usually defined in 'cultural studies' in a way that fits between these two extremes. 'Culture' may be said in this context to refer to concrete sets of *signifying practices* – modes of generating meaning – that create *communication orders* of one kind or another. Understood in this way, 'cultural production' plays an active, constitutive role in the creation of ways of life and overall forms of social organization. 'Culture' in the more lay sense mentioned above is understood as *high culture*, and counterposed to a diversity of popular cultural forms.

The analysis of *media of communication* forms a central component of cultural studies. For the creation of signifying orders depends upon the development of vehicles of communication. The written text is one such communications medium, whether this takes the form of a newspaper, novel, scientific treatise or political pamphlet. Painting and music, while they might not involve print, clearly also are communicative forms. To these we must add the electronic media of communication which have become so important in our day – radio, television, videos, tapes and computer communication systems.

When printed or electronic media reach very large numbers of people, as is commonplace in the modern world, we speak of the existence of *mass media*. The term 'mass' itself needs some elaboration, since it is potentially ambiguous – indeed some have suggested it be abandoned altogether. One of the founders of cultural studies, the American sociologist Herbert Blumer, defined 'mass' in a way which still secures a good deal of support from other scholars. A mass is a large aggregate of people distinct from a 'group', 'crowd' or 'public'. A group consists of people who are in some sort of interaction with one another and who share a sense of common identity. A crowd is a larger collectivity, gathered together in an open space such as a street or a square. Crowds tend to be temporary and, while there may be some sort of sense of solidarity, this is transient. A 'public', like a mass, refers to large numbers of people. A public, however, is more than a mere aggregate. It is a collectivity that engages with issues in political or communal life; as such it is a key component of any modern democratic political order. The public operates in the 'public sphere' – a forum for debate of issues that affect the society as a whole.

A 'mass' is usually very large, numbering up to many millions of people. Some films or television programmes, for example, have been seen by hundreds of millions of viewers. A mass is widely dispersed and its members have no direct contact with one another; it is without any sense of collective identity. It is not necessarily, or normally, an aggregate of isolated individuals, but may consist also of groups and publics; but these do not define the nature of the aggregate as a whole.

The word 'mass' has quite often been used in the context of *mass culture*. Like 'mass' itself, the term 'mass culture' quite often has a negative ring to it; it implies the undiscriminating consumption of pre-packaged entertainment. 'Mass culture' has usually been understood in contrast to high culture, on the one hand, and 'popular culture' on the other. High culture is produced by, and often only accessible to, small minorities working within the framework of definite artistic or literary traditions. 'Popular culture' refers to cultural products created in a spontaneous way within local contexts, rather than being generated by the centralized culture industries. Popular culture includes, but is not limited to, forms of folk culture that pre-date the arrival of the modern mass media. There is, as it were, a tension between these three cultural forms. The development of the mass media has tended to dissolve, or re-shape, many folk arts; it has also tended to corrode certain aspects of high culture.

These conceptual distinctions all remain quite controversial. It is an open question how far high culture can be defined in a value-neutral way, that is, without reference to the standards of discrimination and taste that its proponents supposedly follow. In an era in which relativistic thought has tended to come more and more to the fore, there are many who doubt whether the idea of high culture retains much validity, especially if it is seen as somehow enshrining values that other sectors of cultural production have lost.

Characteristic of the mass media, and therefore of mass culture, is that communication is primarily a one-way process, going from sender to receiver. The consumer, in other words, plays no direct role in the creation of the cultural product to which she or he has access. That product is commercially produced and marketed in much the same way as other types of good in modern societies. The media form a set of 'open' channels of communication, which can be received by anyone in the society (and perhaps well beyond the bounds of any one society). Since the media can affect public opinion, however, they are normally linked not only with the market but with various forms of state regulation or even control.

The field of cultural studies is diverse, but a number of key problem areas may be identified within it. Five such areas of investigation are worth mentioning here:

1 What impact has the emergence of the mass media had upon the wider society?
2 What is the nature of the interaction between the media and their audiences?

3   How does the rise of mass culture, if indeed such a thing exists, interrelate with high and popular culture?
4   How should we analyse culture as a medium of power?
5   What sorts of theoretical position should be adopted in interpreting cultural production and the role of the media in modern society?

The first of these questions opens up a host of important issues. For many years the media, and even culture more generally, were treated in the social sciences as relatively marginal to the main dynamics of modern institutions. Yet such a view does not withstand the least scrutiny. Media of communication may not have had quite the decisive influence given to them by Marshall McLuhan, but they have been constitutively involved in the institutions of modernity from its early beginnings.

The development of printing was a precondition for the emergence of a modern state and modern forms of social and economic organization. Pre-modern civilizations always presumed some form of writing: writing, as the anthropologist Claude Lévi-Strauss showed, developed not just a means of recording information or telling stories; it was above all a medium of power. Writing makes possible the forging of social relations across time and space in ways not open to oral cultures.

The control and storage of information that writing provides for allows social relations to become 'stretched' across large spans of time and space and also creates 'history', because records of past events can be kept and must be interpreted. Printing vastly expands the influence of written communications. Literacy need no longer be confined to a privileged few, while an indefinite array of texts becomes available to large populations of people. The creation of 'publics' in the modern sense, noted earlier, would not have been possible without the widespread diffusion of printing.

The printed word still remains fundamental to the organization of modern societies today. The sales of mass circulation newspapers are declining in many Western countries. However, more books, periodicals and magazines are published globally than ever before. Perhaps more important, modern society depends upon the continued production of a whole host of texts that form part of the regular working of all forms of social organization. From bureaucratic file and memos to gas bills, print remains elemental to the modern order.

Electronic communication has played a more far-reaching and extended role in the development of modern societies than is ordinarily recognized. It dates, not from the era of the radio, but from the invention of the morse telegraph in the nineteenth century. The telegraph initiated a new era in communication and thereby human social organization.

For the first time in history, communication and transportation become separable. Apart from certain local forms of communication system, such as semaphore devices, communication in pre-modern times always demanded transportation. A message could not be carried faster than the swiftest horse or boat. Even relatively rapid communications might take several months to cross a continent. The morse code initiated that 'triumph over space' so characteristic of the modern period. It helped transform such diverse institutions as the stock market and the military; and it was the condition of the emergence of 'global news' such as we know it today.

The development of radio, cinema and particularly television has of course brought further changes of major importance. These media do not just carry messages 'about social life'; they act to alter or transform it. For instance, television reporting today is not simply a means of discussing political events, but in some part establishes and orders what those events actually 'are'. The existence of global satellite networks, in place now for some thirty years or so, has provided for instantaneous electronic communication across the world. Many millions of people can 'see' events immediately they happen. The ever-developing global economy is organized through electronic communication networks. 'Money' today, for instance, is no longer the cash in one's pocket, let alone the gold bars stored in government reserve vaults; it is electronic information stored in the world's computers. Global money markets now operate on a more or less twenty-four hour basis, influencing the fate of individuals on all continents; this also is the result of instantaneous electronic communication.

It would be fair to say that in the early years of media analysis the inherent importance of communications systems for the institutional order of modernity was not fully recognized. Rather, a good deal of research and thinking centred upon the 'effects' of various kinds of media, particularly the mass media, upon the audiences exposed to them. Although today it has become fashionable to be critical of such research, it did generate a good deal of useful material – and research still proceeds along these lines today. The study of media effects has very often been prompted by moral or normative considerations. Thus there has been a continuing concern to discover how far levels of crime, and particularly criminal violence, are affected by media representations. Such research has also been fuelled by more diffuse concerns that the mass media are creating cultural forms that produce a spineless, apathetic citizenry.

Research and thinking on media effects has gone through several main stages. The first, covering the opening three or four decades of this century, consisted in sporadic and relatively unsystematic interpretations of media content. Many people at this time saw the then new mass media as radically shaping the opinions of the 'masses'. Such views reflected not only the extraordinary popularity achieved by some of the new media forms, but the uses to which they were put for direct propaganda by governments and other agencies. A second period, during which more systematic research was initiated, beginning in about the 1940s, was stimulated by a concern with media propaganda. Researchers were interested in how far particular types of programme could be used to influence political opinion or persuade audiences to alter their pre-existing attitudes in a given area.

Such research was valuable, indicating as it did that the ideas and views of audiences are more robust in the face of incoming media symbols and information than many had suggested. This very conclusion, however, combined with an array of methodological objections that were raised to the research procedures used, pushed such studies into the background for some time. Over the past two decades or so, new cycles of research have been initiated, motivated in large part by the growing importance of television among the other media. This third phase of research sees the 'mass' audience as much more differentiated, and active, than the earlier researchers tended to do.

Investigation of the effects of programmes containing violence, or pornographic materials, upon those who watch them has proved as inconclusive as in the former period. But it has come to be recognized that the analysis of media 'effects' has to be placed in an interactive milieu. That is to say, media images form part of a continuity of experience of the individual; one cannot just break into this at a particular point and demonstrate that specific programmes, or even types of programme, have a discernible effect upon attitudes or behaviour. The influence of the media has to be understood in a longer-term, institutional context.

The mass media depend upon what the German thinker Walter Benjamin famously called 'mechanical reproduction'. Both high culture and folk culture were the product, in one sense or another, of the skilled hand. In many forms of folk culture, a long apprenticeship with a master was demanded. High cultural forms sometimes involved a similar phenomenon, but more often developed their specific appeal from the inspiration of exceptional talent or 'genius'. Thus art preserved an 'aura' separating it from more mundane forms of cultural production. The modern media not only invade the territory of folk culture, but threaten to undermine the specific 'distinctiveness' of the work of art. In these circumstances, in the eyes of some observers at least, high culture either largely dissolves or becomes preserved as a series of 'contained' classical endeavours: it exists in museums, theatres and concert halls, but no longer as living and progressing art forms.

Certainly the conditions of the production and dissemination of high cultural forms have changed significantly. 'Classical music' is available to anyone who purchases a disc or tape; *The Best of Mozart* can be purchased alongside any number of competing styles of music and is marketed specifically for mass consumption. Endless reproductions of celebrated paintings appear in books, on posters and on postcards. The 'original' is defined as such no longer in terms of its 'aura' but specifically in relation to a market value; the 'original' may be worth many millions of pounds precisely against the backdrop of a proliferation of reproductions.

The implications of all this are contentious – as is also true of the relation between popular and mass culture. That most forms of folk culture disappear in the face of the advent of modern media is undeniable. Some remain, while others are reinvented; but many of these either become geared themselves to production for markets or are recreated as consciously established forms reacting precisely against such commercialism. Thus ornaments or jewellery may be produced 'by hand', and follow traditional styles, but are not created through craft skills as once they were. A bracelet may be fashioned 'by hand', but using industrially produced silver and gems. Folk cultures that are reinvented, or re-discovered on the point of their extinction, do not normally follow their former patterns. Thus artisanal skills might be re-learned by middle-class professionals as a leisure-time occupation. Traditional customs or arts may be refurbished as tourist attractions.

If folk culture, in its traditional form, largely disappears with the spread of modern media, the same cannot be said of popular culture. Mass culture exists in constant tension with popular cultural forms, and each is symbiotic upon the other. Mass culture is industrialized culture, produced by commercial and state corporations. It is disseminated 'from the top down' by the nature of its specialized technologies. Yet culture by its very nature has to be 'lived' and experienced; it resists reduction to the status of a mere material commodity. The creation and re-creation of local, national and supranational cultures exists in active dialogue with the commercialized media, shaping as it is being shaped.

The mass media produce a 'repertoire' of cultural resources which individuals and groups utilize in their own processes of cultural production. A single media image can be interpreted in very divergent ways, and incorporated within quite contrasting outlooks. Urban aboriginals in Australia might watch Westerns but make of these a text against colonialism rather than seeing what a white American might see there. Street theatre might play upon the themes of a popular television soap opera, turning them, however, into pastiche. The advent of more or less universal consumerism in the highly industrialized societies does not make of everyone a passive recipient of commodified cultural items; opportunities for local cultural reaffirmation are found using the very materials that threaten to eradicate it.

To put things another way, in the cultural domain as in others power is always (in varying degrees) a two-way phenomenon. Studying the relation between cultural production and structures of power is a complex affair. One way of tackling the question is through examining ownership and control of media enterprises. Newspapers, cinema chains, record companies and television corporations are mostly industrial enterprises producing goods for sale in markets. They are subject to the same influences, as well as constraints, as other sorts of industrial organization. Monopoly conditions might prevail where the state assumes exclusive control of a particular medium, as has happened with television in some countries in the past. It is well-known that tendencies towards monopoly or oligopoly operate within capitalistic markets, and media enterprises are no exception. Some media companies have become multinational corporations or parts of conglomerates. A few such firms dominate not just national, but global markets in respect of some cultural products. Individual media tycoons come to control a diversity of media interests combining, for example, ownership of mass-circulation newspapers, television chains and movie companies.

How far such power is used to try to propagate particular types of political or social attitudes is a matter of some debate. Certainly there are many critics who see concentration of ownership in media industries as inimical to a properly democratic public sphere. Yet given the points mentioned above, it is difficult to suppose that those who control the media corporations are able in any simple way to impose their views upon the majority of recipients. Thus *The Sun* newspaper, owned by the entrepreneur Rupert Murdoch, has the largest daily circulation in Britain; but the majority of its subscribers are Labour voters even if the views expressed in the newspaper are normally Conservative. Moreover, whatever their tendencies towards oligopoly, capitalistic markets also allow for many forms of variety and innovation. Tendencies towards decentralization in the sphere of commercial media production go along with those towards concentration.

Studies of patterns of ownership of the media industries are thus of only limited value in analysing the interaction between cultural production and power. More embedded forms of power can only be diagnosed if understood in terms of the constitutive involvement of the media with modern institutions. Thus modes of presentation of news programmes on television might act to preserve certain relations of power in a society by how the 'reality' that is 'reported on' is depicted. What is left out might be as important in this respect as what is included. Subtle, but potentially highly important, means of reproducing power relations can be conveyed in a range of media settings. Thus apparently quite different programme items, such as advertisements, soap operas or game shows, may all contain images of gender that confirm patriarchal systems of power.

The connections between culture and power are the concern of theories of ideology. The concept of ideology is as controversial as any notion within the domain of cultural studies. Although he did not originate the notion, Marx's writings have influenced much subsequent work devoted to it. For Marx 'ideology' is essentially a critical concept – a means of uncovering hidden forms of power in a society. Ideology concerns aspects of cultural production that serve to disguise, and thereby legitimate, systems of domination. Marx never developed his conception of ideology in a full-blown way and his comments on the subject contain various different threads and even inconsistencies. For some who have followed Marx, ideology means 'false consciousness': an erroneous view of what one's true interests are. Others have drawn upon Marx to produce rather more sophisticated views of ideology. Thus Antonio Gramsci, the Italian thinker, employed the notion of 'hegemony' to refer to the overall world-view which, in a given society, acts to support the interests of dominant classes or groups. However it be understood, for many scholars the analysis of ideology is a basic concern for anyone studying cultural production.

Marx's thought has been drawn upon by those who seek to connect the study of ideology to globalization, particularly in respect of so-called 'media imperialism'. Western thought, it has been argued, has been stamped by the impact of colonialism, itself closely bound up with the global spread of capitalism. Media institutions, and cultural diffusion more generally, express the wider relations of power in world society. Thus Third World issues are often referred to in the Western media, it has been suggested, in the context of violence, crisis and poverty – creating quite a slanted view of non-Western cultural forms.

Marxist thinking has influenced the field of cultural studies in other ways also. Thus Marx's discussion of 'the commodity' – a product geared to exchange in a market – has seemed to many authors to offer clues about the nature of culture in modern societies. The commodity is a standardized value; it detaches 'form' from 'content', because its value is not defined by the uses to which it is put but by how much it can be sold for. From Georg Lukács onwards, many have seen commodification as directly related to not just mass culture but high and popular culture too.

As in other areas of the social sciences and humanities, in recent years there has been a move away from Marxist thinking in cultural studies. Although sometimes it has been linked to Marxism, feminist thought has made a major impact upon pre-existing theoretical and empirical perspectives. Feminists as well as other authors have drawn extensively upon structuralist and post-structuralist thought. These traditions tend to stress the pre-eminence of the 'signifier' over the 'signified'. Meaning is generated not by a connection between signs and the world, but by signifying practices internal to language or other semiotic orders. The potential relevance of such an approach to a world in which mediated experience, or non-verbal media imagery, becomes so important is obvious enough.

Structuralism and post-structuralism have fed in a significant way into contemporary debates about whether or not we now live in a 'postmodern' era. Debates about postmodernism have become perhaps even more acute in the domain of cultural studies than elsewhere, because the very notion of postmodernism depends upon attributing fundamental importance to communications media in the structuring of social experience.

If the theorists of postmodernism are correct, Marxism is now irrelevant to current social conditions – as are many comparable 'grand narratives', asserting overall processes of historical change – and the notion of ideology has no part to play. In the postmodern condition, they say, we are dealing with a plurality of values and contexts of action, which obey no general principles. According to some authors, such as Jean Baudrillard, there is in fact no 'reality' separate from media symbols; we find our reality, or our realities, in the communicative exchanges of imagery and information that media create. These claims to many seem extreme. Yet the intense discussion they now provoke is an indication of the degree to which the interpretation of cultural production has moved into the heart of theoretical thinking in social analysis today.

The aim of this collection is to provide a reasonably comprehensive introduction to the area of cultural studies. We have tried to provide a balance between theoretical and more empirical contributions. So far as possible we have sought to choose selections that are accessible to those having little prior knowledge of the field. Each part of the book is prefaced by descriptive material relevant to the selections included. We have kept such material relatively short in order to give primacy of place to the original materials themselves. In order to enhance the readability of the selections references and footnotes have been kept to a minimum. A sufficient number remain in most cases for the interested reader to be able to further pursue questions raised by the various contributions.

An ellipsis has been used whenever material from the original has been omitted. Where more than a paragraph has been excluded, a line space appears above and below [. . .].

PART I

Theoretical Considerations

IN READING 1 John Thompson undertakes a general analysis of the nature of mass communication in modern society. Mass communication involves the production and distribution of 'symbolic goods' to audiences who are not themselves the producers of those goods. Such communication differs from the conversations in which individuals engage in local contexts of action, because there is a 'break' between the producer and receiver. The media of mass communication also circulate in a public domain.

A key feature of the symbolic forms transmitted through mass communication is that they can be multiply reproduced. Many copies are created and made available. Such symbolic forms are also commodified – bought and sold in a market. The mass media are thus directly bound up with two main characteristics of modern capitalistic societies: standardized production, and a system of commodity exchange. The mass media decisively alter our relation to time and space. Media of communication, such as books, have long affected the organization of social relations across time–space contexts. A book can be read by individuals or groups widely separated in time and space from the author. The development of electronic communication, however, furthers this process in a massive way. There occurs what Marshall McLuhan has called an 'implosion' of cultural forms, within the framework of a globalizing order; space is no longer a determinant of the availability of information.

The idea of a 'public' is a creation of modern society. The invention of a 'public domain' depended upon the emergence of an arena of public debate and policy making, fuelled first of all by the spread of printed media. The sphere of 'public knowledge' is further expanded with the development of electronic media, although some of the standardizing characteristics of such media may also limit the degree to which the mass of the population in any effective way participate in the public arena. The spread of the different forms of media also influences the relation between public and private domains. Thus today it is common for the private lives of individuals to be publicly scrutinized in the mass media, while public events, via the newspapers or television, can be experienced in private settings.

The works of Ferdinand de Saussure have had a very wide influence in cultural studies (see Hodge and Kress, Reading 2). Saussure was a Swiss linguist, writing just after the turn of the century, who pioneered a new approach to problems of language and meaning. He drew a celebrated distinction between *langue* and *parole* – language and speech. Linguistics before Saussure had concentrated upon the study of the second of these, that is, the spoken or written word. Saussure argued that a concentration on *parole* misses the most distinctive features of linguistic communication, which derive from *langue*. *Langue* refers to sets of rules and syntactical properties which speakers draw upon to produce particular speech acts or forms of writing. In studying *langue* Saussure distinguished between the *signifier* and the *signified*. The signifier is the vehicle of communication: in the case of speaking, the sounds which come tumbling from the mouth, or in the case of writing, the marks that a person makes on paper or some other material. The signified is the meaning of whatever is said or written.

Meaning, according to Saussure, does not derive from the relation between language and the world. The meaning of the word 'table', for instance, is not the object, the table. Rather, meaning derives from the internal system of differences which constitute *langue*. We know the meaning of 'table' only in so far as we learn to understand the difference between 'table', 'chair', 'stool' and so on.

Since meaning is created by differences between signifiers, it follows that any vehicle of difference can serve as a medium of communication, not just verbal sounds or written marks. Saussure called the study of non-verbal modes of communication *semiology*, although many authors today prefer the term *semiotics*. Semiotics or semiology studies the whole universe of signs. Thus clothing can carry meanings, as can the various foods on a menu, or the visual images of television programmes and advertisements.

Hodge and Kress offer a critical analysis of Saussure's ideas. Saussure is rightly regarded as the founder of semiotics; although he wrote rather little directly on the subject, his works provide a systematic basis for semiotic studies. Hodge and Kress find major limitations in Saussure's ideas, which nevertheless serve them as a basic point of departure for their consideration of the nature of semiotic interpretation.

Pierre Bourdieu (Reading 3) presents a general theory of cultural production which is quite different from most semiotic approaches. Bourdieu emphasizes that, whether in the arenas of high or popular culture, cultural production always takes place within specific contexts or 'fields'. Symbolic products, to put things another way, can never be understood in isolation but only in relation to other such products and producers. A literary or artistic field, according to Bourdieu, is a 'field of forces' and also a 'field of struggles' between producers occupying different positions. Consider for example, Bourdieu says, 'classic works'. It might be thought that the distinctive property of a 'classic' is that it remains unchanged through its various readings. However, the repetition of a classic work will have different implications depending upon the fields of cultural production within which it takes place. If it is simply repeated without modification, for example, a 'classic' play may become a parody. One of the major difficulties in studying cultural production, according to Bourdieu, is that of reconstructing the positions and spaces of cultural fields, because these go largely unremarked at the time at which the cultural products are first created.

Fields of cultural production intersect with larger systems of political and economic power. The struggles which characterize an array of artistic fields thus serve to shape not just what is produced but how it is received. Struggles to define the 'autonomy' of art, or even of aesthetics more generally, often have to be interpreted in terms of wider divisions of power and interests.

The theme of power is also central to the contribution from W.F. Haug (Reading 4). In Haug's view the nature of cultural production in modern societies has to be understood in terms of the centrality of commodification. Capitalism, as Marx stressed, depends upon the commodity. A commodity is any product that can be bought and sold on a market and therefore has exchange value. A commodity for Marx always involves a certain 'illusion'. Commodities seem to relate to human needs but actually serve the concerns of the wider system, which tends to assess all value in terms of values of exchange.

Haug aims to uncover the illusory nature of commodity exchange. The more developed the system of commodification, the more surface values which provide for easy exchange – such as packaging or advertising images – come to the fore. The aesthetic qualities of goods, including cultural as well as more material goods, become separated from the object of exchange itself. Packaging and surface appearances become everything. The commodity, as Haug puts it, 'becomes completely disembodied and drifts unencumbered like a multicoloured spirit of the commodity into every household . . .'. Illusion replaces reality or, rather, reality is created through the illusory character of the commodity.

Like Haug, Theodor Adorno, whose work is discussed in the contribution from Douglas Kellner (Reading 5), writes as a critic of the commodified society of modern capitalism. Human beings are the true producers of commodities, but commodification is such a pervasive influence that individuals tend to become 'slaves' to it. They are deluded, he says, by surface values and lack a full understanding of their own needs. Modern culture seems to be stamped by a high degree of individuality, but in fact such individuality is a sham; it is manufactured as part of mass consumption processes. For Adorno, as for Marx, modern capitalism creates enormous wealth, but the emancipatory potential of such wealth cannot be actualized because of the shallow and limited forms of life which capitalism allows. A more humane society would both overcome our contemporary obsession with material productivity and separate use-value from exchange-value.

The view of Jürgen Habermas (Reading 6) is different from that of Adorno. Modern capitalism creates mass markets and is marked by the prevalence of commodification, but it also opens spheres of public communication and debate that were unavailable in pre-existing forms of social order. The existence of a public sphere is of vital importance because it represents a domain where policy issues and values can be openly debated by the members of a community or society. The word 'public', Habermas notes, is somewhat ambiguous. A 'public building', for example, is simply a building owned by or involved with the state; the state is sometimes referred to as the 'public authority'. When we speak of '*a* public' or '*the* public', on the other hand, we refer to a court of opinion and controversy formed through the impact of communications media.

The 'public' in this sense emerged in the first phases of the development of bourgeois society and was first of all quite restricted. Those who participated in public dialogue were limited to aristocratic or political notables and to the small spectrum of the literate. The emergence of universal literacy, coupled to the development of new means of mass communication, extended the domain of the public to include the majority of the population. Much of the interest of contemporary media studies, for Habermas, centres upon the dilemmas involved in the development of an 'open' public sphere – and the constraints to which it is subject as a result of the one-way nature of most mass communication.

In Reading 7 John Thompson subjects Habermas's theory of the public sphere to a critical appraisal. Since it first appeared, Habermas's work has been widely criticized – although it has also been very influential. Habermas, it has been pointed out, uses a narrow definition of the public sphere which neglects other forms of public communication that existed in Europe from the seventeenth century onwards. There were various forms of popular movement, for example, which developed public modes of discourse; and these often set themselves up in opposition to the 'public authorities' upon whom Habermas concentrates.

Habermas has recognized the force of this criticism, as he has also critiques coming from feminist circles. For as he defines it the public sphere is a male affair, reflecting in its very development the marginalizing of women and the re-shaping of patriarchal power. Some feminist scholars have argued that the exclusion of women from the public sphere was much more than just a by-product of its development; it was integral to it. For the public sphere was seen as a domain of universal reason, in which men are suited to participate, but from which women must be barred because of their 'emotional' or 'irrational' character.

According to Habermas, with the development of the mass media in the nineteenth and twentieth centuries, the public sphere went into decline. The mass media became subject to centralized control and largely 'imposed' views upon their audiences. Habermas, however, Thompson concludes, has a defective and limited conception of modern communications media and their possibilities. The development of the media, from print onwards, has created forums of 'publicness' quite distinct from that identified by Habermas. Modern media are 'non-dialogical', but they create modes of communication – stretching across large spans of space and time – generating novel modes of public experience and discourse, rather than just diminishing the public sphere.

In Reading 8 Mulgan analyses the significance of electronic networks in the development of modernity. Traditional civilizations, he says, have always had quite developed communications systems. In traditional China, for example, an extensive complex of post-houses was maintained whereby messages were transmitted by carriers on horseback across large areas of the country. However, electronic communication introduces something new in human social development: for the first time large-scale processes of communication are possible without transportation. Moreover with the development of satellite systems such communication becomes immediate.

The telegraph was the first form of communication to break the connection with transportation. Telegraphy set various patterns followed by subsequent forms of electronic communication. There are close connections between communications networks and financial power; the New York and Philadelphia stock exchanges were the sites of the first commercial use of the telegraph. Telegraphic technology was also early on commodified and came under the control of monopolies and cartels. Electronic communication has ever since become subject to the push and pull of government intervention on the one side and commercial interests on the other.

Electronic networks have today become transformed by their integration with computers. Such networks now service large areas of industrial production and government organization. Airline booking and navigation systems, for instance, depend upon the instantaneous communication of computerized information across the globe. The integration of computers and electronic communication systems is by no means limited to the dissemination of information. Such systems have been introduced into industrial production itself, and have revolutionized many forms of production technology; they have also brought about changes in typical forms of business organization, usually promoting greater flexibility.

Jean Baudrillard (Reading 9) is the most adventurous and perhaps most controversial theorist of media writing today. His ideas echo some of the themes elaborated by authors like Haug or Adorno, but he does not believe that these express specific features of a capitalist system. On the contrary, the profusion of signs and images has become so intense that we can no longer discern a 'reality' behind them. Illusion here has replaced reality, in a much more complete sense even than that specified by Haug. We live now in a world of 'hyperreality' where there is literally nothing beyond the universe of surface appearances. Thus Baudrillard separates himself both from what he calls the 'pessimistic' (or Marxist) interpretation of the media and the 'optimist' view (associated with McLuhan among others).

As an example of his viewpoint he offers the case of opinion polls. Such polls might seem to involve the manipulation of need and consumption in much the way Haug and Adorno argue is characteristic of a commodified society as a whole. This would be so if there were, as Habermas believes, a distinct 'public opinion' to be sampled. Yet 'public opinion' is in some large part actually *created* through opinion polling; the taking of opinion polls does not simply relate to a pre-given subject matter.

This point can be generalized. Those who claim that the media manipulate needs and those who argue that the media offer new opportunities for mass participation are both deluding themselves. We live today within a universe of mediated experience which no longer has any 'outside'. This is exactly what the term 'hyperreality' refers to. In a world of endless information, publicity and symbolism, we can no longer be alienated, but neither can we impose our will to produce a collectively organized future. The 'silence' or de-politicizing of the masses is not the outcome of commodification; nor is it just passivity. The members of society often see through what Baudrillard calls 'the obscenity' of information that is constantly used to feed upon itself; a distanced or ironic attitude may be much more subversive than the sorts of oppositional standpoint offered by those who try to correct the 'flaws' in the system.

Does modern culture stimulate individualism and the formation of personal identity, or does it tend to stifle them? The issue remains a much debated one. Pluralism is said by many to characterize the cultural field today. In theoretical terms an emphasis upon diversity and pluralism finds expression in theories of postmodernism or postmodernity (terms which are often, although not always, used interchangeably). In earlier phases of modern social development, so it is argued, there were strong tendencies towards standardization, in areas of economic production as well as in architecture, art and literature. High culture from this point of view became a sort of defensive reaction to such stand-ardizing influences. But the further development of modern societies leads to a world of multiple values in which universal value standards, including those involved in the aesthetic judgements of high culture, become inoperable.

Stuart Hall (Reading 10) approaches this issue in a developmental way. There is a clear sense in which 'the individual' was invented during the course of the seventeenth and eighteenth centuries with the early formation of modern culture. The individual conscience was set free from traditional dogma and the human subject was placed at the centre of the universe. Over the period since 'the individual' came to be the centre-point of modern civilization, Hall says, several sorts of 'decentring' have subsequently taken place. Marx showed that human social life is strongly influenced by historical conditions of which individuals are only partly the authors, while Freud demonstrated that the individual con-sciousness is constrained by unconscious forces. Saussure provided a further decentring by showing that *langue* is not created by any indi-vidual language speaker but is a property of the social community. The French historian Michel Foucault has indicated how the 'individual' was created through a system of disciplinary power of a collective kind. Finally, new social movements of various sorts, including in particular feminism, have questioned divisions between the 'personal' and 'imper-sonal' in such a way as to alter the boundaries between them.

This analysis suggests that we should make a distinction between individualism and personal identity. Individualism is essentially an ideo-logy of a society breaking free from the limitations of imposed religion and tradition. As a cultural form, and an intellectual outlook, individual-ism has today become contested by the intellectual developments which Hall identifies. On the other hand, the opportunities for the development of personal identity in a world which has become more pluralistic might actually become heightened.

Mark Poster (Reading 11) makes use of Baudrillard's ideas to con-sider the nature of TV ads. Baudrillard's writings can usefully be under-stood against the backdrop of Saussure's linguistics. Normally a sign is thought of as composed of signifier and signified: the signified allows us to have reference to an outside world of reality even if its meaning is not determined by that world. The development of a highly commodified consumer society alters the relation between signifier and signified. Meaning becomes organized through a chain of signifiers which have no point of reference outside themselves. Advertising offers an excellent example. An ad develops meanings that have no intrinsic relation to the objects being promoted and thereby creates a new 'language' of its own.

It does not make any sense to 'believe' or 'disbelieve' the ad, because it establishes a new set of meanings that only make sense in their own terms. Advertising expresses that situation which Baudrillard refers to as the 'end of the social'. Social life is no longer oriented in terms of collective ambitions or policies of a long-term sort; we are all adrift in a swirling universe of floating signifiers.

According to Scott Lash and John Urry (Reading 12), the circumstances described by Baudrillard are related to the emergence of 'disorganized capitalism' and postmodernism. Postmodern culture is in effect the cultural expression of capitalism in a condition of disorganization. During the earlier stages of its development, capitalism produced strong tendencies towards centralization, in the shape of the development of large-scale bureaucracies, consolidated industrial production and distribution. Today, however, as a result of the emergence of global markets and the development of 'flexible production systems', a more chaotic and decentred order reigns.

Modernism in art, literature and architecture, Lash and Urry say, was the characteristic cultural accompaniment – in the area of high culture at least – of the phase of organized capitalism. With the shift to a more disorganized world, postmodern culture comes to the fore. The terms 'modernism' and 'postmodernism' are much debated. For Lash and Urry, postmodernism signals the disappearance of that 'aura' which Walter Benjamin saw as characteristic of high culture in the modern era. The 'aura' refers to the air of originality and distinctiveness that surrounds the art object. In postmodern culture, art can no longer lay claim to such singularity; the differentiation between high and mass culture essentially evaporates. The cultural forms of postmodernism reject any distinction between 'art' and 'life', while the boundary (as Baudrillard says) between reality and illusion is more and more thoroughly transgressed. In postmodern culture the consumption of images becomes of foremost importance and the visual imagery of the spectacle – as in the TV ad – replaces structured meaning.

Peter Bürger (Reading 13) interprets the decline of modernism in somewhat different terms. He agrees that, whether or not we label it 'postmodernism', a major transition has taken place over the past two or three decades in aesthetic sensitivities. Bürger approaches this issue through an interrogation of the writings of Adorno. Before blithely speaking of the emergence of postmodernism, he argues, we should give some attention to whether modernism itself has in the past been accurately interpreted. What might seem to be a decline of modernism might, first of all, be a demand not to place art upon a pedestal. From this point of view the 'aura' would be a sort of mysticism which could in fact be questioned and a demand for a rational interpretation of artistic distinctiveness made.

Modernism might have been identified too much with one particular cultural production, modern art. Such a view implicitly devalues other artistic movements and thereby sees a decline where there was only a pluralism. Modernism contains internal dialectics, or oppositions, whose implications are only now being explored. For these reasons it might be more accurate to speak of the exploration of modernism rather than the emergence of postmodern culture.

1

Social Theory, Mass Communication and Public Life

John Thompson

Let me begin by analysing some of the general characteristics of what is commonly called 'mass communication'. It has often been pointed out that, while 'mass communication' is a convenient label for referring to a broad range of media institutions and products, the term is misleading in certain respects. It is worth dwelling for a moment on some of the respects in which this term can lead astray. The expression 'mass' derives from the fact that the messages transmitted by the media industries are generally available to relatively large audiences. This is certainly the case in some sectors of the media industries and at some stages in their development, such as the mass circulation newspaper industry and the major television networks. However, during other periods in the development of the media industries (e.g. the early newspaper industry) and in some sectors of the media industries today (e.g. some book and magazine publishers), the audiences were and remain relatively small and specialized. Hence the term 'mass' should not be construed in narrowly quantitative terms; the important point about mass communication is not that a given number or proportion of individuals receive the products, but rather that the products are available in principle to a plurality of recipients. Moreover, the term 'mass' is misleading in so far as it suggests that the audiences are like inert, undifferentiated heaps. This suggestion obscures the fact that the messages transmitted by the media industries are received by specific individuals situated in particular social–historical contexts. These individuals attend to media messages with varying degrees of concentration, actively interpret and make sense of these messages and relate them to other aspects of their lives. Rather than viewing these individuals as part of an inert and undifferentiated mass, we should leave open the possibility that the reception of media messages is an active, inherently critical and socially differentiated process.

If the term 'mass' may be misleading in this context, the term 'communication' may also be, since the kinds of communication generally involved in mass communication are quite different from those involved in ordinary conversation. I shall examine some of these differences in the course of the following discussion. Here I shall call attention to one important difference: namely, that mass communication generally involves a one-way flow of messages from the transmitter to the receiver. Unlike the dialogical situation of a conversation, in which a listener is also a potential respondent, mass communication institutes a fundamental *break* between the producer and receiver, in such a way that recipients have relatively little capacity to contribute to the course and content of the communicative process. Hence it may be more appropriate to speak of the 'transmission' or 'diffusion' of messages rather than of 'communication' as such. Yet even in the circumstances of mass communication, recipients do have some capacity to contribute, in so far as recipients are also consumers who may sometimes choose between various media products and whose views are sometimes solicited or taken into account by the organizations concerned with producing and diffusing these products. Moreover, it is possible that new technological developments – such as those associated with fibre optic cables – will increase the interactive capacity of the medium of television and give viewers greater control over the transmission process, although the extent to which this will become a practical reality remains to be seen.

In the light of these preliminary qualifications, I want to offer a broad conceptualization of mass communication and to highlight some of its key characteristics. We may broadly conceive of mass communication as *the institutionalized production and generalized diffusion of symbolic goods via the transmission and storage of information/communication.* By conceiving of mass communication in terms of the production and diffusion of symbolic goods, I wish to stress the importance of viewing mass communication in relation to the institutions concerned with the commodification of symbolic forms. What we now describe as mass communication is a range of phenomena and processes that emerged historically through the development of institutions seeking to exploit new opportunities for the fixation and reproduction of symbolic forms. I now want to analyse mass communication in a more theoretical way by focusing on the following four characteristics: the institutionalized production and diffusion of symbolic goods; the instituted break between production and reception; the extension of availability in time and space; and the public circulation of symbolic forms.

The first characteristic of mass communication is *the institutionalized production and diffusion of symbolic goods*. Mass communication presupposes the development of institutions – that is, relatively stable clusters of social relations and accumulated resources – concerned with the large-scale production and generalized diffusion of symbolic goods. These activities are 'large-scale' in the sense that they involve the production and diffusion of multiple copies or the provision of materials to numerous recipients. This is rendered possible by the fixation of symbolic forms in technical media and by the reproducibility of the forms. *Fixation* may involve processes of encoding whereby symbolic forms are translated into information which can be stored in a particular medium or material substratum; the symbolic forms may be transmitted as information and then decoded for the purposes of reception or consumption. The symbolic forms diffused by mass communication are inherently *reproducible* in the sense that multiple copies may be produced or made available to numerous recipients. The reproduction of forms is generally controlled as strictly as possible by the institutions of mass communication, since it is one of the principal means by which symbolic forms are subjected to economic valorization. Forms are reproduced in order to be exchanged on a market or through a regulated type of economic transaction. Hence they are *commodified* and treated as objects to be sold, as services to be paid for or as media which can facilitate the sale of other objects or services. In the first instance, therefore, mass communication should be understood as part of a range of institutions concerned, in varying ways, with the fixation, reproduction and commodification of symbolic forms.

A second characteristic of mass communication is that *it institutes a fundamental break between the production and reception of symbolic goods*. These goods are produced for recipients who are generally not physically present at the place of production and transmission or diffusion; they are, literally, *mediated* by the technical media in which they are fixed and transmitted. This characteristic is not, of course, unique to mass communication: the fixation and transmission of symbolic forms on papyrus or stone also involved a break between production and reception. But with the rise of mass communication, the range of producers and receivers affected by this process has greatly expanded. Moreover, the mediation of symbolic forms via mass communication generally involves a one-way flow of messages from the producer to the recipient, such that the capacity of the recipient to influence or intervene in the processes of production and transmission or diffusion is strictly limited. One consequence of this condition is that the processes of production and transmission or diffusion are characterized by a distinctive form of *indeterminacy*. Symbolic forms are produced for audiences and transmitted or diffused in order to reach the audiences, but these processes generally take place in the absence of a direct and continuous monitoring of the audiences' responses. In contrast to face-to-face interaction, where the interlocutors can question one another and observe one another's responses, in mass communication the personnel involved in the production and transmission or diffusion are generally deprived of immediate feedback from the recipients. Since the economic valorization of mass-mediated symbolic forms may depend crucially on the nature and extent of reception, the personnel involved typically employ a variety of strategies to cope with this indeterminacy. They draw upon past experience and use it as a guide to likely future outcomes; they use well-tried formulas which have a predictable audience appeal; or they try to obtain information about recipients through market research or through the routine monitoring of audience size and response. These and other techniques are institutionalized mechanisms which enable personnel to reduce the indeterminacy stemming from the break between production and reception, and to do so in a way which concurs with the overall aims of the institutions concerned.

A third characteristic of mass communication is that *it extends the availability of symbolic forms in time and in space*. Again, this characteristic is not unique to mass communication: all forms of cultural transmission involve some degree of space–time distanciation. But the media of mass communication generally involve a relatively high degree of distanciation in both space and time; and, with the development of telecommunications, space–time distanciation is severed from the physical transportation of symbolic forms. The transmission of symbolic forms via telecommunications – for example, via a network of terrestrial and satellite relays – enables the institutions of mass communication to achieve a high degree of spatial distanciation in a minimal amount of time. Moreover, since the symbolic forms are generally fixed in a relatively durable medium, such as paper, photographic film or electromagnetic tape, they also have extended availability in time and can be preserved for subsequent use. The space–time distanciation involved in mass communication is also affected by the conditions under which symbolic forms are received and consumed. By virtue of the instituted break between production and reception, the nature and extent of distanciation may depend on the social practices and technical conditions of reception. For example, the extension of availability of a book in time and space may depend as much on the ways in which the book is received – whether it is recommended or ignored, incorporated into curricula or actively suppressed, and so on – as on the channels of diffusion and the nature of the technical medium itself. Similarly, the extension of availability of a television programme or film may depend on whether potential recipients have the technical means to receive the programme, whether the scheduling concurs with the social organization of their everyday lives, and so on.

A fourth characteristic of mass communication is that *it involves the public circulation of symbolic forms*. The products of mass communication are produced in principle for a plurality of recipients. In this respect, mass communication differs from forms of communication – such as telephone conversations, teleconferencing, or private video recordings of various kinds – which employ the same technical media of fixation and transmission but which are oriented towards a single or a highly restricted range of recipients. This basic difference between established forms of mass communication and other forms of electronically mediated interaction may be called into question by the increasing deployment of new communication technologies, but this is a development which has yet to be fully realized. As the institutions of mass communication have developed hitherto, their products circulate within a 'public domain', in the sense that they are available in principle to anyone who has the technical means, abilities and resources to acquire them. While the nature and scope of this public domain may be unlimited in principle, it is always limited in practice by the social–historical conditions of production, transmission and reception. The institutions of mass communication often aim to reach as large an audience as possible, since the size of the audience may directly affect the economic valorization of the products concerned. Today the audiences for some films and television programmes may amount to hundreds of millions of viewers worldwide; a single Christmas Day television broadcast can command more than 30 million viewers in Britain alone. The nature and scope of the audiences for the products of mass communication vary enormously from one medium to another, and from one product to another within the same medium. The ways in which these products are appropriated by the recipients – whether, for example, they are appropriated by a collective gathering in a cinema or by a private viewing in the home – also vary considerably, depending on the medium, the product, the channels of diffusion and the social and technical conditions of reception. One consequence of the intrinsically public character of media products is that the development of mass communication has been accompanied by attempts to exercise control, on the part of state authorities and other regulatory bodies, over the institutions of mass communication. The very capacity of these institutions to make symbolic forms available to a potentially vast audience is a source of concern for authorities which seek to maintain order and regulate social life within the territories under their jurisdiction.

[···]

By making messages available to audiences which are extended and dispersed in time and space, the deployment of technical media of mass communication also serves to reconstitute the boundaries between public and private life. The private lives of individuals can be turned into public events by being publicized through the mass media; and public events can be experienced in private settings, as happens when affairs of state are watched or read about in the privacy of the home. The nature of what is public and what is private, and the demarcation between these domains, are transformed in certain ways by the development of mass communication, and this in turn has implications for the ways in which political power, at the level of state institutions, is acquired, exercised and sustained in modern societies.

In order to examine these issues further, we have to draw some broad distinctions between the public and private domains. The terms 'public' and 'private' have acquired a wide variety of senses in modern social and political discourse, and any attempt to identify broad distinctions is bound to be a selective and simplifying task. Nevertheless, this task is worthwhile and important for analysing the nature and impact of mass communication. Although the public–private dichotomy can be traced back to the philosophical debates of Classical Greece and to the early development of Roman law, here I shall focus on some of the senses which this dichotomy has come to assume in early modern and modern Western societies characterized by capitalist economic relations and a constitutional state incorporating democratic institutions.[1] In this context, we can distinguish between two basic senses of the public–private dichotomy. According to the first sense, the public–private dichotomy refers to the distinction between, on the one hand, the domain of institutionalized political power which was increasingly vested in the hands of a sovereign state, and, on the other, the domains of private economic activity and personal relations which fell outside the direct control of the state. Of course, this broad distinction was never rigid or clear-cut; the early development of capitalist economic activity was a process that took place within a legal framework that was established and continuously modified by state authorities, and the activities of the state were, in turn, influenced and constrained in varying degrees by the development of the capitalist economy. Moreover, since the late nineteenth century, a range of economic and welfare organizations has been created within, or brought into, the public domain, as a result of policies of state intervention aimed partly at offsetting the erratic character of capitalist economic growth, thus rendering the distinction between private and public domains more complex.

[⋯]

The public–private dichotomy, as it has emerged in Western social and political discourse, has a second basic sense which must be separated off from the distinction elaborated above. According to this second sense, 'public' means 'open' or 'available to the public'. What is public, in this sense, is what is visible or observable, what is performed in front of spectators, what is open for all (or many) to see or hear or hear about; what is private, by contrast, is what is hidden from view, what is said or done in privacy or secrecy or among a restricted circle of people. In this sense, the public–private dichotomy has to do with *publicness versus privacy*, with *visibility versus invisibility*. This second sense of the dichotomy does not coincide with the first, but rather overlaps with it in complex and historically varying ways. In the traditional monarchical states of medieval and early modern Europe, the affairs of state were conducted in the relatively closed circles of the court, in ways that were largely invisible to most of the subject population. When officials of the state appeared before their subjects, they did so in ways that were carefully staged and managed: their principal aim was to affirm their power publicly (visibly), not to render public (visible) the grounds and deliberations which entered into their decision-making processes. The privacy of their decision-making processes was justified by recourse to the *arcana imperii* – that is, to the doctrine of state secrecy, which held that the power of the prince is more effective and true to its aim if it is hidden from the gaze of the people and, like divine will, invisible.[2] The invisibility of power was assured institutionally by the fact that decision-making processes took place in a closed space, the secret cabinet, and by the fact that decisions themselves were only occasionally and selectively made public. With the development of the modern constitutional state, however, the invisibility of power and the privacy of decision-making processes were limited in certain ways. The secret cabinet was replaced or supplemented by a range of political institutions that were more open and accountable to the people, and the doctrine of *arcana imperii* was transformed into the modern principle of official secrecy and restricted in its application to those issues regarded as vital to the security and stability of the state. Power was rendered more visible and decision-making processes became more public, although this broad trend was neither uniform nor complete: new forms of invisibility and privacy have emerged, and the exercise of state power in modern societies remains in many ways shrouded in secrecy and hidden from the public gaze.

Against the backcloth of these distinctions, we can consider the ways in which the development of mass communication has reconstituted the boundaries between public and private life. The basis for this reconstitution is that, *with the development of mass communication, the publicness (visibility) of events or individuals in the public and private domains is no longer linked directly with the sharing of a common locale*, and hence events or individuals can acquire a publicness which is independent of their capacity to be observed or heard directly by a plurality of individuals. The development of mass communication has thus facilitated and promoted the emergence of two types of events which have distinctive characteristics and consequences: we can describe these as *mediated public events* and *mediated private events*. Mediated public events are events which originally take place in an institutional setting within the public domain, but which acquire a new status by virtue of the fact that they are recorded in a technical medium of transmission and thereby made available to a range of recipients who were not present to witness the original occurrence of the event. Similarly, mediated private events are events which originally take place in the private domain, but which acquire a new status by being recorded and diffused through the media of mass communication.

[···]

While both public and private events can be given a new publicness by mediazation, these mediated events are generally experienced by others within their own private domains. The development of mass communication, and especially of television, is characterized by what we may describe as *the privatized reception of mediated events*. Events which take place in public and private domains can be experienced in private domestic settings which are remote in space and perhaps distant in time from the contexts in which the events originally took place. By virtue of the technical media of mass communication *the private domain of modern societies – in particular, the private domestic setting – has become a principal site of mediated publicness*. In modern societies most individuals typically experience events which take place in the public domain, and events which take place in those regions of the private domain which are beyond their immediate milieu, by watching, reading or hearing about these events in the context of their private domestic settings: their experience is both mediated and privatized. The privatized reception of mediated events is also typically *fragmentary*, in the sense that receptive activities typically take place in locales which are segregated and dispersed in time and space; but this does not mean that receptive activities are non-social. On the contrary, the privatized reception of mediated events involves two distinctive kinds of interaction: the quasi-interaction characteristic of the reception process, and what we may call *the discursive elaboration of media messages*. Through mediated quasi-interaction, individuals situated in private domestic contexts are able to experience public and private events. But the nature of this experience is peculiar, since the flow of messages is predominantly one-way and the capacity for recipients to respond to the principal communicator is limited. Hence individuals are able to experience events which take place in the public and private domains without directly participating in these domains; their participation is, at most, a 'quasi-participation' in which there are definite limits on the range of responses available to recipients. The messages received via television and other media are commonly subjected to discursive elaboration: they are discussed by individuals in the course of their everyday lives, both within the primary reception region and in a variety of other interactive contexts in the private and public domains. In this way mediated messages may acquire an additional audience of secondary recipients who did not themselves participate in the mediated quasi-interaction, but who assimilate some version of the message through interaction with the primary recipients. The messages may also be taken up by media organizations and incorporated in new media messages, a process that may be described as *extended mediazation*. Through discursive elaboration and extended mediazation, messages received via the media are adapted and dispersed to an ever-widening circle of secondary recipients, who may thereby acquire information about events which they neither experienced directly nor witnessed via the media.

Thus the development of mass communication has not only facilitated the process of making public the events or individuals which take place or who act in the public or private domains, but it has also enabled the publicness of events or individuals to be experienced or otherwise received in the domestic settings of the private domain. The experience of publicness no longer requires individuals to share a common locale. The severing of publicness from the context of co-presence involves a transformation in the nature of publicness and in the ways in which individuals participate in it. Since access to publicness is no longer dependent on physical co-presence, a wider range of individuals, and especially individuals in so far as they inhabit private domestic settings, are able to experience a greater spectrum of events in the public and private domains. The advent of television has been particularly important in this regard, since the codes and conventions of access are often less restrictive than is the case with other media of transmission, such as books and newspapers. *Hence any individual situated in a private domestic setting equipped with a television set has potential access to the sphere of publicness created and mediated by television.* It is the very accessibility of mediated publicness which has given rise to new opportunities as well as new problems – new opportunities, in the sense that the greater accessibility of mediated publicness may enable a wider range of individuals to participate, in a certain way, in spheres of information and communication. Thanks to the development of new modes of mass communication, especially television, more individuals than ever before are able to experience events which take place in spatially and temporally remote regions, and to participate in an ever-widening and increasingly global sphere of mediated publicness. But these opportunities may also present new problems, for greater accessibility and participation may make it more difficult for those who exercise power, whether in the public or the private domain, to control and restrict access to information, a control upon which their power may, to some extent, depend. This is part of what is at stake in the continuing debate about children and television, for the debate is, in part, about what can and should be transmitted on a medium which enables reception to take place in the relatively uncontrolled and uncontrollable contexts of private domestic life. With the advent of television, children have acquired a new and accessible means of learning about the events and activities which take place in public and private domains, including those forms of behaviour which adults generally reserve for the back regions of the private domestic context. And this in turn may present new problems for adults, who may feel that mediated messages intended primarily for themselves have become, by virtue of the accessibility of the medium, a source of information, entertainment or harm for children, and hence have come into conflict with their perceived responsibility to regulate and control the educative process of children. The levelling of access to material transmitted via television creates new problems for those individuals who, rightly or wrongly, are concerned with the regulation of access to information and communication, whether this bears on the education of children or, more generally, on the knowledge and experience of the population at large.

I have argued that the development of mass communication has transformed the nature and experience of publicness in the modern world. By severing publicness from the sharing of a common locale, it has rendered more events more public (more visible) and has rendered their publicness more accessible to more people. But there are some commentators who would interpret the development of mass communication as a largely negative force in the historical unfolding of public life. These commentators see the privatized and fragmentary character of the reception process as a sign that public life in modern societies is all but dead – not that the development of mass communication by itself has killed public life, but that the deployment of technical media, with their one-way flow of messages pouring into the privacy of the home, has sealed the coffin of a once-thriving public sphere.[3] This interpretation would, I think, be an overly negative view of the significance of mass communication in the modern world. It is true that the reception of mediated messages is generally a fragmentary and privatized process, but from this it does not follow that reception is non-social: on the contrary, the reception of mediated messages generally involves, as I have indicated, a range of distinctive social activities, including the discursive elaboration of mediated messages. It is true that mass communication generally involves a one-way flow of messages, in such a way that those who receive mediated messages have relatively little capacity to respond. But from this it does not follow that recipients have no control over the communicative process, nor that the process of reception does not involve some form of participation – albeit a distinctive and limited form. On the contrary, as I have suggested, the process of reception is a much more active, creative and critical process than many commentators are inclined to assume.

The most serious shortcoming of the argument that the development of mass communication has destroyed a once-thriving public sphere is that it fails to take account of the ways in which the deployment of technical media has transformed the very nature of publicness. The argument is based on a notion of publicness which is essentially *spatial* and *dialogical* in character: that is, publicness implies an ensemble of individuals meeting in an open place, a public space, within which they can directly discuss issues of common concern. This is a notion of publicness derived from the assemblies of the Classical Greek city-states, a notion which could still be applied to some extent to the salons and coffee-houses of early modern Europe. But with the development of mass communication, and especially television, the nature of publicness has changed. An individual need no longer be present at an event in order to witness it; the publicness (visibility) of an event no longer depends on the sharing of a common locale. Hence the notion of publicness has become de-spatialized and increasingly divorced from the idea of a dialogical conversation in a shared locale. Publicness has become increasingly linked to the distinctive kind of visibility produced by, and achievable through, the technical media of mass communication. Television and other media have generated a new type of public realm which has no spatial limits, which is not necessarily tied to dialogical conversation and which is accessible to an indefinite number of individuals who may be situated within privatized domestic settings. Rather than sounding the death knell of public life, the development of mass communication has created a new kind of publicness and has transformed fundamentally the conditions under which most people are able to experience what is public and participate today in what could be called a public realm.

It is important to emphasize that, with regard to the exercise of institutionalized political power, the kind of publicness or visibility created by the development of mass communication is a double-edged sword. In the new political arena produced and sustained by the media of mass communication, political leaders are able to appear before their subjects in a way and on a scale that has never existed previously. The relationship between political leaders and subjects becomes increasingly mediated by mass communication, that is, becomes a form of technically mediated quasi-interaction, through which bonds of loyalty and affection (as well as feelings of repugnance) can be formed. Skilful politicians exploit this circumstance to their advantage. They seek to create and sustain a basis of support for their power and their policies by controlling their self-presentation, by *managing the visibility which they have within the mediated arena of modern politics*. Today the management of visibility is widely recognized as a fundamental aspect of institutionalized politics. From fireside chats to party conventions, from local walkabouts to superpower summits, political leaders and their organizations preoccupy themselves with the management of visibility and with the nurturing of a relationship produced and sustained by mediated quasi-interaction. By virtue of the very nature of mass communication, this management activity is not localized in time or in space. Political leaders appear before an audience which extends well beyond those individuals who may be assembled within a common locale. The audience may extend to the boundaries of a nation-state and beyond, for the mediated arena of modern politics is potentially global in character.

While the development of mass communication has created unprecedented opportunities for the management of visibility, it has also created unprecedented risks for political leaders and for the exercise of political power. Prior to the advent of mass communication, political leaders could restrict the activity of managing visibility to the relatively closed circle of the assembly or the court, while generally maintaining a distance and aloofness from the population as a whole. The legitimacy of their power was sustained, to some extent, by the very distance they maintained from the subjects over whom they ruled, a distance which nourished the cultivated aura of regality. Today it is no longer possible to restrict the management of visibility in this way. The mediated arena of modern politics is open and accessible in a way that traditional assemblies and courts were not. Moreover, given the nature of mass communication, the messages transmitted by the media may be received in ways that cannot be directly monitored and controlled by communicators. Hence the visibility created by mass communication may also be the source of a new kind of fragility: *however much political leaders may seek to manage their visibility, the very phenomenon of visibility may slip out of their control and undermine whatever support they may have or may seek.* Political leaders can be destroyed by an emotional outburst, an impromptu remark or an ill-judged action: the fall from power can be breathtakingly quick. More importantly, the exercise of political power today takes place in an arena which is increasingly *open to view*, however hard political leaders may try to control and restrict the visibility. Hence the deployment of American troops in Southeast Asia or Central America, or the suppression of demonstrations in China, South Africa or the West Bank, are activities which take place in a new kind of public realm: they are visible, observable, capable of being witnessed simultaneously by millions of individuals dispersed across the globe. The exercise of political power is subjected to a kind of *global scrutiny* which simply did not exist prior to the advent of mass communication, and especially of television. Given the possibility of such scrutiny, political actions carry unprecedented risks and may expose a regime to international condemnation and to political and economic isolation. The visibility created by mass communication is a double-edged sword: today political leaders must seek continuously to manage it, but they cannot completely control it. Mediated visibility is an unavoidable condition of institutionalized politics in the modern era, but it has uncontrollable consequences for the exercise of political power.

Notes and references

1   For more extended discussions of the nature and development of this dichotomy, see Jürgen Habermas, *The Structural Transformation of the Public Sphere: An Inquiry into a Category of Bourgeois Society*, tr. Thomas Burger with Frederick Lawrence (Polity, Cambridge, 1989), and Norberto Bobbio, *Democracy and Dictatorship: The Nature and Limits of State Power*, tr. Peter Kennealy (Polity, Cambridge, 1989).

2   See Bobbio, *Democracy and Dictatorship*, ch. 1.
3   See, for example, Richard Sennett, *The Fall of Public Man* (Cambridge University Press, Cambridge, 1974), pp. 282ff. Sennett's argument converges in some respects with that developed by Habermas in *The Structural Transformation of the Public Sphere*.

2

Saussure and the Origin of Semiotics

Robert Hodge and Gunther Kress

Like any social activity semiotics has a past which acts on its present and its future, and which is also constructed in histories which make the contingencies of the past and present seem inevitable and unchallengeable. We want to contest one particular version of history which underpins a specific and limiting conception of what semiotics was and is, and should be and do. We will refer to this as the dominant tradition without implying either that it is all of a piece or continuous with itself as it reached back to claim its past. What we want to do is neither to break with the past (if that were possible) nor to reunite it and appropriate its potency. Instead we will try to restore to it some possibilities that have been foreclosed, emphasizing some fissures and contradictions that were prematurely and illicitly resolved. We have talked of 'traditional semiotics' so far as though it could be neatly opposed to 'social semiotics', but that is an oversimplification. In practice the 'tradition' of traditional semiotics is not monolithic or even an agreed body of theories and concepts, and it by no means repudiates the social dimension unequivocally. In coming to terms with so amorphous and shifting an entity, we will not try to offer a tidy survey, which would be superficial and tendentious at best. Instead, we will look critically at the work of some key figures who were producing their ideas at a crucial stage in the formulation of the semiotics project.

One figure we cannot ignore in such an approach is Ferdinand de Saussure, who in all accounts of semiotics is named as a founding father of the discipline. Sometimes his name is bracketed with that of C.S. Peirce, but his thought was undoubtedly far more influential. As professor of general linguistics at Geneva University, with pupils later occupying chairs in prestigious universities in Europe, he was ideally placed to exert influence, even posthumously. His legacy shaped modern structural linguistics as well as structuralist semiotics. Peirce, on the other hand, produced his ideas from the peripheries of the American academic system in the late nineteenth century, and some of his early disciples were too eminent in their own right to feel they had to be faithful to his thought. Some accounts of semiotics suggest that there are two traditions stemming from these two founding fathers: continental semiotics (or semiology), a rationalist, structuralist form deriving from Saussure, and American semiotics, more behaviourist and positivistic and deriving from Peirce. But though American semiotics does have its characteristic forms, the seeming deference to Peirce is not a decisive factor in it. Peirce's observations on semiotics, scattered through his collected works (1940–65), are potentially far more subtle and fluid than the mechanistic theories of those who claim to follow him. There is not a Peircean counter-tradition, with solid achievements planted in American soil, ready to confront the European semiology of Saussure. But there *is* Peirce's own work, unsystematic but full of sharp and illuminating observations on semiosis and thought, still waiting to be properly assimilated into a general semiotic theory.

Peirce was a philosopher, in so far as he was an academic at all. Philosophy, at that stage in the institutionalization of knowledge, had a wide scope, addressing itself to general problems of language and thinking. Peirce actually used the term 'semiotic'; other philosophers reflected productively on problems of language and meaning without invoking the term. Thinkers like Husserl, in the phenomenological tradition, and Wittgenstein were developing semiotic notions which have largely remained outside the semiotic tradition. These of course have not been without their influence and their followers, but that influence was labelled 'philosophy'. Linguistics subsequently did without either semiotics or a philosophy of language, while linguistic philosophy, cut off from a broader range of semiotic phenomena, was reduced to endless analysis of the language of philosophy as its proper subject matter.

Two other thinkers must be included even in so limited an inventory of 'founding fathers'. One is Freud. Although he produced his ideas from as marginal a position as Peirce, there is no question of the magnitude of his general influence today. Since Lacan's advocacy his status as a proto-semiotician has been recognized, although Lacan's versions of both Freud and semiotics are not definitive or exhaustive, and the place of Freud's thought in a general semiotics is far from settled. Even more important, in the reconstitution of semiotics that we envisage, is the work of Voloshinov and the school of Bakhtin. Voloshinov's major work (1973),[1] produced in Russia in the 1920s, offered a contemporary critique of Saussure that has only recently begun to have its effect in the

West and to be recognized as a potentially decisive theoretical intervention. Voloshinov drew heavily on Marxism, a tradition which was
effectively excluded in West European and American theories of language in the 1930s. But he and others in that group were also silenced
for decades by Stalinism. The rediscovery of Voloshinov in effect makes
a contemporary of Saussure as well, giving new life to the issues he set
in motion, providing a powerful impetus and orientation to a new form
of semiotics.

Saussure's *Course in General Linguistics* is at first glance a surprising
text to have precipitated semiotics. Saussure's explicit references to
'semiology' amount to three pages. Most of his book draws on a very
narrow range of semiotic phenomena. The examples come mainly from
his field of special competence, the history of changes in sounds in the
Indo-European group of languages. This contradiction is at the centre
of the problematic legacy of Saussure. On the one hand he projected
a discipline with the widest possible scope, while on the other he laid
down a set of strictures which split his heritage in two, deforming linguistics, and preventing the coming of semiotics for decades.

    We can see his contradiction in many aspects of Saussure's work. He
was trained in the precise and scholarly tradition of comparative philo-
logy, whose primary goal was the historical reconstruction of the Indo-
European group of languages, but that tradition had virtually run out of
feasible tasks. Bally and Sechehaye, editors of the *Course*, described his
motives as follows: 'We have often heard Ferdinand de Saussure lament
the dearth of principles and methods that marked linguistics during his
developmental period. Throughout his lifetime, he stubbornly continued to search out the laws that would give direction to his thought amid
the chaos.' In the *Course* Saussure set himself the task of constituting
a new and broader field of study, and so he devised a simple, clear and
comprehensive map, in terms of which the close, narrow work he found
congenial could proceed again with the certainty he so desired. His
basic strategy was to project a large, undifferentiated field, then divide
it up by successive sharp dichotomies; and then proceed to eliminate
one half of each dichotomy. The result was a set of boundaries, each regarded as absolute, and a successive narrowing of linguistics and semiotics. What needs to be challenged are the exclusions enforced by those
boundaries; the original scope of these claims must be re-examined, in
the coming to terms with Saussure which semiotics needs even today.
The Saussurean scalpel cut deep, and his need for limits has found
echoes in many others who have set up sterile barriers, in linguistics and
in many other fields of cultural studies.

His famous pairs of categories are often discussed in isolation, but they must be understood both as part of a rigorous scheme and as successive stages in a progression through that scheme. We will summarize that progression in our summary of his thought. In the search for a pure object of study, he first made a distinction between that which was internal to language, and that which was external to it although essential to an interest in language phenomena: ethnology, political and social history, history of institutions, geography. Having posited this first division, he proposed to exclude 'external linguistics' – even though he also insisted elsewhere that language is irreducibly a 'social fact'. The class of objects that was left he put together, and he proposed it as a larger object of study, that of sign systems generally. That study he named 'semiology', and prophesied its existence in advance, while not in fact studying it himself.

Verbal language as such (*langage*) he designated as one such sign system. This object he then categorized into two: *langue* (the abstract system of rules underlying speech) and *parole* (human speech: literally 'words'), conceived of as an intrinsically unordered morass, an infinite and arbitrary combination of the elements of *langue* by individual speakers. He discarded *parole* as an impossible object for systematic study. *Langue* was then divided into two: the *synchronic*, the study of stages of language (the system as it exists at any one time, for a particular language community), and the *diachronic*, the study of changes in the system over time. Most of Saussure's lifetime had been spent on diachronic studies, but he categorized these as defeating systematization. Diachronic change, for him, was essentially piecemeal and irrational. He then described synchronic language phenomena on two axes: the plane of combination and the plane of selection, which he called the associative plane (Hjelmslev (1953)[2] later renamed these the syntagmatic and the paradigmatic planes respectively). Synchronic linguistics deals with signs which have a value, that is, a place in a system or structure, syntagmatic or paradigmatic, and a signification, that is, a relation of reference, existing outside language. For reasons that are consistent with the rest of the scheme, he opted for considerations of value (relations in a system) rather than signification. Signs themselves have a double form, consisting of signifiers (carriers of meaning) and signifieds, the concept or meaning. Saussure did not entirely neglect consideration of signifieds, but his main interest was with signifiers. The signifier, too, has a double form, made up of a material entity (e.g. a stroke of the pen, a physical sound) and an image of that entity, which is a mental event. Characteristically, Saussure relegated the study of the material sign to a discipline outside linguistics. The full scheme, then, looks like this:

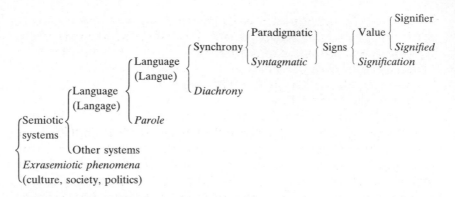

The italics in this schema indicate the contents of Saussure's rubbish bin, what he chose to reject or seemed to minimize. So important are the things that he excluded that it is tempting to see him as that useful phenomenon, the person who is *always* wrong. On that reasoning, if Saussure rejects something it must be important. But that of course is too simple. His acts of exclusion, acts of repression, always see the return of the repressed. The repressed is the dynamic principle of his system. That repressed is invariably energy, movement, process: whatever changes, or causes or describes change. So he affirmed the social over the individual, but only as an abstract, immobilized version of the social order, potentially threatened by actions of innumerable individuals. At the level of language, however, he studied mainly words or phrases, not larger structures of discourse. This could be seen as a concern with the individual word, rather than with the structures in which words exist. But at a deeper level that concern betrays the same desire to stay with that which can be fixed and therefore known, even if the price is to see only chaos in the life and discourse that swirls outside the domain of linguistics or semiotics; in *parole*, in society, in history, in the intractable material world of objects and events. The strength of this attempt to escape the world of processes reveals his fascinated recognition of these forces, even if they appear in his theory only as negations.

Using Saussure as an antiguide, we can invert his prohibitions and rewrite them as basic premises for an alternative semiotics (an alternative which is implicit in his work). This alternative semiotics will incorporate the study of at least the following components:

1   culture, society and politics as intrinsic to semiotics;
2   other semiotic systems alongside verbal language;
3   *parole*, the act of speaking, and concrete signifying practices in other codes;

4 diachrony, time, history, process and change;
5 the processes of signification, the transactions between signifying systems and structures of reference;
6 structures of the signified;
7 the material nature of signs.

Voloshinov, writing in 1929, turned Saussure's doctrines on their head in essentially the same terms as we do above. His critique has an exemplary lucidity, and still repays close attention. He labelled the Saussurean tradition as 'abstract objectivism', and he diagnosed its central mistake, its *proton pseudos*, as follows: 'Abstract objectivism, by taking the system of language and regarding it as the entire crux of linguistic phenomena, rejected the speech act – the utterance – as something individual . . . [But] *The utterance is a social phenomenon. . . .*' This sees the separation of *langue* and *parole*, and the rejection of *parole* as too individual to be an object of theory, as the decisive error in Saussure's thought. Voloshinov also reconstituted the unity of semiotic phenomena, against Saussure's fatal dichotomies, in three propositions asserting the material and social dimensions as essential to semiotic analysis.

1 Ideology may not be divorced from the material reality of the sign.
2 Signs may not be divorced from the concrete forms of social intercourse (seeing that the sign is part of organized social intercourse and cannot exist, as such, outside it).
3 Communication and the forms of communication may not be divorced from the material basis.

Voloshinov's own position on the social determination of signs is not without problems of the relation of individual and collective structures: 'The form of signs is conditioned above all by the social organization of the participants involved and also by the immediate conditions of their interaction.'[3] This 'also' links the general social organization and the immediate conditions of interaction, though it makes light of the problems a social semiotics must face in accounting for the constraints and determinations acting on participants in a semiotic act. Voloshinov's work foregrounds the speech act as an exchange between individuals whose consciousness is already socially constructed. It emphasizes the plane of production as decisive for semiotic analysis. His formulation, however, leaves unexplored the nexus of relationships between speech roles and social relationships in a class society, the complex structures of the logonomic systems at various levels. Moreover, a general semiotic theory must try to theorize the full range of semiotic acts, including writing, art, film and the mass media, where the relationships between participants are more complex and abstract than is the case with a face-to-face conversational exchange. But this is only to say that Voloshinov has left important tasks for social semiotics to explore. In that exploration, the two formulations 'social organization of participants' and 'immediate conditions of interaction' seem to us as good as any currently available.

Voloshinov makes a close link between semiotics and the study of ideology. 'Without signs there is no ideology. . . . Everything ideological possesses semiotic value.'[4] He uses the word 'ideology' here in a specific sense which we will examine later. The point to stress is that, for him, neither ideology nor language are monolithic phenomena, imposing their irresistible unity on a helpless society. On the contrary, society for him is characterized by struggle and conflict and constantly renegotiated relations, and semiosis reflects this process in its typical forms. Here his concept of the 'accent' is useful. An accent is a particular inflection which gives a different social meaning to an apparently common set of signs, just as happens with various accents of speech which mark class and regional identity. As well as this, for Voloshinov they affect the force and meaning of signs, by connecting them with different life experiences and values. He sees language systems as typically 'multi-accentual', with a seemingly common code refracted by different class or group positions. From this perspective it becomes impossible to see an ideology as a unitary set of meanings or texts, imposed from above in an absolute take-it-or–leave-it kind of way. For Saussure, language had to be a totally collective phenomenon, or it would be asocial and incomprehensible. For Voloshinov the processes of struggle, negotiation, and creation and resolution of differences are both social and comprehensible, and indeed are at the centre of semiotic inquiry.

We believe that as an outline Voloshinov's sketch of the basis for a social semiotics is essentially sound. The task that remains is to build on this basis, and confront the difficulties of implementing the programme. But it is worth pointing out moments in the Western European tradition which could have led in this kind of direction. C.S. Peirce, for instance, had a dialogic conception of language and signs. 'Every thought is a sign', he declared; 'All thinking is dialogic in form. Your self of one instant appeals to your deeper self for his assent.'[5] Unlike Voloshinov, he has internalized the transaction that constitutes thought, presenting it as a fact of personal psychology without explicit roots in the social process, and this is an important weakness in Peirce's theory. But otherwise, this is essentially the same kind of account of thinking processes as was developed later by the Russian psychologist Vygotsky, himself influenced by Voloshinov and the Bakhtin group.

Peirce also stressed process in the study of signs. 'Semiotic' for him was 'the doctrine of the essential nature and fundamental varieties of semiosis'.[6] And semiosis here is a process, 'the action of a sign', not a language structure or a code. 'By semiosis I mean an action, an influence, which is, or involves, a co-operation of *three* subjects, such as a sign, its object and its interpretant, this tri-relative influence not being in any way resolvable into actions between pairs.'[7] Exactly what Peirce meant by 'interpretant' is not clear, and his theory has been disputed. But it is clear that semiosis involves a transaction, a process linking object, sign, and 'interpretants'. Interpretants are further ideas linked to a sign. 'The interpretant of a proposition is its predicate.'[8] The process of generation of interpretants is seemingly limitless, an infinite semiosis, rather like the process of free association. But Peirce insists on two limits to this freedom and infinitude. The relation between 'sign' and 'interpretant' is still controlled by the relations with the object, with material existence. And the endless flux of interpretants is also controlled by what he called 'habits', culturally specific rules of thought and inference that correspond to what we have called logonomic systems. So, unlike Saussure, Peirce sees meaning as intrinsically a process, not a quality of signs or texts, and he sees a place for both the material determinations of meaning and general social cultural constraints on individual thought.

Even Saussure should not be seen as unequivocally opposed to a social basis for semiotics. In fact his work shows a deep division on precisely this topic, a contradiction that runs throughout his work. For instance he lists three aims that determine the scope of linguistics:

1   to describe and trace the history of all observable languages ...,
2   to determine the forces that are universally at work in all language, and to deduce the general laws to which all specific historical phenomena can be reduced, and
3   to delimit and define itself.

Aims (1) and (2) foreground the study of historical and social forces on language; aim (3) then attempts to cut linguistics off from semiotics, and from social and historical explanation. This set of aims does not show a hostility to this wider scope for the subject so much as a profound ambivalence towards that project. Saussure did not in fact dismiss what he called 'external linguistics': 'I believe that the study of external linguistic phenomena is most fruitful; but to say that we cannot understand the internal linguistic organism without studying external phenomena is wrong.'[9] This statement explicitly recognizes the value and importance of external linguistics, while making a plea for internal linguistics as well. Saussure has been invoked by later semioticians to justify a clear rejection of 'external linguistics' in the name of an abstract, autonomous internal linguistics. This is not entirely fair to him, although he was certainly not unambivalent about the issue.

How signs work

Saussure's confusion about the relations between semiosis and society affected some of his most influential pronouncements, even where that problem does not seem at issue. One example is his doctrine that the linguistic sign is *arbitrary*: by which he meant that (in verbal languages at least) there is no necessary or 'natural' connection between a signified and its signifier (e.g. the words 'horse', *equus* (Latin) and *hippos* (Greek) all refer to the same species of animal). There could therefore be no natural connection between the concept of 'horseness' and any of these words (and many others in other languages). Clearly this observation makes good sense, so far as it goes. However, Saussure's treatment of this topic attaches a surprising degree of importance to it. He declared it to be 'the first principle of language signs', no less.

This has proved a very influential and damaging overstatement. In practice, as some influential semioticians have argued, it is not absolutely and invariably true even of the sound of words. It certainly is not true of all signs in verbal language: Saussure himself recognized that syntactic patterns, for instance, are often what he called 'motivated', that is, connected in some rational, 'natural' way to their meaning. For example, the subject of a sentence in English comes first, which is a 'motivated' signifier of its importance. Outside verbal language, so many important classes of signs so obviously have some rationale (as Saussure himself recognized) that it becomes difficult to justify this doctrine as a universal doctrine in semiotics. Peirce had a more helpful classification of signs. He had three major types: *icon* (based on identity or likeness: e.g. road signs), *index* (based on contiguity or causality: e.g. smoke as a sign of fire) and *symbol* (a merely conventional link, as in Saussure's 'arbitrary' sign). The first two of these types are 'motivated' in Saussure's terms. Looking at the full range of sign types it seems incontrovertible that there is a continuum in signs, from more to less 'arbitrary' or 'motivated'. A dogmatic assertion that signs are all and equally 'arbitrary' is unjustifiable and unhelpful for general semiotics. Even Saussure's terms 'arbitrary' and 'motivated' have misleading implications. We will use instead the term 'transparent' to indicate a signifier whose connection with a signified can be seen easily by a user, whether producer or receiver, with the orientation always important. So the same sign could be transparent to a producer and not to a receiver, or vice versa. We will call the opposite quality 'opaque', again relative to specific agents.

But this alternative proposal does not explain why Saussure felt it necessary to insist on arbitrariness in the first place. Paradoxically, his motive was his sense of the overwhelming power of society in determining verbal semiotic systems. The logic of that position is as follows. Applying his habitually dichotomous ways of thinking to the relation between signifiers and signifieds, he saw two possibilities. Either there is a natural connection between signifiers and signifieds, based on their physical nature, or there is not. His interests, as we mentioned earlier, were largely confined to the study of sounds and of words. Scanning languages of the past and the present he saw such a variety of words corresponding to what he thought of as the same concept, and such continuous changes over time, that he felt forced to conclude that there was no natural bond to resist these social and historical forces. So the doctrine of the arbitrariness of the linguistic sign expresses, in a masked form and by negation, the principle of the social determination of the sign, in as strong a form as Voloshinov.

But the form of Saussure's version of this principle is not as helpful as Voloshinov's, and unsurprisingly has prevented the development of social semiotics in practice. This is because Saussure saw the social determination of language as not simply unlimited but also inherently incomprehensible. That is why he used the term 'arbitrary', as though the bonds between signifier and signified were subject to the whims of an inscrutably powerful collective being, Society. To call these signs 'conventional', as many including Saussure have done, is not much better, since it still attributes the source of determination to society without encouraging a study of how that determination works in practice. Voloshinov's work offers a clear framework for exploring the nature of the process of signification, by setting this process in a wider setting in which the action of social forces is powerful but by no means incomprehensible.

[···]

Semiotics and reality

Equally important, a practical semiotics should have some account of the relationship of semiosis and 'reality', that is, the material world that provides the objects of semiosis and semiotic activity. Unless semiotics confronts this relationship, it can have no relevance to the world of practical affairs with its confident assumptions about 'reality', and it cannot account for the role of semiotic systems in that world.

[···]

As long as the general relationship of semiosis and reality is avoided as too problematic, the study of strategies for relating specific acts of semiosis to reality also tends to be deferred or ignored. But for practical purposes, it is important to have ways of detecting different kinds of error, and different kinds of lie – or conversely, to develop ever more devious ways of lying or concealing ignorance of the truth. Saussure did not consider this class of problem. Peirce did give it some consideration. From logic he took the category of 'modality', that is, the kind of truth value attached to a proposition. There are three types of modality for Peirce: actuality, necessity, and possibility (i.e. actually true, logically necessary, and hypothetical). He considered tense as part of modality, something that linguists did not realize for over fifty years. His classi- fication of signs into icons, indices and symbols also had a modality- value built in. Icons, as picture-like signs which either are or resemble what they signify, have the modality of direct perception, and hence are the most persuasive of signs (as modern advertisers and news editors are aware). Indexical signs are formed from cause–effect chains (e.g. smoke–fire) or contiguity linkages (e.g. an arm for the person). These have a high modality (i.e. a close fit between sign and meaning), but since they are still based on an act of judgement or inference they have a lower modality than icons. Symbols, which relate sign to object by bonds of convention (like Saussure's linguistic sign) have the lowest modality, though Peirce also saw semiosis using symbols as the highest mode of thought, in an evolutionary schema.

Peirce's treatment of modality is fairly rudimentary. Three forms of modality, and three kinds of sign, are not adequate to account for the full range of strategies that are deployed in this area, and semioticians tend to overuse Peirce's terms for want of anything better. But at least Peirce has put this topic on the agenda for semiotic theory. And in so far as Eco is right to call semiotics a 'theory of the lie', it cannot afford to neglect this whole class of strategies for lying more effectively by posi- tioning readers and messages in different ways to normative accounts of reality. At the same time semiotics must also consider the means for controlling lies and their effects.

Notes and references

1   V.N. Voloshinov, *Marxism and the Philosophy of Language* (Seminar Press, New York, 1973).
2   L. Hjelmslev, *Prolegomena to a Theory of Language* (Indiana University Press, Bloomington, Ind., 1953).
3   Voloshinov, *Marxism*, p. 21.
4   Ibid., p. 9.
5   C.S. Peirce, *Collected Papers* (Belknap Press, Cambridge, Mass., 1940–65), vol. 6, p. 338.
6   Ibid., vol. 5, p. 488.
7   Ibid., vol. 5, p. 484.
8   Ibid., vol. 5, p. 473.
9   F. de Saussure, *Course in General Linguistics*, ed. J. Culler tr. W. Baskin (Fontana, London, 1974).

3

The Field of Cultural Production

Pierre Bourdieu

Few areas more clearly demonstrate the heuristic efficacy of *relational* thinking than that of art and literature. Constructing an object such as the literary field requires and enables us to make a radical break with the substantialist mode of thought (as Ernst Cassirer calls it) which tends to foreground the individual, or the visible interactions between individuals, at the expense of the structural relations – invisible, or visible only through their effects – between social positions that are both occupied and manipulated by social agents which may be isolated individuals, groups or institutions. There are in fact very few other areas in which the glorification of 'great individuals', unique creators irreducible to any condition or conditioning, is more common or uncontroversial – as one can see, for example, in the fact that most analysts uncritically accept the division of the corpus that is imposed on them by the names of authors ('the work of Racine') or the titles of works (*Phèdre* or *Bérénice*).

To take as one's subject of study the literary or artistic field of a given period and society (the field of Florentine painting in the quattrocento or the field of French literature in the Second Empire) is to set the history of art and literature a task which it never completely performs, because it fails to take it on explicitly, even when it does break out of the routine of monographs which, however interminable, are necessarily inadequate (since the essential explanation of each work lies outside each of them, in the objective relations which constitute this field). The task is that of constructing the space of positions and the space of the position-takings (*prises de position*) in which they are expressed. The science of the literary field is a form of *analysis situs* which establishes that each position – e.g. the one which corresponds to a genre such as the novel or, within this, to a sub-category such as the 'society novel' (*roman mondain*) or the 'popular' novel – is subjectively defined by the system of distinctive properties by which it can be situated relative to other positions; that every position, even the dominant one, depends for its very existence, and for the determinations it imposes on its occupants, on the other positions constituting the field; and that the structure of the field, i.e. of the space of positions, is nothing other than the structure of the distribution of the capital of specific properties which governs success in the field and the winning of the external or specific profits (such as literary prestige) which are at stake in the field.

The *space of literary or artistic position-takings*, i.e. the structured set of the manifestations of the social agents involved in the field – literary or artistic works, of course, but also political acts or pronouncements, manifestos or polemics, etc. – is inseparable from the *space of literary or artistic positions* defined by possession of a determinate quantity of specific capital (recognition) and, at the same time, by occupation of a determinate position in the structure of the distribution of this specific capital. The literary or artistic field is a *field of forces*, but it is also a *field of struggles* tending to transform or conserve this field of forces. The network of objective relations between positions subtends and orients the strategies which the occupants of the different positions implement in their struggles to defend or improve their positions (i.e. their position-takings), strategies which depend for their force and form on the position each agent occupies in the power relations (*rapports de force*).

Every position-taking is defined in relation to the *space of possibles* which is objectively realized as a *problematic* in the form of the actual or potential position-takings corresponding to the different positions; and it receives its distinctive *value* from its negative relationship with the coexistent position-takings to which it is objectively related and which determine it by delimiting it. It follows from this, for example, that a position-taking changes, even when the position remains identical, whenever there is change in the universe of options that are simultaneously offered for producers and consumers to choose from. The meaning of a work (artistic, literary, philosophical, etc.) changes automatically with each change in the field within which it is situated for the spectator or reader.

This effect is most immediate in the case of so-called classic works, which change constantly as the universe of coexistent works changes. This is seen clearly when the simple *repetition* of a work from the past in a radically transformed field of compossibles produces an entirely automatic *effect of parody* (in the theatre, for example, this effect requires the performers to signal a slight distance from a text impossible to defend as it stands; it can also arise in the presentation of a work corresponding to one extremity of the field before an audience corresponding structurally to the other extremity – e.g. when an avant-garde play is performed to a bourgeois audience, or the contrary, as more often happens). It is significant that breaks with the most orthodox works of the past, i.e. with the belief they impose on the newcomers, often take the form of *parody* (intentional, this time), which presupposes and confirms *emancipation*. In this case, the newcomers 'get beyond' ('*dépassent*') the dominant mode of thought and expression not by explicitly denouncing it but by repeating and reproducing it in a sociologically non-congruent context, which has the effect of rendering it incongruous or even absurd, simply by making it perceptible as the arbitrary convention it is. This form of heretical break is particularly favoured by ex-believers, who use pastiche or parody as the indispensable means of objectifying, and thereby appropriating, the form of thought and expression by which they were formerly possessed.

> This explains why writers' efforts to control the reception of their own works are always partially doomed to failure (one thinks of Marx's 'I am not a Marxist'); if only because the very effect of their work may transform the conditions of its reception and because they would not have had to write many things they did write and write them as they did – e.g. resorting to rhetorical strategies intended to 'twist the stick in the other direction' – if they had been granted from the outset what they are granted retrospectively.

One of the major difficulties of the social history of philosophy, art or literature is that it has to reconstruct these spaces of original possibles which, because they were part of the self-evident givens of the situation, remained unremarked and are therefore unlikely to be mentioned in contemporary accounts, chronicles or memoirs. It is difficult to conceive of the vast amount of information which is linked to membership of a field and which all contemporaries immediately invest in their reading of works: information about institutions – e.g. academies, journals, magazines, galleries, publishers, etc. – and about persons, their relationships, liaisons and quarrels, information about the ideas and problems which are 'in the air' and circulate orally in gossip and rumour. (Some intellectual occupations presuppose a particular mastery of this information.) Ignorance of everything which goes to make up the 'mood of the age' produces a derealization of works: stripped of everything which attached them to the most concrete debates of their time (I am thinking in particular of the connotations of words), they are impoverished and transformed in the direction of intellectualism or an empty humanism.

This is particularly true in the history of ideas, and especially of philosophy. Here the ordinary effects of derealization and intellectualization are intensified by the representation of philosophical activity as a summit conference between 'great philosophers'; in fact, what circulate between contemporary philosophers, or those of different epochs, are not only canonical texts, but a whole philosophical doxa carried along by intellectual rumour – labels of schools, truncated quotations, functioning as slogans in celebration or polemics – by academic routine and perhaps above all by school manuals (an unmentionable reference), which perhaps do more than anything else to constitute the 'common sense' of an intellectual generation. Reading, and *a fortiori* the reading of books, is only one means among others, even among professional readers, of acquiring the knowledge that is mobilized in reading.

It goes without saying that, in both cases, change in the space of literary or artistic possibles is the result of change in the power relation which constitutes the space of positions. When a new literary or artistic group makes its presence felt in the field of literary or artistic production, the whole problem is transformed, since its coming into being, i.e. into difference, modifies and displaces the universe of possible options; the previously dominant productions may, for example, be pushed into the status either of outmoded (*déclassé*) or of classic works.

This theory differs fundamentally from all 'systemic' analyses of works of art based on transposition of the phonological model, since it refuses to consider the field of position-takings in itself and for itself, i.e. independently of the field of positions which it manifests. This is understandable when it is seen that it applies relational thinking not only to symbolic systems, whether language (like Saussure) or myth (like Lévi-Strauss), or any set of symbolic objects, e.g. clothing, literary works, etc. (like all so-called 'structuralist' analyses), but also to the *social relations* of which these symbolic systems are a more or less transformed expression. Pursuing a logic that is entirely characteristic of symbolic structuralism, but realizing that no cultural product exists by itself, i.e. outside the relations of interdependence which link it to other products, Michel Foucault gives the name 'field of strategic possibilities' to the regulated system of differences and dispersions within which each individual work defines itself. But – and in this respect he is very close to semiologists such as Trier and the use they have made of the idea of the 'semantic field' – he refuses to look outside the 'field of discourse' for the principle which would cast light on each of the discourses within it: 'If the Physiocrats' analysis belongs to the same discourses as that of the Utilitarians, this is not because they lived in the same period, not because they confronted one another within the same society, not because their interests interlocked within the same economy, but because their two options sprang from one and the same distribution of the points of choice, one and the same strategic field.'[1] In short, Foucault shifts on to the plane of possible position-takings the strategies which are generated and implemented on the sociological plane of positions; he thus refuses to relate works in any way to their social conditions of production, i.e. to positions occupied within the field of cultural production. More precisely, he explicitly rejects as a 'doxological illusion' the endeavour to find in the 'field of polemics' and in 'divergences of interests and mental habits' between individuals the principle of what occurs in the 'field of strategic possibilities', which he sees as determined solely by the 'strategic possibilities of the conceptual games'.[2] Although there is no question of denying the specific determination exercised by the possibilities inscribed in a given state of the space of position-takings – since one of the functions of the notion of the relatively autonomous field with its own history is precisely to account for this – it is not possible, even in the case of the scientific field and the most advanced sciences, to make the cultural order (*épistème*) a sort of autonomous, transcendent sphere, capable of developing in accordance with its own laws.

The same criticism applies to the Russian formalists, even in the interpretation put forward by Itamar Even-Zohar in his theory of the 'literary polysystem', which seems closer to the reality of the texts, if not to the logic of things, than the interpretation which structuralist readings (especially by Todorov) have imposed in France.[3] Refusing to consider anything other than the system of works, i.e. the 'network of relationships between texts', or 'intertextuality', and the – very abstractly defined – relationships between this network and the other systems functioning in the 'system-of-systems' which constitutes the society (we are close to Talcott Parsons), these theoreticians of cultural semiology or culturology are forced to seek in the literary system itself the principle of its dynamics. When they make the process of 'banalization' and 'debanalization' the fundamental law of poetic change and, more generally, of all cultural change, arguing that a 'deautomatization' must necessarily result from the 'automatization' induced by repetitive use of the literary means of expression, they forget that the dialectic of orthodoxy which, in Weber's terms, favours a process of 'routinization', and of heresy, which 'deroutinizes', does not take place in the ethereal realm of ideas, and in the confrontation between 'canonized' and 'non-canonized' texts. More concretely, they forget that the existence, form and direction of change depend not only on the 'state of the system', i.e. the 'repertoire' of possibilities which it offers, but also on the balance of forces between social agents who have entirely real interests in the different possibilities available to them as stakes and who deploy every sort of strategy to make one set or the other prevail. When we speak of a *field* of position-takings, we are insisting that what can be constituted as a *system* for the sake of analysis is not the product of a coherence-seeking intention or an objective consensus (even if it presupposes unconscious agreement on common principles) but the product and prize of a permanent conflict; or, to put it another way, that the generative, unifying principle of this 'system' is the struggle, with all the contradictions it engenders (so that participation in the struggle – which may be indicated objectively by, for example, the attacks that are suffered – can be used as the criterion establishing that a work belongs to the field of position-takings and its author to the field of positions).

In defining the literary and artistic field as, inseparably, a field of positions and a field of position-takings we also escape from the usual dilemma of internal ('tautegorical') reading of the work (taken in isolation or within the system of works to which it belongs) and external (or 'allegorical') analysis, i.e. analysis of the social conditions of production of the producers and consumers which is based on the – generally tacit – hypothesis of the spontaneous correspondence or deliberate matching of production to demand or commissions. And by the same token we escape from the correlative dilemma of the charismatic image of artistic activity as pure, disinterested creation by an isolated artist, and the reductionist vision which claims to explain the act of production and its product in terms of their conscious or unconscious external functions, by referring them, for example, to the interests of the dominant class or, more subtly, to the ethical or aesthetic values of one or another of its fractions, from which the patrons or audiences are drawn.

Here one might usefully point to the contribution of Becker who, to his credit, constructs artistic production as a collective action, breaking with the naïve vision of the individual creator. For Becker, 'works of art can be understood by viewing them as the result of the co-ordinated activities of all the people whose co-operation is necessary in order that the work should occur as it does'.[4] Consequently the inquiry must extend to all those who contribute to this result, i.e. 'the people who conceive the idea of the work (e.g. composers or playwrights); people who execute it (musicians or actors); people who provide the necessary equipment and material (e.g. musical instrument makers); and people who make up the audience for the work (playgoers, critics, and so on)'.[5] Without elaborating all the differences between this vision of the 'art world' and the theory of the literary and artistic field, suffice it to point out that the artistic field is not reducible to a *population*, i.e. a sum of individual agents, linked by simple relations of *interaction* – although the agents and the *volume* of the *population* of producers must obviously be taken into account (e.g. an increase in the number of agents engaged in the field has specific effects).

But when we have to re-emphasize that the principle of position-takings lies in the structure and functioning of the field of positions, this is not done so as to return to any form of economism. There is a specific economy of the literary and artistic field, based on a particular form of belief. And the major difficulty lies in the need to make a radical break with this belief and with the deceptive certainties of the language of celebration, without thereby forgetting that they are part of the very reality we are seeking to understand, and that, as such, they must have a place in the model intended to explain it. Like the science of religion, the science of art and literature is threatened by two opposite errors, which, being complementary, are particularly likely to occur since, in reacting diametrically against one of them, one necessarily falls into the other. The work of art is an object which exists as such only by virtue of the (collective) belief which knows and acknowledges it as a work of art. Consequently, in order to escape from the usual choice between celebratory effusions and the reductive analysis which, failing to take account of the fact of belief in the work of art and of the social conditions which produce that belief, destroys the work of art as such, a rigorous science of art must, *pace* both the unbelievers and iconoclasts and also the believers, assert the possibility and necessity of understanding the work in its reality as a fetish; it has to take into account everything which helps to constitute the work as such, not least the discourses of direct or disguised celebration which are among the social conditions of production of the work of art *qua* object of belief.

> The production of discourse (critical, historical, etc.) about the work of art is one of the conditions of production of the work. Every critical affirmation contains, on the one hand, a recognition of the value of the work which occasions it, which is thus designated as a worthy object of legitimate discourse (a recognition sometimes extorted by the logic of the field, as when, for example, the polemic of the dominant confers participant status on the challengers), and on the other hand an affirmation of its own legitimacy. All critics declare not only their judgement of the work but also their claim to the right to talk about it and judge it. In short, they take part in a struggle for the monopoly of legitimate discourse about the work of art, and consequently in the production of the value of the work of art. (And one's only hope of producing scientific knowledge – rather than weapons to advance a particular class of specific interests – is to make explicit to oneself one's position in the sub-field of the producers of discourse about art and the contribution of this field to the very existence of the object of study.)

The science of the social representation of art and of the appropriate relation to works of art (in particular, through the social history of the process of autonomization of the intellectual and artistic field) is one of the prerequisites for the constitution of a rigorous science of art, because belief in the value of the work, which is one of the major obstacles to the constitution of a science of artistic production, is part of the full reality of the work of art. There is in fact every reason to suppose that the constitution of the aesthetic gaze as a 'pure' gaze, capable of considering the work of art in and for itself, i.e. as a 'finality without an end', is linked to the *institution* of the work of art as an object of contemplation, with the creation of private and then public galleries and museums, and the parallel development of a corps of professionals appointed to conserve the work of art, both materially and symbolically. Similarly, the representation of artistic production as a 'creation' devoid of any determination or any social function, though asserted from a very early date, achieves its fullest expression in the theories of 'art for art's sake'; and, correlatively, in the representation of the legitimate relation to the work of art as an act of 're-action' claiming to replicate the original creation and to focus solely on the work in and for itself, without any reference to anything outside it.

> The actual state of the science of works of art cannot be understood unless it is borne in mind that, whereas external analyses are always liable to appear crudely reductive, an internal reading, which establishes the charismatic, creator-to-creator relationship with the work that is demanded by the social norms of reception, is guaranteed social approval and reward. One of the effects of this charismatic conception of the relation to the work of art can be seen in the cult of the virtuoso which appeared in the late nineteenth century and which leads audiences to expect works to be performed and conducted from memory – which has the effect of limiting the repertoire and excluding avant-garde works, which are liable to be played only once.

The educational system plays a decisive role in the generalized imposition of the legitimate mode of consumption. One reason for this is that the ideology of 're-creation' and 'creative reading' supplies teachers – *lectores* assigned to commentary on the canonical texts – with a legitimate substitute for the ambition to act as *auctores*. This is seen most clearly in the case of philosophy, where the emergence of a body of professional teachers was accompanied by the development of a would-be autonomous science of the history of philosophy, and the propensity to read works in and for themselves (philosophy teachers thus tend to identify philosophy with the history of philosophy, i.e. with a pure *commentary* on past works, which are thus invested with a role exactly opposite to that of suppliers of problems and instruments of thought which they would fulfil for original thinking).

Given that works of art exist as symbolic objects only if they are known and recognized, that is, socially instituted as works of art and received by spectators capable of knowing and recognizing them as such, the sociology of art and literature has to take as its object not only the material production but also the symbolic production of the work, i.e. the production of the value of the work or, which amounts to the same thing, of belief in the value of the work. It therefore has to consider as contributing to production not only the direct producers of the work in its materiality (artist, writer, etc.) but also the producers of the meaning and value of the work – critics, publishers, gallery directors and the whole set of agents whose combined efforts produce consumers capable of knowing and recognizing the work of art as such, in particular teachers (but also families, etc.). So it has to take into account not only, as the social history of art usually does, the social conditions of the production of artists, art critics, dealers, patrons, etc., as revealed by indices such as social origin, education or qualifications, but also the social conditions of the production of a set of objects socially constituted as works of *art*, i.e. the conditions of production of the field of social agents (e.g. museums, galleries, academies, etc.) which help to define and produce the value of works of art. In short, it is a question of understanding works of art as a *manifestation* of the field as a whole, in which all the powers of the field, and all the determinisms inherent in its structure and functioning, are concentrated.

The literary and artistic field is contained within the field of power, while possessing a relative autonomy with respect to it, especially as regards its economic and political principles of hierarchization. It occupies a *dominated position* (at the negative pole) in this field, which is itself situated at the dominant pole of the field of class relations. It is thus the site of a double hierarchy. The *heteronomous* principle of hierarchization, which would reign unchallenged if, losing all autonomy, the literary and artistic field were to disappear as such (so that writers and artists became subject to the ordinary laws prevailing in the field of power, and more generally in the economic field), is *success*, as measured by indices such as book sales, number of theatrical performances, etc. or honours, appointments, etc. The *autonomous* principle of hierarchization, which would reign unchallenged if the field of production were to achieve total autonomy with respect to the laws of the market, is *degree specific consecration* (literary or artistic prestige), i.e. the degree of recognition accorded by those who recognize no other criterion of legitimacy than recognition by those whom they recognize. In other words, the specificity of the literary and artistic field is defined by the fact that the more autonomous it is, i.e. the more completely it fulfils its own logic as a field, the more it tends to suspend or reverse the dominant principle of hierarchization; but also that, whatever its degree of independence, it continues to be affected by the laws of the field which encompasses it, those of economic and political profit. The more autonomous the field becomes, the more favourable the symbolic power balance is to the most autonomous producers and the more clear-cut is the division between the field of restricted production, in which the producers produce for other producers, and the field of large-scale production (*la grande production*), which is *symbolically* excluded and discredited (this symbolically dominant definition is the one that the historians of art and literature *unconsciously* adopt when they exclude from their object of study writers and artists who produced for the market and have often fallen into oblivion). Because it is a good measure of the degree of autonomy, and therefore of presumed adherence to the disinterested values which constitute the specific law of the field, the degree of public success is no doubt the main differentiating factor. But lack of success is not in itself a sign and guarantee of election, and *poètes maudits*, like 'successful playwrights', must take account of a secondary differentiating factor whereby some *poètes maudits* may also be 'failed writers' (even if exclusive reference to the first criterion can help them to avoid realizing it), while some box-office successes may be recognized, at least in some sectors of the field, as genuine art.

Thus, at least in the most perfectly autonomous sector of the field of cultural production, where the only audience aimed at is other producers (as with Symbolist poetry), the economy of practices is based, as in a generalized game of 'loser wins', on a systematic inversion of the fundamental principles of all ordinary economies: that of business (it excludes the pursuit of profit and does not guarantee any sort of correspondence between investments and monetary gains), that of power (it condemns honours and temporal greatness), and even that of institutionalized cultural authority (the absence of any academic training or consecration may be considered a virtue).

One would have to analyse in these terms the relations between writers or artists and publishers or gallery directors. The latter are equivocal figures, through whom the logic of the economy is brought to the heart of the sub-field of production-for-fellow-producers; they need to possess, simultaneously, economic dispositions which, in some sectors of the field, are totally alien to the producers and also properties close to those of the producers whose work they valorize and exploit. The logic of the structural homologies between the field of publishers or gallery directors and the field of the corresponding artists or writers does indeed mean that the former present properties close to those of the latter, and this favours the relationship of trust and belief which is the basis of an exploitation presupposing a high degree of misrecognition on each side. These 'merchants in the temple' make their living by tricking the artist or writer into taking the consequences of his or her statutory professions of disinterestedness.

This explains the inability of all forms of economism, which seek to grasp this anti-economy in economic terms, to understand this upside-down economic world. The literary and artistic world is so ordered that those who enter it have an interest in disinterestedness. And indeed, like prophecy, especially the prophecy of misfortune, which, according to Weber, demonstrates its authenticity by the fact that it brings in no income, a heretical break with the prevailing artistic traditions proves its claim to authenticity by its disinterestedness. As we shall see, this does not mean that there is not an economic logic to this charismatic economy based on the social miracle of an act devoid of any determination other than the specifically aesthetic intention. There are economic conditions for the indifference to economy which induces a pursuit of the riskiest positions in the intellectual and artistic avant-garde, and also for the capacity to remain there over a long period without any economic compensation.

The literary or artistic field is at all times the site of a struggle between the two principles of hierarchization: the heteronomous principle, favourable to those who dominate the field economically and politically (e.g. 'bourgeois art'), and the autonomous principle (e.g. 'art for art's sake'), which those of its advocates who are least endowed with specific capital tend to identify with degree of independence from the economy, seeing temporal failure as a sign of election and success as a sign of compromise. The state of the power relations in this struggle depends on the overall degree of autonomy possessed by the field, that is, the extent to which it manages to impose its own norms and sanctions on the whole set of producers, including those who are closest to the dominant pole of the field of power and therefore most responsive to external demands (i.e. the most heteronomous); this degree of autonomy varies considerably from one period and one national tradition to another, and affects the whole structure of the field. Everything seems to indicate that it depends on the value which the specific capital of writers and artists represents for the dominant fractions, on the one hand in the struggle to conserve the established order and, perhaps especially, in the struggle between the fractions aspiring to domination within the field of power (bourgeoisie and aristocracy, old bourgeoisie and new bourgeoisie, etc.), and on the other hand in the production and reproduction of economic capital (with the aid of experts and cadres). All the evidence suggests that, at a given level of overall autonomy, intellectuals are, other things being equal, proportionately more responsive to the seduction of the powers that be, the less well endowed they are with specific capital.

The struggle in the field of cultural production over the imposition of the legitimate mode of cultural production is inseparable from the struggle within the dominant class (with the opposition between 'artists' and 'bourgeois') to impose the dominant principle of domination (that is to say – ultimately – the definition of human accomplishment). In this struggle, the artists and writers who are richest in specific capital and most concerned for their autonomy are considerably weakened by the fact that some of their competitors identify their interests with the dominant principles of hierarchization and seek to impose them even within the field, with the support of the temporal powers. The most heteronomous cultural producers (i.e. those with least symbolic capital) can offer the least resistance to external demands, of whatever sort. To defend their own position, they have to produce weapons, which the dominant agents (within the field of power) can immediately turn against the cultural producers most attached to their autonomy. In endeavouring to discredit every attempt to impose an autonomous principle of hierarchization, and thus serving their own interests, they serve the interests of the dominant fractions of the dominant class, who obviously have an interest in there being only one hierarchy. In the struggle to impose the legitimate definition of art and literature, the most autonomous producers naturally tend to exclude 'bourgeois' writers and artists, whom they see as 'enemy agents'. This means, incidentally, that sampling problems cannot be resolved by one of those arbitrary decisions of positivist ignorance which are dignified by the term 'operational definition': these amount to blindly arbitrating on debates which are inscribed in reality itself, such as the question as to whether such and such a group ('bourgeois' theatre, the 'popular' novel, etc.) or such and such an individual claiming the title of writer or artist (or philosopher, or intellectual, etc.) belongs to the population of writers or artists or, more precisely, as to who is legitimately entitled to designate legitimate writers or artists.

The preliminary reflections on the definitions of the object and the boundaries of the population, which studies of writers, artists and, especially, intellectuals often indulge in so as to give themselves an air of scientificity, ignore the fact, which is more than scientifically attested, that the definition of the writer (or artist, etc.) is an issue at stake in struggles in every literary (or artistic, etc.) field. In other words, the field of cultural production is the site of struggles in which what is at stake is the power to impose the dominant definition of the writer and therefore to delimit the population of those entitled to take part in the struggle to define the writer. The established definition of the writer may be radically transformed by an enlargement of the set of people who have a legitimate voice in literary matters. It follows from this that every survey aimed at establishing the hierarchy of writers predetermines the hierarchy by determining the population deemed worthy of helping to establish it. In short, the fundamental stake in literary struggles is the monopoly of literary legitimacy, i.e. *inter alia* the monopoly of the power to say with authority who are authorized to call themselves writers; or, to put it another way, it is the monopoly of the power to consecrate producers or products (we are dealing with a world of belief and the consecrated writer is the one who has the power to consecrate and to win assent when he or she consecrates an author or a work – with a preface, a favourable review, a prize, etc.).

While it is true that every literary field is the site of a struggle over the definition of the writer (a universal proposition), the fact remains that scientific analysts, if they are not to make the mistake of universalizing the particular case, need to know that they will only ever encounter historical definitions of the writer, corresponding to a particular state of the struggle to impose the legitimate definition of the writer. There is no other criterion of membership of a field than the objective fact of producing effects within it. One of the difficulties of orthodox defence against heretical transformation of the field by a re-definition of the tacit or explicit terms of entry is the fact that polemics imply a form of recognition; adversaries whom one would prefer to destroy by ignoring them cannot be combated without consecrating them. The '*Théâtre libre*' effectively entered the sub-field of drama once it came under attack from the accredited advocates of bourgeois theatre, who thus helped to produce the recognition they sought to prevent. The '*nouveaux philosophes*' came into existence as active elements in the philosophical field – and no longer just that of journalism – as soon as consecrated philosophers felt called upon to take issue with them.

The *boundary* of the field is a stake of struggles, and the social scientist's task is not to draw a dividing line between the agents involved in it by imposing a so-called operational definition, which is most likely to be imposed on him by his own prejudices or presuppositions, but to describe a *state* (long-lasting or temporary) of these struggles and therefore of the frontier delimiting the territory held by the competing agents. One could thus examine the characteristics of this boundary, which may or may not be institutionalized, that is to say, protected by conditions of entry that are tacitly and practically required (such as a certain cultural capital) or explicitly codified and legally guaranteed (e.g. all the forms of entrance examination aimed at ensuring a *numerus clausus*). It would be found that one of the most significant properties of the field of cultural production, explaining its extreme dispersion and the conflicts between rival principles of legitimacy, is the extreme permeability of its frontiers and, consequently, the extreme diversity of the 'posts' it offers, which defy any unilinear hierarchization. It is clear from comparison that the field of cultural production demands neither as much inherited economic capital as the economic field nor as much educational capital as the university sub-field or even sectors of the field of power such as the top civil service – or even the field of the 'liberal professions'. However, precisely because it represents one of the *indeterminate sites* in the social structure, which offer ill-defined posts, waiting to be made rather than ready made, and therefore extremely elastic and undemanding, and career paths which are themselves full of uncertainty and extremely dispersed (unlike bureaucratic careers, such as those offered by the university system), it attracts agents who differ greatly in their properties and dispositions but the most favoured of whom are sufficiently secure to be able to disdain a university career and to take on the risks of an occupation which is not a 'job' (since it is almost always combined with a private income or a 'bread-and-butter' occupation).

The 'profession' of writer or artist is one of the least professionalized there is, despite all the efforts of 'writers' associations', 'Pen Clubs', etc. This is shown clearly by (*inter alia*) the problems which arise in classifying these agents, who are able to exercise what they regard as their main occupation only on condition that they have a secondary occupation which provides their main income (problems very similar to those encountered in classifying students).

The most disputed frontier of all is the one which separates the field of cultural production and the field of power. It may be more or less clearly marked in different periods, positions occupied in each field may be more or less totally incompatible, moves from one universe to the other more or less frequent and the overall distance between the corresponding populations more or less great (e.g. in terms of social origin, educational background, etc.).

The field of cultural production produces its most important effects through the play of the *homologies* between the fundamental opposition which gives the field its structure and the oppositions structuring the field of power and the field of class relations. These homologies may give rise to ideological effects which are produced automatically whenever oppositions at different levels are superimposed or merged. They are also the basis of partial alliances: the struggles within the field of power are never entirely independent of the struggle between the dominated classes and the dominant class, and the logic of the homologies between the two spaces means that the struggles going on within the inner field are always overdetermined and always tend to aim at two birds with one stone. The cultural producers, who occupy the economically dominated and symbolically dominant position within the field of cultural production, tend to feel solidarity with the occupants of the economically and culturally dominated positions within the field of class relations. Such alliances, based on homologies of position combined with profound differences in condition, are not exempt from misunderstandings and even bad faith. The structural affinity between the literary avant-garde and the political vanguard is the basis of rapprochements, between intellectual anarchism and the Symbolist movement for example, in which convergences are flaunted (e.g. Mallarmé referring to a book as an '*attentat*' – an act of terrorist violence) but distances prudently maintained. The fact remains that the cultural producers are able to use the power conferred on them, especially in periods of crisis, by their capacity to put forward a critical definition of the social world, to mobilize the potential strength of the dominated classes and subvert the order prevailing in the field of power.

> The effects of homology are not all and always automatically granted. Thus whereas the dominant fractions, in their relationship with the dominated fractions, are on the side of nature, common sense, practice, instinct, the upright and the male, and also order, reason, etc., they can no longer bring certain aspects of this representation into play in their relationship with the dominated classes, to whom they are opposed as culture to nature, reason to instinct. They need to draw on what they are offered by the dominated fractions, in order to justify their class domination, to themselves as well. The cult of art and the artist (rather than of the intellectual) is one of the necessary components of the bourgeois 'art of living', to which it brings a '*supplément d'âme*', its spiritualistic point of honour.

Even in the case of the seemingly most heteronomous forms of cultural production, such as journalism, adjustment to demand is not the product of a conscious arrangement between producers and consumers.

It results from the correspondence between the space of the producers, and therefore of the products offered, and the space of the consumers, which is brought about, on the basis of the homology between the two spaces, only through the competition between the producers and through the strategies imposed by the correspondence between the space of possible position-takings and the space of positions. In other words, by obeying the logic of the objective competition between mutually exclusive positions within the field, the various categories of producers tend to supply products adjusted to the expectations of the various positions in the field of power, but without any conscious striving for such adjustment.

If the various positions in the field of cultural production can be so easily characterized in terms of the audience which corresponds to them, this is because the encounter between a work and its audience (which may be an absence of immediate audience) is, strictly speaking, a *coincidence* which is not explained either by conscious, even cynical adjustment (though there are exceptions) or by the constraints of commission and demand. Rather, it results from the homology between positions occupied in the space of production, with the correlative position-takings, and positions in the space of consumption; that is, in this case, in the field of power, with the opposition between the dominant and the dominated fractions, or in the field of class relations, with the opposition between the dominant and the dominated classes. In the case of the relation between the field of cultural production and the field of power, we are dealing with an almost perfect homology between two chiastic structures. Just as, in the dominant class, economic capital increases as one moves from the dominated to the dominant fractions, whereas cultural capital varies in the opposite way, so too in the field of cultural production economic profits increase as one moves from the 'autonomous' pole to the 'heteronomous' pole, whereas specific profits increase in the opposite direction. Similarly, the secondary opposition which divides the most heteronomous sector into 'bourgeois art' and 'industrial art' clearly corresponds to the opposition between the dominant and the dominated classes.

Notes and references

1   M. Foucault, 'Réponse au cercle d'épistémologie', *Cahiers pour l'analyse*, 9 (1968), p. 29.
2   Ibid., p. 37.
3   I. Even-Zohar, 'Polysystem theory', Poetics Today, 1 (93) (1979), pp. 65–74.
4   H. S. Becker, 'Art worlds and social types', *American Behavioral Scientist*, 19 (6) (1976), p. 703.
5   Ibid., pp. 703–4.

4

Critique of Commodity Aesthetics

W.F. Haug

The production and great importance of mere illusion are rooted in capitalist society in the fundamental contradiction which permeates it at all levels. Capitalism is based on a systematic *quid pro quo*: all human goals, even life itself, matter only as means and pretexts (not just in theory but in economic fact) in the functioning of the system. The standpoint of capital valorization as an end in itself, to which all human endeavours, longings, instincts and hopes are just exploitable means (and motivations which people can relate to and on whose research and usage a whole branch of the social sciences is working), this valorization standpoint which dominates absolutely in capitalist society, is diametrically opposed to what people are and want autonomously. Taken in the abstract, the mediation between people and capital can thus be but an illusion: of necessity, capitalism is rooted in this illusory world. In other words, the generality of human goals under capitalism, so long as they are content to remain under its control, can never be more than a bad illusion which, nevertheless, attains a high status in such a society.

The valorization standpoint of capital pursues its claim to absolute domination in an ambivalent relationship to the sensuality of the human being. In so far as this being puts up resistance to the domination of capital, human independence is destroyed by it; and in so far as the domination of capital is mediated by moments of sensual and instinctual life, these elements are persistently made to seem dependent and incongruous. The individuals whom capital conditions to be either its functionaries, capitalists themselves, or its wage labourers, share, at least formally, a common instinctual fate in spite of their radical differences: their sensual immediacy must be disrupted and rendered absolutely controllable. Unless people are driven to work for others by brute force, this is only possible if one natural urge is directed against another; for example, the illusion of a controlled sensuality is employed as a reward for conforming. For it is not only the great goals of humanity which become lost in the reality of capitalism, and therefore have to be re-captured through the medium of illusion, but this applies also to the individual's instinctual aims.

Now we need to investigate more deeply the structure, effect, and dynamics of the capitalistic use of illusion. The abstraction of use-value, as a consequence of and precondition for the establishment of exchange-value and its standpoint, paves the way for corresponding abstractions, which will make them both theoretically and above all practically valorizable. The functional vacuum, that is to say the demand of the system, is there even before the capabilities needed to fill it exist.

One of these abstractions is fundamental to the natural sciences, i.e. the abstraction of use-values into qualities, for example, detaching the mere spatial extension of objects so that they become just that – mere *res extensae* – reduced at the same time to comparable quantity rela-tions. It seems logical that Descartes, the pioneer of this abstract theoretical thought, should introduce aesthetic abstraction into the technique of de-realizing the sensual reality of the world. He makes the assumption that there is an almighty god of manipulation who, by means of some omnipresent television programme for the gullible, deceives the whole sensual world. Here, all shapes, colours, sounds, and 'all exter-nals', are only a delusion. 'Myself,' he writes, 'I will regard as someone with neither hands nor eyes, neither flesh nor blood, nor any senses,'[1] but merely as a consciousness deceived by a technique in every way superior to humankind.

Descartes also gives more prosaic examples which amount to the same thing. First, a figure of given shape and colour, when held close to the heat, begins to melt, changes form and hue, and proves to be wax or some such plastic material which can be moulded into all kinds of sensual forms. Second, someone in the street walks past the window and for all we know it could easily be an automaton disguised in human clothes.

All these examples and assumptions are intended to introduce the doctrine, henceforth termed a science, that in the first place only one thing is certain: that the processes of consciousness themselves do exist, but that their content can be falsified. Thus people are reduced to these falsifiable processes of consciousness. But what of inanimate objects? They are reduced to something 'extended in space, but flexible, and mutable' (*Extensum, quid flexibile, mutabile*).

This is not the moment to develop the involuntary dialectic in this kind of early bourgeois theory, which begins with the aim of emancipating the individual from deception (especially pre-bourgeois deception), and ends with mere domination on one side and deception on the other. Instead, it is crucial to consider, within the mediating context of economic and technological developments, that process we called the 'aesthetic abstraction'.

The contradiction of interests between buyer and seller, use-value and exchange-value (or valorization), which ultimately dominates the unleashed commodity–cash nexus, exposes the object of use, which was made and acts as a carrier of value, to a field of antagonistic forces: in this dissection, to which the commodity is subjected under the calculated control of the valorization standpoint, the commodity's surface appearance and its meaning detach themselves and form a hybrid which performs a highly specific function. This hybrid is the expression, and carries out the function, of a social relationship as it appears in the relationship of the character-masks worn by buyer and seller. This antagonistic relationship constitutes the function: the economic function in turn leads to the emergence of the techniques and phenomena which become their carrier. In concrete terms this process can be imagined as a situation where everything functional contributes to phenomenal economic successes, which, once established and consciously repeated, go on to cripple economically anything which does not further this development. The function leading to the aesthetic abstraction of the commodity is realization, which, through the aesthetic promise of use-value, creates the means that trigger the sale.

The aesthetic abstraction of the commodity detaches both sensuality and meaning from the object acting as a carrier of exchange-value and makes the two separately available. At first the functionally already separate form and surface, which already have their own manufacturing processes, remain with the commodity to develop as naturally as skin covers a body. Yet functional differentiation is preparing the actual process of replacement, and the beautifully designed surface of the commodity becomes its package: not the simple wrapping for protection during transportation, but its real countenance, which the potential buyer is shown first instead of the body of the commodity and through which the commodity develops and changes its countenance, like the fairytale princess who is transformed through her feathered costume in which she seeks her fortune in the marketplace. As an example of this, a US bank, in order to facilitate the exchange of money, recently changed even the design of its cheques to make use of new psychedelic colours.

But to return to the commodity: now that its surface has been detached and become its second skin, which as a rule is incomparably more perfect than the first, it becomes completely disembodied and drifts unencumbered like a multicoloured spirit of the commodity into every household, preparing the way for the real distribution of the commodity. No one is safe any longer from its amorous glances, which the realization motive casts at the consumers with the detached yet technically perfect appearance of a highly promising use-value. For the time being at least, the customers' wallets still hold the equivalent of this disguised exchange-value.

[· · ·]

The people, as in monopoly capitalist society, are faced with a commodity world of attractive and seductive illusion and here, despite the outrageous deception, something very strange occurs, the dynamics of which are greatly underestimated. An innumerable series of images are forced upon the individual, like mirrors, seemingly empathetic and totally credible, which bring their secrets to the surface and display them there. In these images, people are continually shown the unfulfilled aspects of their existence. The illusion ingratiates itself, promising satisfaction: it reads desires in one's eyes, and brings them to the surface of the commodity. While the illusion with which commodities present themselves to the gaze gives the people a sense of meaningfulness, it provides them with a language to interpret their existence and the world. Any other world, different from that provided by the commodities, is almost no longer accessible to them.

How can people behave, or change themselves, when continually presented with a collection of dream-images that have been taken from them? How can people change when they continue to get what they want, but only in the form of illusion? Commodity aesthetics' ideal would be to invent something which enters one's consciousness unlike anything else; something which is talked about, which catches the eye and which cannot be forgotten; something which everyone wants and has always wanted. Encountering little resistance, the consumer is being served, be it by way of the latest, and the most sensational, or the most modest, the most comfortable of things. Thus both greed and laziness are cultivated with equal care.

Commodity aesthetics, by determining the direction an individual's being takes, seems to warp the progressive tendency in human instincts, their desire for satisfaction, enjoyment and happiness. Human motivation appears to have been shackled to a drive towards conformism. Many critical observers of contemporary culture see this as an all-embracing corruption of the entire species. Gehlen speaks of its degeneration as it adjusts to 'all-too-convenient living conditions'. Indeed, there is a deceitfulness in the servile flattery of commodities; their dominant tendency is the desire to serve in this way. Those served by capitalism are, in the end, unconsciously its servants – not merely pampered, distracted, fed and bribed by it.

[⋯]

Do instincts and needs still have any progressive value under these conditions? Does any essential trace of people's material needs still remain? That which has occasionally been called repressive satisfaction now appears as corrupting use-value. In particular this dominates the area of illusion which concerns commodities. The corrupting use-value feeds back to the needs-structure of the consumers, whom it brings down to a corrupt standpoint of use-value. These corrupting influences, although only a side-effect of the dynamics of capitalist profit, are catastrophic to an almost anthropological extent. People seem to have had their consciousnesses bought off. They are conditioned daily to enjoy that which betrays them, to celebrate their own defeat, in the enjoyment of identifying with their superiors. Even the genuine use-values they receive carry within them a tremendous power of destruction. The private car, together with the running-down of public transport, carves up the towns no less effectively than saturation bombing, and creates distances that can no longer be crossed without a car.

It would be pointless and premature to describe this process in terms of a systematic theory for corrupting the masses. For the ideal of commodity aesthetics is to deliver the absolute minimum of use-value, disguised and staged by a maximum of seductive illusion, a highly effective strategy because it is attuned to the yearnings, and desires, of the people. But despite commodity aesthetics' ideal, real use-value (whose effects require separate investigation) does not disappear. This contradiction is contained in commodity aesthetics as such. The agents of capital cannot do what they like with it, but rather they are dependent on the condition that they create, or appear to create, what the consumers want.

The dialectic of master and slave within the flirtation of commodity aesthetics remains ambiguous: certainly, capital dominates in the sphere where commodity aesthetics plays a role in affecting public consciousness and behaviour, and finally, worms its way in via the exchange-value

in their pockets; thus a seemingly servile power becomes in effect dominant. Of course those who are supposedly served are being subjugated.
But the fact that the dominance through a corrupting and illusory service creates its own dynamic can be illustrated by examining the consequences caused by using sexual illusion as a commodity in its own right,
as well as the sexualization of many other commodities.

The ambiguity of commodity aesthetics is shown by its use of the sex-
ually stimulating illusion. As we have already seen, it is a means of solving
certain problems in valorization and capital realization. At the same
time it is only an illusory solution to the contradiction of use-value and
exchange-value.

Sex as a commodity appears at historically different, and very dispar-
ate, stages of development. Prostitution remains on the level of simple
commodity production or rather a service industry, with the pimp as
capitalist agent and the brothel as factory. What all these forms of
sexual commodification have in common is that their use-value is still
realized in direct sensual or physical contact. Sexuality is only valorizable
at an industrial capitalist level in the form of aesthetic abstraction – if
one overlooks certain necessary props. The mere picture or sound, or
a combination of both, can be recorded and reproduced on a mass
basis, on a technically unlimited scale, which is restricted in practice
only by the market.

In a situation of general sexual repression, or at least of isolation, the
use-value of mere sexual illusion lies in the satisfaction which voyeurism can provide. This satisfaction through a use-value, whose specific
nature is as an illusion, can be called illusory satisfaction. The characteristics of this satisfaction through sexual illusion is that it simultaneously reproduces further demand alongside satisfaction, and produces a
compulsive fixation. If guilt feelings and the *angst* they arouse block the
way to the sexual object, then the commodity of sexual illusion acts as
its replacement, mediating excitement and a certain satisfaction which
might be difficult to develop in actual sensual and physical contact. This
type of seemingly unhindered satisfaction threatens to cut off completely
the possibility of direct pleasure. Here the form of use-value as specifically employed for large-scale valorization feeds back on to the structure of needs. Thus a general voyeurism is reinforced, habituated, and
determines the human instinctual structure.

The suppression of instincts plus the simultaneous illusory satisfaction of instincts tend towards a general sexualization of the human
condition, called by Max Scheler *Gehirnsinnlichkeit* or 'sensuality on the
brain'. The response of the commodities is to reflect sexual images from

all sides. Here it is not the sexual object which takes on the commodity form, but the tendency of all objects of use in commodity form to assume a sexual form to some extent. That is, the sensual need and the means by which it is satisfied are rendered non-specific. In a certain way, they come to resemble money, which Freud compared with anxiety in this respect: triggered by almost anything, they become freely convertible into stimulation from any source. Thus by taking on sexuality as an assistant, exchange-value transforms itself into sexuality. All manner of goods are enveloped by its surface, and this background of sexual enjoyment becomes the commodity's most popular attire, or perhaps the gilded backdrop against which the commodity appears. The general sexualization of commodities has also included people. It provides an outlet for expressing previously suppressed sexual urges. Adolescents, most of all, make use of this possibility, and their demand generates a further supply. With the help of new fashions it is possible to advertise oneself as, above all, a sexual being.

Inherent in all this lies a remarkable return to our socio-historical point of departure. Just as the commodities once borrowed their seductive language from people, so now they return in a language of clothes conveying sexual feelings. And, even though the capital in the textile industry makes a profit from this, the power of the tentatively developing sexual liberation will not be restricted unconditionally again.

So long as the economically determined function of commodity aesthetics exists, and continues to be driven by the profit motive, it will retain its ambiguous tendency: by serving people, in order to ensure *their* service, it brings an unending stream of desires into the open. Seen merely as commodity aesthetics, it can offer only an illusory satisfaction, which does not feed but causes hunger. And as a false solution to the contradiction, commodity aesthetics reproduces the contradiction in another form, which is perhaps even more far-reaching.

Note

1 Descartes, 'Meditatio Prima', in *Meditationes De Prima Philosophia* (Amsterdam, 1642), pp. 13f.

5

Critical Theory and the Consumer Society

Douglas Kellner

Adorno's early studies of music showed how the production and consumption of popular music followed the logic of commodity production. In a 1938 article entitled 'On the fetish character of music and the regression of listening', he throws a characteristic swipe at consumer culture in the midst of his critical reflections on popular music:

> The couple out driving who spend their time identifying every passing car and being happy if they recognize the trademarks speeding by, the girl whose satisfaction consists solely in the fact that she and her boyfriend 'look good,' the expertise of the jazz enthusiast who legitimizes himself by having knowledge about what is in any case inescapable: all this operates according to the same command. Before the theological caprices of commodities, the consumers become temple slaves. Those who sacrifice themselves nowhere else can do so here, and here they are fully betrayed.[1]

After his arrival in the United States in 1938, Adorno observed the extent to which commodity production pervaded culture and how the new culture of consumption was colonizing everyday life, while producing a consumer society. One of Adorno's 1940s essays analyzed the diagnosis of an early critic of the culture of consumption, Thorstein Veblen. He begins: 'Veblen's *Theory of the Leisure Class* became famous for its doctrine of conspicuous consumption, according to which the consumption of goods, from the very early "predatory" stage of history to the present, has served not so much to satisfy men's true needs or to provide what Veblen chooses to call the "fullness of life" as to maintain social prestige – status.'[2] Adorno sets out Veblen's theory of history, his sources and his method, and finds salutary elements of a critique of the consumer society. For Adorno, 'Veblen's basic experience may be characterized as that of pseudo-uniqueness' (p. 78).[3] In an era of mass production and consumption, standardization reigns, and individuation (of goods and individual thought and behavior) declines. Pseudo-individuality emerges, to compensate for the actual decline of individuality, and takes the forms of kitsch for the middle classes and conspicuous consumption for the upper classes. Veblen sees both the pathetic attempts of the middle classes to emulate upper-class ostentation with kitsch reproductions, ornaments and artifacts and the waste and excess involved in conspicuous consumption as fundamentally irrational signs of modern 'barbarism'. Veblen championed a rational technocratic organization of society in opposition to a society organized around conspicuous consumption, while presenting cultivation of 'the work instinct' as an alternative to the emerging world of consumer capitalism. Competition, lust for acquisition and conspicuous consumption are attacked by Veblen as remnants of a primitive, 'predatory spirit', and he criticizes 'pecuniary capital' as a wasteful, irrational economic form.

Adorno sharply criticizes Veblen's idolization of production and his failure to see that the mode of consumption which he criticizes is integrally part of the mode of production and that the industrial capital whose 'instincts' Veblen praises is interconnected with 'pecuniary capital' and conspicuous consumption, as part of the same capitalist system. Yet Adorno appreciates many insights in Veblen's work concerning the structure and façade of the emerging consumer society. For example, he is impressed by Veblen's analysis of how the ostentation and ornamentation of contemporary architecture express a predatory capitalist (and in some cases imperialist) spirit, and applauds Veblen's characterization of sports in terms of a predatory regression to barbarism. Adding some thoughts of his own to Veblen's critique of sports, Adorno concludes: 'Modern sports, one will perhaps say, seek to restore to the body some of the functions of which the machine has deprived it. But they do so only in order to train men all the more inexorably to serve the machine. Hence sports belong to the realm of unfreedom, no matter where they are organized' (p. 81).[4]

Adorno also appreciates Veblen's concern with the 'woman question' and his analyses of the ways in which women are oppressed by a society which enslaves them so that they can serve and become ostentatious elements of display to enhance their husbands' status and prestige. Adorno believes that there is a rudimentary 'dialectic of women' in Veblen's analysis, which presents women both as relatively independent of the economic system, and thus free from the 'predatory spirit', and as potentially conservative by virtue of exclusion from the production process and the public sphere. Reflecting on this situation, Adorno writes:

Following this line of thought, one might reach the conclusion that women have escaped the sphere of production only to be absorbed all the more entirely by the sphere of consumption, to be captivated by the immediacy of the commodity world no less than men are transfixed by the immediacy of profit. Women mirror the injustice masculine society has inflicted on them – they become increasingly like commodities. Veblen's insight indicates a change in the utopia of emancipation. Hope cannot aim at making the mutilated social character of women identical to the mutilated social character of men; rather, its goal must be a state in which the face of the grieving woman disappears simultaneously with that of the bustling, capable man, a state in which all that survives the disgrace of the difference between the sexes is the happiness that difference makes possible.[5]

Adorno especially objects to Veblen's image of the good life, which 'is based not on the ideal of happiness but on that of work. Happiness enters his field of vision only as the fulfillment of the 'work instinct', his supreme anthropological category. He is a puritan *malgré lui-même*. While he never tires of attacking taboos, his criticism stops at the sacredness of work.'[6] Adorno defends the values of leisure, happiness and freedom from utility, whereas Veblen criticizes the waste, luxury and irrationality of the leisure class, while celebrating the values of work, utility and industry. These values, Adorno points out, are fundamental values of the capitalist economic system itself. Thus, while Veblen powerfully denounces the 'residues' and 'culture' of capitalism, he fails to provide adequate critical perspectives on capitalism itself. Against Veblen's undialectical and splenetic denunciation of the epiphenomena of conspicuous consumption, Adorno concludes: 'The only adequate response to the present technical situation, which holds out the promise of wealth and abundance to men, is to organize it according to the needs of a humanity which no longer needs violence because it is its own master. . . . Today, adjustment to what is possible no longer means adjustment; it means making the possible real.'[7]

Adorno assumed here a distinction central to Critical Theory between the possible and the actual, between the possibility of meeting needs and fulfilling potentialities with existing social wealth, contrasted with the actual suffering and inequality in current society. The problem was that existing wealth was utilized in the interests of maintaining the current organization of society and class domination, rather than in fulfilling human needs. In an article on Aldous Huxley's *Brave New World*, Adorno intensified his own critique of the consumer society. For Adorno, Huxley's dystopia depicts the ways in which standardization and homogenization massify and destroy individual thought and action. In Huxley's sketch of a society constituted by mass reproduction, massive social conditioning and controlled consumption and sexuality:

> 'Community, Identity, and Stability' replaces the motto of the French Revolution. Community defines a collectivity in which each individual is unconditionally subordinated to the functioning of the whole (the question of the point of this whole is no longer permitted or even possible in the New World). Identity means the elimination of individual differences, standardization even down to biological constitution; stability, the end of all social dynamics.[8]

Huxley attacks the eradication of culture, tradition, individuality and spirituality from a society which worships only production and consumption. Adorno's analysis and critique of Huxley provide some revealing insights into his own complex views of the consumer society. On one hand, the consumer society comes to control even thought and communication:

> The degeneration of talk is due to objective tendencies. The virtual transformation of the world into commodities, the predetermination by the machinery of society of everything that is thought or done, renders speaking illusory. . . . The ladies of *Brave New World* – and in this case extrapolation is hardly required – converse only as consumers. In principle, their conversation concerns nothing but what is in any case to be found in the catalogues of the ubiquitous industries, information about available commodities. Objectively superfluous, it is the empty shell of dialogue, the intention of which was once to find out what was hitherto unknown. Stripped of this idea, dialogue is ripe for extinction.[9]

In a subtle critique of Huxley's harsh condemnation of the hedonism of *Brave New World*, Adorno suggests that Huxley fails to perceive that the sexual libertarianism and gratification of individual impulses with which individuals are integrated into Huxley's dystopia contain a utopian potentiality of genuine gratification of individual needs. Adorno fears that Huxley's negative portrayal of admittedly socially administered happiness contains a puritan condemnation of happiness as such. Crucially, 'His anger at false happiness sacrifices the idea of true happiness as well.'[10] Adorno also objects to Huxley's implicit celebration of ideal values – spiritual transcendence in this case – over material ones. Against such ascetic condemnation of the consumer society, Adorno maintains an uncompromising defense of the importance of satisfying material needs. Quoting a passage by Horkheimer, Adorno concludes:

We criticize mass culture not because it gives men too much or makes their life too secure – that we may leave to Lutheran theology – but rather because it contributes to a condition in which men get too little and what they get is bad, a condition in which whole strata inside and out live in frightful poverty, in which men come to terms with injustice, in which the world is kept in a condition where one must expect on the one hand gigantic catastrophes and on the other clever elites conspiring to bring about a dubious peace.[11]

Adorno thus defends the value of happiness against ascetic attacks, but insists that true happiness can be envisaged only in a new social order. In his essay on Huxley, Adorno provides one of only a few glimpses into how he envisages human life might be when 'existing property relations' and 'the market and competition' – that is, capitalism – are abolished:

When this static situation comes to an end needs will look completely different. If production is redirected towards the unconditional and un-limited satisfaction of needs, including precisely those produced by the hitherto prevailing system, needs themselves will be decisively altered. The indistinguishability of true and false needs is an essential part of the present phase. . . . One day it will be readily apparent that men do not need the trash provided them by the culture industry or the miserable high-quality goods proffered by the more substantial industries. The thought, for instance, that in addition to food and lodging the cinema is necessary for the reproduction of labour power is 'true' only in a world which prepares men for the reproduction of their labour power and con-strains their needs in harmony with the interests of supply and social control.[12]

In this passage Adorno combines critique of the culture industries with critique of consumption in his attack on the consumer society. He envisages a condition which would at once satisfy individual needs and provide true happiness. Such a social order would require an economy (socialism) oriented toward the satisfaction of the material needs of all its members and aimed at the abolition of scarcity, poverty and human suffering. If material needs could be satisfied, Adorno imagines a condition in which the antithesis between production and consumption would be overcome and individuals could attain happiness in all dimen-sions of their lives. Such a society would also transcend the obsession with material goods and imperatives toward productivity and utility that define the capitalist social order (that is, that productivity is an end in itself, and that only goods and activities that have a market value and utility are valuable *per se*).

In *Dialectic of Enlightenment*, written during the same period as the essays on Veblen and Huxley, Horkheimer and Adorno focus their critique of contemporary society on mass culture. In a key passage they indicate how technological and material forces of progress can be used to foster domination and regression:

> The fallen nature of modern man cannot be separated from social progress. On the one hand the growth of economic productivity furnishes the conditions for a world of greater justice; on the other hand it allows the technical apparatus and the social groups which administer it a dispro- portionate superiority to the rest of the population. The individual is wholly devaluated in relation to the economic powers, which at the same time press the control of society over nature to hitherto unsuspected heights. Even though the individual disappears before the apparatus which he serves, that apparatus provides for him as never before. In an unjust state of life, the impotence and pliability of the masses grow with the quantitative increase in commodities allowed them.[13]

Horkheimer and Adorno point to similarities between industrial and cultural production and a growing social unification based on increasing homogenization and control:

> The ruthless unity in the culture industry is evidence of what will happen in politics. Marked differentiations such as those of A and B films, or of stories in magazines in different price ranges, depend not so much on subject matter as on classifying, organizing, and labelling consumers. Something is provided for all so that none may escape; the distinctions are emphasized and extended. The public is catered for with a hierarch- ical range of mass-produced products of varying quality, thus advancing the rule of complete quantification. Everybody must behave (as if spon- taneously) in accordance with his previously determined and indexed level, and choose the category of mass product turned out for his type. Con- sumers appear as statistics on research organization charts, and are di- vided by income groups into red, green, and blue areas; the technique is that used for any type of propaganda.[14]

Later in the chapter Horkheimer and Adorno describe the blend between mass culture, advertising and consumption in the consumer society. They argue:

> The assembly-line character of the culture industry, the synthetic, planned method of turning out its products (factory-like not only in the studio but, more or less, in the compilation of cheap biographies, pseudodocumentary novels, and hit songs) is very suited to advertising: the important individual

points, by becoming detachable, interchangeable, and even technically alienated from any connected meaning, lend themselves to ends external to the work. The effect, the trick, the isolated repeatable device, have always been used to exhibit goods for advertising purposes, and today every monster close-up of a star is an advertisement for her name, and every hit song a plug for its tune. Advertising and the culture industry merge technically as well as economically. In both cases the same thing can be seen in innumerable places, and the mechanical repetition of the same cultural product has come to be the same as that of the propaganda slogan. In both cases the insistent demand for effectiveness makes technology into psycho-technology, into a procedure for manipulating men. In both cases the standards are the striking yet familiar, the easy yet catchy, the skillful yet simple; the object is to overpower the customer, who is conceived as absent-minded or resistant.[15]

Throughout *Minima Moralia*, written just after the completion of *Dialectic of Enlightenment* in the mid-1940s, Adorno presents frequent criticisms of the culture industry and the consumer society – which are two aspects of the same new configuration of capitalism and have similar effects on personality structure and behavior. This text is full of criticisms of the new forms of mass culture which were emerging in the United States. Adorno reflects on conspicuous consumption and advertising, travel, the media and obsession with new products:

The fascinated eagerness to consume the latest process of the day not only leads to indifference towards the matter transmitted by the process, but encourages stationary rubbish and calculated idiocy. It confirms the old kitsch in ever new paraphrases as *haute nouveauté*. The concomitant of technical progress is the narrow-minded determination at all costs to buy nothing that is not in demand, not to fall behind the careering production process, never mind what the purpose of the product might be. Keeping up, crowding and queuing everywhere take the place of what were to some extent rational needs.[16]

While Adorno's melancholy reflections on a bad social order were deeply pessimistic, they occasionally included glimpses of the positive values by means of which Critical Theory criticized the current state of capitalism, principal of which was the fulfillment of basic needs and values such as peace, security and freedom from anxiety, as well as freedom from the competition and the administered consumption and production which define the contemporary stage of capitalism. In a revealing passage, Adorno attacks the values of hustle and bustle associated with capitalism and affirms opposing values:

The concept of dynamism, which is the necessary complement of bourgeois 'a-historicity', is raised to an absolute, whereas it ought, as an anthropological reflex of the laws of production, to be itself critically confronted, in an emancipated society, with need. The conception of unfettered activity, of uninterrupted procreation, of chubby insatiability, of freedom as frantic bustle, feeds on the bourgeois concept of nature that has always served solely to proclaim social violence as unchangeable, as a piece of healthy eternity. It was in this, and not in their alleged levelling-down, that the positive blue-prints of socialism, resisted by Marx, were rooted in barbarism. It is not man's lapse into luxurious indolence that is to be feared, but the savage spread of the social under the mask of universal nature, the collective as a blind fury of activity.[17]

Notes and References

1   T. Adorno, 'On the fetish character of music', in *The Frankfurt School Reader*, ed. Andrew Arato and Eike Gebhardt (Continuum, New York, 1982), p. 280.
2   T. Adorno, *Prisms* (Neville Spearman, London, 1967), p. 75.
3   Ibid., p. 78.
4   Ibid., p. 81.
5   Ibid., p. 82.
6   Ibid., p. 83.
7   Ibid., pp. 93–4.
8   Ibid., p. 99.
9   Ibid., p. 102.
10 Ibid., p. 103.
11 Ibid., p. 109.
12 Ibid., pp. 109–10.
13 M. Horkheimer and T. Adorno, *Dialectic of Enlightenment* (Herder and Herder, New York, 1972), pp. xiv–xv.
14 Ibid., p. 123.
15 Ibid., p. 163.
16 T. Adorno, *Minima Moralia: Reflections from a Damaged Life* (New Left Books, London, 1974), p. 118.
17 Ibid., pp. 155–6.

6

The Emergence of the Public Sphere

Jürgen Habermas

The Question

The usage of the words "public" and "public sphere" betrays a multiplicity of concurrent meanings. Their origins go back to various historical phases and, when applied synchronically to the conditions of a bourgeois society that is industrially advanced and constituted as a social-welfare state, they fuse into a clouded amalgam. Yet the very conditions that make the inherited language seem inappropriate appear to require these words, however confused their employment. Not just ordinary language (especially as it bears the imprint of bureaucratic and mass media jargon) but also the sciences – particularly jurisprudence, political science, and sociology – do not seem capable of replacing traditional categories like "public" and "private," "public sphere," and "public opinion," with more precise terms. Ironically, this dilemma has first of all bedeviled the very discipline that explicitly makes public opinion its subject matter. With the application of empirical techniques, the object that public-opinion research was to apprehend has dissolved into something elusive; nevertheless sociology has refused to abandon altogether these categories; it continues to study public opinion.

We call events and occasions "public" when they are open to all, in contrast to closed or exclusive affairs – as when we speak of public places or public houses. But as in the expression "public building," the term need not refer to general accessibility; the building does not even have to be open to public traffic. "Public buildings" simply house state institutions and as such are "public." The state is the "public authority." It owes this attribute to its task of promoting the public or common welfare of its rightful members. The word has yet another meaning when one speaks of a "public [official] reception"; on such occasions a powerful display of representation is staged whose "publicity" contains an element of public recognition. There is a shift in meaning again when we say that someone has made a name for himself, has a public reputation. The notion of such personal prestige or renown originated in epochs other than that of "polite society."

None of these usages, however, has much affinity with the meaning most commonly associated with the category – expressions like "public opinion," an "outraged" or "informed public," "publicity," "publish," and "publicize." The subject of this publicity is the public as carrier of public opinion; its function as a critical judge is precisely what makes the public character of proceedings – in court, for instance – meaningful. In the realm of the mass media, of course, publicity has changed its meaning. Originally a function of public opinion, it has become an attribute of whatever attracts public opinion: public relations and efforts recently baptized "publicity work" are aimed at producing such publicity. The public sphere itself appears as a specific domain – the public domain versus the private. Sometimes the public appears simply as that sector of public opinion that happens to be opposed to the authorities. Depending on the circumstances, either the organs of the state or the media, like the press, which provide communication among members of the public, may be counted as "public organs."

A social–historical analysis of the syndrome of meanings possessed by "public" and "publicity" could uncover the essential sociological characteristics of the various historical language strata. The first etymological reference to the public sphere is quite revealing. In German the noun *Öffentlichkeit* was formed from the older adjective *öffentlich* during the eighteenth century, in analogy to "*publicité*" and "publicity"; by the close of the century the word was still so little used that Heynatz could consider it objectionable. If the public sphere did not require a name of its own before this period, we may assume that this sphere first emerged and took on its function only at that time, at least in Germany. It was specifically a part of "civil society," which at the same time established itself as the realm of commodity exchange and social labor governed by its own laws. Notions concerning what is "public" and what is not – that is, what is "private" – however, can be traced much further back into the past.

We are dealing here with categories of Greek origin transmitted to us bearing a Roman stamp. In the fully developed Greek city-state the sphere of the *polis*, which was common (*koine*) to the free citizens, was strictly separated from the sphere of the *oikos*; in the sphere of the *oikos*, each individual is in his own realm (*idia*). The public life, *bios politikos*, went on in the market place (*agora*), but of course this did not mean that it occurred necessarily only in this specific locale. The public sphere was constituted in discussion (*lexis*), which could also assume the forms of consultation and of sitting in the court of law, as well as in common action (*praxis*), be it the waging of war or competition in athletic games. (Strangers were often called upon to legislate, which was not properly one of the public tasks.) The political order, as is well known, rested on a patrimonial slave economy. The citizens were thus set free from productive labor; it was their private autonomy as masters of households, however, on which their participation in public life depended. The private sphere was attached to the house not by (its Greek) name only. Movable wealth and control over labor power were no more substitutes for being the master of a household and of a family than, conversely, poverty and a lack of slaves would in themselves prevent admission to the *polis*. Exile, expropriation, and the destruction of the house amounted to one and the same thing. Status in the *polis* was therefore based upon status as the unlimited master of an *oikos*. The reproduction of life, the labor of the slaves, and the service of the women went on under the aegis of the master's domination; birth and death took place in its shadow; and the realm of necessity and transitoriness remained immersed in the obscurity of the private sphere. In contrast to it stood, in Greek self-interpretation, the public sphere as a realm of freedom and permanence. Only in the light of the public sphere did that which existed become revealed, did everything become visible to all. In the discussion among citizens issues were made topical and took on shape. In the competition among equals the best excelled and gained their essence – the immortality of fame. Just as the wants of life and the procurement of its necessities were shamefully hidden inside the *oikos*, so the *polis* provided an open field for honorable distinction: citizens indeed interacted as equals with equals (*homoioi*), but each did his best to excel (*aristoiein*). The virtues, whose catalogue was codified by Aristotle, were ones whose test lies in the public sphere and there alone receive recognition.

Since the Renaissance this model of the Hellenic public sphere, as handed down to us in the stylized form of Greek self-interpretation, has shared with everything else considered "classical" a peculiarly normative power. Not the social formation at its base but the ideological template itself has preserved continuity over the centuries – on the level of intellectual history. To begin with, throughout the Middle Ages the categories of the public and the private and of the public sphere understood as *res publica* were passed on in the definitions of Roman law. Of course, they found a renewed application meaningful in the technical, legal sense only with the rise of the modern state and of that sphere of civil society separated from it. They served the political self-interpretation as well as the legal institutionalization of a public sphere that was bourgeois in a specific sense. Meanwhile, however, for about a century the social foundations of this sphere have been caught up in a process of decomposition. Tendencies pointing to the collapse of the public sphere are unmistakable, for while its scope is expanding impressively, its function has become progressively insignificant. Still, publicity continues to be an organizational principle of our political order. It is apparently more and other than a mere scrap of liberal ideology that a social democracy could discard without harm. If we are successful in gaining a historical understanding of the structures of this complex that today, confusedly enough, we subsume under the heading "public sphere," we can hope to attain thereby not only a sociological clarification of the concept but a systematic comprehension of our own society from the perspective of one of its central categories.

[···]

The aristocratic "society" that emerged from that Renaissance society no longer had to represent its own lordliness (i.e. its manorial authority), or at least no longer primarily; it served as a vehicle for the representation of the monarch. Only after national and territorial power states had arisen on the basis of the early capitalist commercial economy and shattered the feudal foundations of power could this court nobility develop the framework of a sociability – highly individuated, in spite of its comprehensive etiquette – into that peculiarly free-floating but clearly demarcated sphere of "good society" in the eighteenth century. The final form of the representative publicness, reduced to the monarch's court and at the same time receiving greater emphasis, was already an enclave within a society separating itself from the state. Now for the first time private and public spheres became separate in a specifically modern sense.

[···]

The major tendencies that prevailed by the end of the eighteenth century are well known. The feudal powers, the Church, the prince, and the nobility, who were the carriers of the representative publicness, disintegrated in a process of polarization; in the end they split into private elements, on the one hand, and public ones, on the other. The status of the Church changed as a result of the Reformation; the anchoring in divine authority that it represented – that is, religion – became a private matter. The so-called freedom of religion historically

secured the first sphere of private autonomy; the Church itself continued to exist as one corporate body among others under public law. The
first visible mark of the analogous polarization of princely authority was
the separation of the public budget from the territorial ruler's private
holdings. The bureaucracy, the military (and to some extent also the
administration of justice) became independent institutions of public
authority separate from the progressively privatized sphere of the court.
Out of the estates, finally, the elements of political prerogative developed into organs of public authority: partly into a parliament, and partly
into judicial organs. Elements of occupational status group organization,
to the degree that they were already involved in the urban corporations
and in certain differentiations within the estates of the land, developed
into the sphere of "civil society" that as the genuine domain of private
autonomy stood opposed to the state.

[· · ·]

On the Genesis of the Bourgeois Public Sphere

With the emergence of early finance and trade capitalism, the elements
of a new social order were taking shape. From the thirteenth century on
they spread from the northern Italian city-states to western and northern Europe and caused the rise first of Dutch centers for staple goods
(Bruges, Lüttich, Brussels, Ghent, etc.) and then of the great trade fairs
at the crossroads of long-distance trade. Initially, to be sure, they were
integrated without much trouble by the old power structure. That initial
assimilation of bourgeois humanism to a noble courtly culture, as we
observe it paradigmatically during the rise of Florentine Renaissance
society, much also be seen against this background. Early capitalism
was conservative not only as regards the economic mentality so vividly
described by Sombart (a characteristic way of doing business typified by
"honorable" gain) but also as regards politics. As long as it lived from
the fruits of the old mode of production (the feudal organization of
agricultural production involving an enserfed peasantry and the petty
commodity production of the corporatively organized urban craftsmen)
without transforming it, it retained ambivalent characteristics. On the
one hand this capitalism stabilized the power structure of a society organized in estates, and on the other hand it unleashed the very elements
within which this power structure would one day dissolve. We are speaking of the elements of the new commercial relationships: the *traffic in
commodities and news* created by early capitalist long-distance trade.

The towns, of course, had local markets from the beginning. In the hands of the guilds and the corporations, however, these remained strictly regulated, serving more as instruments for the domination of the surrounding areas than for free commodity exchange between town and country. With the rise of long-distance trade, for which – according to Pirenne's observations – the town was only a base of operations, markets of a different sort arose. They became consolidated into periodic trade fairs and, with the development of techniques of capitalist financing (it is known that letters of credit and promissory notes were in use at the trade fairs of the Champagne as early as the thirteenth century), were established as stock exchanges. In 1531 Antwerp became a "permanent trade fair." This commercial exchange developed according to rules which certainly were manipulated by political power; yet a far-reaching network of horizontal economic dependencies emerged that in principle could no longer be accommodated by the vertical relationships of dependence characterizing the organization of domination in an estate system based upon a self-contained household economy. Of course, the political order remained unthreatened by the new processes which, as such, had no place in the existing framework, as long as the members of the old ruling stratum participated in them only as consumers. When they earmarked an increasing portion of what was produced on their lands for the acquisition of luxury goods made available through long-distance trade, this by itself did not bring traditional production – and hence the basis of their rule – into dependence on the new capital.

The traffic in news that developed alongside the traffic in commodities showed a similar pattern. With the expansion of trade, merchants' market-oriented calculations required more frequent and more exact information about distant events. From the fourteenth century on, the traditional letter carrying by merchants was for this reason organized into a kind of guild-based system of correspondence for their purposes. The merchants organized the first mail routes, the so-called ordinary mail, departing on assigned days.

[· · ·]

Civil society came into existence as the corollary of a depersonalized state authority. Activities and dependencies hitherto relegated to the framework of the household economy emerged from this confinement into the public sphere. Schumpeter's observation "that the old forms that harnessed the whole person into systems of supraindividual purpose had died and that each family's individual economy had become the center of its existence, that therewith a private sphere was born as a distinguishable entity in contrast to the public"[1] only captures one side of the process – the privatization of the process of economic reproduction. It glances over the latter's new "public" relevance. The economic activity that had become private had to be oriented toward a commodity market that had expanded under public direction and supervision; the economic conditions under which this activity now took place lay outside the confines of the single household; for the first time they were of general interest. Hannah Arendt refers to this *private sphere of society that has become publicly relevant* when she characterizes the modern (in contrast to the ancient) relationship of the public sphere to the private in terms of the rise of the "social": "Society is the form in which the fact of mutual dependence for the sake of life and nothing else assumes public significance, and where the activities connected with sheer survival are permitted to appear in public."[2]

The changed conditions of the times were reflected in the transformation of the economics handed down from antiquity into political economy. Indeed the term "economic" itself, which until the seventeenth century was limited to the sphere of tasks proper to the *oikodespotes*, the *pater familias*, the head of the household, now, in the context of a practice of running a business in accord with principles of profitability, took on its modern meaning. The duties of the household head were narrowed and "economizing" became more closely associated with thriftiness. Modern economics was no longer oriented to the *oikos*; the market had replaced the household, and it became "commercial economics" (*Kommerzienwirtschaft*). Significantly, in eighteenth-century cameralism (whose name derives from *camera*, the territorial ruler's treasure chamber) this forerunner of political economy was part of "police-science," that is, of administrative science proper, together with the science of finance on the one hand and with agricultural technology on the other (which was becoming differentiated from traditional economics). This shows how closely connected the private sphere of civil society was to the organs of the public authority.

Within this political and social order transformed during the mercantilist phase of capitalism (and whose new structure found its expression precisely in the differentiation of its political and social aspects) the second element of the early capitalist commercial system, the press, in turn developed a unique explosive power. The first journals in the strict sense, ironically called "political journals," appeared weekly at first, and daily as early as the middle of the seventeenth century. In those days private correspondence contained detailed and current news about Imperial Diets, wars, harvests, taxes, transports of precious metals, and, of course, reports on foreign trade. Only a trickle of this stream of reports passed through the filter of these "news letters" into printed journals. The recipients of private correspondence had no interest in their contents becoming public. On the one hand, therefore, the political journals responded to a need on the part of the merchants; on the other hand, the merchants themselves were indispensable to the journals. They were called *custodes novellarum* among their contemporaries precisely because of this dependence of public reporting upon their private exchange of news. It was essentially news from abroad, of the court, and of the less important commercial events that passed through the sieve of the merchants' unofficial information control and the state administrations' official censorship. Certain categories of traditional "news" items from the repertoire of the broadsheets were also perpetuated – the miracle cures and thunderstorms, the murders, pestilences, and burnings. Thus, the information that became public was constituted of residual elements of what was actually available; nevertheless, it requires explanation why at this particular time they were distributed and made generally accessible, made public at all. It is questionable whether the interests of those who made a living by writing news pamphlets would have provided a sufficiently strong impetus; still, they *did* have an interest in publication. For the traffic in news developed not only in connection with the needs of commerce; the news itself became a commodity. Commercial news reporting was therefore subject to the laws of the same market to whose rise it owed its existence in the first place. It is no accident that the printed journals often developed out of the same bureaus of correspondence that already handled hand-written newsletters. Each item of information contained in a letter had its price; it was therefore natural to increase the profits by selling to more people. This in itself was already sufficient reason periodically to print a portion of the available news material and to sell it anonymously, thus giving it publicity.

The interest of the new (state) authorities (which before long began to use the press for the purposes of the state administration), however, was of far greater import. Inasmuch as they made use of this instrument to promulgate instructions and ordinances, the addressees of the authorities' announcements genuinely became "the public" in the proper sense. From the very beginning, the political journals had reported on the journeys and returns of the princes, on the arrival of foreign dignitaries, on balls, "special events" (*Solennitäten*) at court, appointments, etc.; in the context of this news from the Court, which can be thought of as a kind of transposition of the publicity of representation into the new form of public sphere, there also appeared "sovereign ordinances in the subjects' best interest." Very soon the press was systematically made to serve the interests of the state administration.

[· · ·]

The authorities addressed their promulgations to "the" public, that is, in principle to all subjects. Usually they did not reach the "common man" in this way, but at best the "educated classes." Along with the apparatus of the modern state, a new stratum of "bourgeois" people arose which occupied a central position within the "public." The officials of the rulers' administrations were its core – mostly jurists (at least on the continent, where the technique of the received Roman law was adopted as an instrument for the rationalization of social organization). Added to them were doctors, pastors, officers, professors, and "scholars," who were at the top of a hierarchy reaching down through schoolteachers and scribes to the "people."

For in the meantime the genuine "burghers," the old occupational orders of craftsmen and shopkeepers, suffered downward social mobility; they lost their importance along with the very towns upon whose citizens' rights their status was based. At the same time, the great merchants outgrew the confining framework of the towns and in the form of companies linked themselves directly with the state. Thus, the "capitalists," the merchants, bankers, entrepreneurs, and manufacturers (at least where, unlike in Hamburg, the towns could not maintain their independence from the territorial rulers) belonged to that group of the "bourgeois" who, like the new category of scholars, were not really "burghers" in the traditional sense. This stratum of "bourgeois" was the real carrier of the public, which from the outset was a reading public. Unlike the great urban merchants and officials who, in former days, could be assimilated by the cultivated nobility of the Italian Renaissance courts, they could no longer be integrated *in toto* into the noble culture at the close of the Baroque period. Their commanding status in the new sphere of civil society led instead to a tension between "town" and "court."

In this stratum, which more than any other was affected *and* called upon by mercantilist policies, the state authorities evoked a resonance leading the *publicum*, the abstract counterpart of public authority, into an awareness of itself as the latter's opponent, that is, as the public of the now emerging *public sphere of civil society*. For the latter developed to the extent to which the public concern regarding the private sphere of civil society was no longer confined to the authorities but was considered by the subjects as one that was properly theirs.

[· · ·]

The history of words preserved traces of this momentous shift. In Great Britain, from the middle of the seventeenth century on, there was talk of "public," whereas until then "world" or "mankind" was usual. Similarly, in France *le public* began to denote what in the eighteenth century, according to Grimm's *Wörterbuch*, also gained currency throughout Germany as *Publikum* (its use spreading from Berlin). Until then one spoke of the "world of readers" (*Lesewelt*), or simply of the "world" (*Welt*) in the sense still used today: all the world, *tout le monde*. Adelung draws a distinction between the public that gathered as a crowd around a speaker or actor in a public place, and the *Lesewelt* (world of readers). Both, however, were instances of a "critical (*richtend*) public." Whatever was submitted to the judgment of the public gained *Publizität* (publicity). At the end of the seventeenth century the English "publicity" was borrowed from the French *publicité*; in Germany the word surfaced in the eighteenth century. Criticism itself was presented in the form of *öffentliche Meinung*, a word formed in the second half of the eighteenth century in analogy to *opinion publique*. In Great Britain "public opinion" arose at about the same time; the expression "general opinion," however, had been in use long before.

Notes and references

1   J. Schumpeter, *Die Krise des Steuerstaates* (Leuschner, Graz, and Lubensky, Leipzig, 1918), p. 16.
2   H. Arendt, *The Human Condition* (University of Chicago Press, Chicago, 1959), p. 46.

7

The Theory of the Public Sphere: A Critical Appraisal

John Thompson

Undoubtedly part of the rhetorical force of *The Structural Transformation of the Public Sphere* stems from the way that Habermas weaves together historical analysis and normative critique – a feature that has bothered some commentators over the years. I shall not object in principle to this aspect of Habermas's work, but I will try to distinguish the substantive issues from the normative ones and to deal with each separately. In this discussion I shall focus on four problems (or sets of problems).

1 Let us begin by considering, from a historical point of view, the adequacy and plausibility of Habermas's account of the emergence of the bourgeois public sphere in early modern Europe. One of the criticisms that has been made most frequently of this account is that, by focusing attention on the *bourgeois* public sphere, Habermas tends to neglect the significance of other forms of public discourse and activity which existed in seventeenth-, eighteenth- and nineteenth-century Europe, forms which were not part of, and in some cases were excluded from or opposed to, the forms of bourgeois sociability. This point is made very effectively by Geoff Eley, though somewhat similar criticisms can be found in earlier German literature.[1] As Eley remarks, the work of E.P. Thompson, Christopher Hill and others has highlighted the significance of a variety of popular social and political movements in the early modern period, and it cannot be assumed that these movements were either derivative of, or organized along similar lines to, the activities which took place in the bourgeois public sphere. On the contrary, argues Eley, the relation between the bourgeois public sphere and popular social movements was often a conflictual one. Just as the emerging bourgeois public sphere

defined itself in opposition to the traditional authority of royal power, so too it was confronted by the rise of popular movements which it sought to contain. The bourgeois public sphere was, from the outset, embedded in a field of conflictual social relations which shaped its formation and development.

This is a forceful line of criticism. In the Preface to *Structural Transformation*, Habermas had explained that his account would be limited to, as he put it, 'the liberal model of the bourgeois public sphere', and that he would leave aside that 'variant' of the liberal model – what he called 'the plebeian public sphere' – which had briefly appeared on the stage of the French Revolution but which was subsequently suppressed in the historical process. But it seems clear that his schematic way of characterizing popular social and political movements was not satisfactory. Returning to these issues thirty years later, Habermas concedes that his earlier account would have to be substantially revised today.[2] Not only were popular movements much more important in the early modern period than he had previously allowed, but it is also clear that they cannot be adequately understood as mere variants of the liberal model of the bourgeois public sphere (any more than popular culture can be understood as a derivative of dominant cultural forms). Habermas acknowledges that we need a more flexible approach to popular social movements and popular cultural forms, an approach which does not prejudge their character and which allows for the possibility that they may have a shape and dynamic of their own.

2 Let us now focus on the model of the bourgeois public sphere itself, quite apart from the question of whether this model provided a satisfactory way of thinking about the character of non-bourgeois social movements. It is clear that this model was regarded by Habermas as an idealization of actual historical processes. Although the bourgeois public sphere was based on the principle of universal access, in practice it was restricted to those individuals who had the education and the financial means to participate in it. What does not emerge very clearly from Habermas's account, however, is the extent to which the bourgeois public sphere was not only restricted to educated and propertied elites, but was also a predominantly *male* preserve. Habermas was not unaware of the marginalization of women in the bourgeois public sphere and of the patriarchal character of the bourgeois family; but it could be argued very plausibly that, at the time of writing *Structural Transformation*, he did not appreciate the full significance of this issue.

In recent years a number of feminist scholars have examined the gendered character of the public sphere and political discourse in the early modern period, and have brought sharply into focus a set of issues which remained rather blurred in Habermas's account. Particularly interesting in this regard is Joan Landes's *Women and the Public Sphere in the Age of the French Revolution*.[3] Landes is concerned with the relation of women to the public sphere in France in the period from 1750 to 1850. Her central argument is that the exclusion of women from the public sphere was not simply a contingent historical circumstance, one of the many respects in which the public sphere in practice fell short of the ideal; rather, the exclusion of women was constitutive of the very notion of the public sphere. For the notion of the public sphere, as it was articulated in the political discourse of the time, was juxtaposed to the private sphere in a gender-specific way. The public sphere was generally understood as a domain of reason and universality in which men were uniquely well equipped to participate, while women, being inclined (supposedly) to particularity and to mannered, frivolous talk, were commonly thought to be better suited to domestic life. Hence the masculine character of the bourgeois public sphere was not an incidental aspect: it was a fundamental feature of a public sphere which, in its very conception, was shaped by a deeply rooted set of assumptions about gender differences.

It is to Habermas's credit that, in reconsidering these issues today, he is swayed by the force of this line of argument. He accepts that, while workers and peasants as well as women were largely excluded from the bourgeois public sphere, the exclusion of women needs to be thought about differently, precisely because this exclusion had, as Habermas now puts it, 'structuring significance'. This shift in Habermas's approach is important, but one might reasonably remain a little sceptical about the extent to which Habermas has taken account of gender issues. For, as Nancy Fraser has shown, a somewhat similar line of argument can be developed with regard to Habermas's more recent work. It may be that, while Habermas is certainly sympathetic to the issues raised by feminist critics, these issues remain somewhat tangential to the basic assumptions and priorities that shape his way of conceptualizing the social world.[4]

3 The weakest parts of *Structural Transformation* are probably not the sections concerned with the emergence of the bourgeois public sphere, but rather the sections concerned with its alleged decline. Surprisingly, Habermas's arguments concerning the transformation of the public sphere in the nineteenth and twentieth centuries are not addressed in any detail by the contributors to *Habermas and the Public Sphere,* though they are reconsidered by Habermas himself in his reply. If one re-reads today Habermas's account of the changes which have occurred over

the last two centuries, one will find many details to dispute and some empirical material which is now well out of date. But the important question is whether Habermas was right to interpret these changes broadly in the way that he did – as a sign that the public sphere of debating citizens had collapsed into a fragmented world of consumers who are enthralled by the media spectacles unfolding before them and manipulated by media techniques. Is there any substance to this interpretation and, more specifically, to the thesis of the refeudalization of the public sphere?

I doubt it. Certainly this account has some prima facie plausibility. One need only watch a few party political broadcasts to remind oneself of the extent to which the conduct of politics today has become inseparable from the activity of public relations management. But if we press beyond the level of initial observations, it is clear that there are serious deficiencies to Habermas's account. Let me highlight two. In the first place, it is very doubtful whether the recipients of media products can plausibly be regarded as enthralled and manipulated consumers. In developing this argument, Habermas was betraying his debt to the work of Horkheimer and Adorno, whose theory of mass culture provided part of the inspiration for his own account. Today it is clear, however, that this kind of argument exaggerates the passivity of individuals and takes far too much for granted concerning the process of reception; a more contextualized and hermeneutically sensitive approach would show that the process of reception is a much more complicated and creative activity than the Frankfurt School theorists supposed. Habermas now accepts the force of this criticism and acknowledges that, if he were to rework his account of the transformation of the public sphere, he would have to give more attention to recent work on the reception of media products.

A second problem in Habermas's account concerns the thesis of the refeudalization of the public sphere. It is not difficult to see why Habermas had argued that the public sphere was being 'refeudalized': the showiness characteristic of mediated politics today, and its concern to cultivate personal aura rather than to stimulate critical debate, does seem, at least at first glance, to resemble the kind of representative publicness typical of the Middle Ages. But the similarity here is more apparent than real, and the fact that Habermas could seriously make this comparison suggests that he had not really appreciated the quite profound impact that the mass media have had on the modern world. For the development of the media – and especially of the various types of electronic communication – has created new forms of social interaction and information diffusion which exist on a scale and are organized in a

manner that preclude any serious comparison with the theatrical practices of feudal courts. Whereas courtly behaviour in the Middle Ages
was largely oriented towards individuals who shared the same spatial–
temporal context, today it is common for political leaders to appear
before millions of recipients who are widely dispersed in space (and
perhaps also in time); and the kinds of relationship established through
mediated communication are quite different from the face-to-face interaction which takes place in a shared locale. I shall return to these issues
below. Here it will suffice to say that, if we wish to understand how
public life in the modern world had been reshaped by the development
of the media (among other things), we would be well advised to put
aside the thesis of the refeudalization of the public sphere and to think
about these issues in a different way.

4 I mentioned earlier that *Structural Transformation* could be viewed
as an initial attempt to outline a theory of democracy that would be relevant to the conditions of twentieth-century Western societies. Although
the bourgeois public sphere has long since declined, the critical principle
of publicity retains some relevance as a normative ideal and could be
used to guide institutional change. In the closing pages of *Structural
Transformation,* Habermas put forward a few ideas about how the critical
principle of publicity could be implemented within the organizations and
interest groups which had assumed an ever-increasing role in political
affairs. In sketching these proposals for a kind of 'intra-organizational
democratization', Habermas was indebted to the work – little known
in the English-speaking world – of Wolfgang Abendroth. (Habermas's
Habilitationschrift, having apparently been received unfavourably by
Horkheimer and Adorno, was submitted to Abendroth at Marburg, and
the book was subsequently dedicated to him.) But the proposals put
forward by Habermas were, at best, exceedingly vague; and Habermas
himself gradually came to the view that, given the complexity of modern,
internally differentiated societies, such proposals would be largely un-
workable in practice.

   In recent decades Habermas has continued to pursue the question of
how a theory of democracy, informed by the ideas once embodied in the
bourgeois public sphere, could be developed and applied to the conditions of modern societies. This has involved two parallel lines of argument. In the first place, Habermas has tried to show that the notion of
a discursive formation of the will through a process of reasoned debate
can be given a firmer foundation than it had in *Structural Transformation,* and that this notion forms the core of a discourse-centred theory
of democracy in which questions of a moral–practical character can be

resolved in a rational manner. Certainly this line of argument has not won universal assent. Even Habermas's most sympathetic critics find much with which to disagree in his account of practical discourse; and many have doubted whether, in view of the plurality of evaluative and interpretative standpoints characteristic of modern societies, it makes sense to try to build a political theory based on the possibility of rational consensus. Habermas's arguments concerning the theory of practical discourse and its political application have given us a great deal to think about and will, no doubt, continue to generate much debate. But it seems to me that, at least in some respects, his critics are justified, and it would probably be sensible for Habermas to tone down some of his stronger claims in favour of a more modest approach.

The second line of argument developed by Habermas has involved a substantial revision of his theory of society, culminating in the distinction between system and lifeworld elaborated in *The Theory of Communicative Action*.[5] This distinction has major implications for Habermas's theory of democracy. He now accepts that the state and economy are systematically organized fields of action which can no longer be transformed democratically from within: to attempt to do so would be to threaten their capacity to function according to their distinctive logic, with potentially disastrous consequences. The task today of a radical programme of democratization should be, instead, to push back the colonizing intrusion of system imperatives into the lifeworld and to achieve thereby a new balance between forms of societal integration, so that the practically oriented demands of the lifeworld can prevail over the exercise of economic and administrative power.

Not everyone will be convinced that, with the notions of system and lifeworld, Habermas has found the most compelling way to reformulate the political programme of radical democratization. Some will doubt whether the state and economy should be insulated from democratic processes in the manner proposed, and many will wonder what all of this amounts to in practice. Moreover, in developing his theory of society in recent years, Habermas seems largely to have lost sight of a theme that concerned him in his earlier work – namely, the importance of communication media and their structuring impact on social and political life . . .

I have considered some of the criticisms that have been made of Habermas's early writings on the public sphere and some of the reasons why Habermas subsequently modified his views. However, there is one issue which has not figured prominently in the debate sparked off by Habermas's work, and yet which is, in my view, of considerable significance for any attempt to rethink the changing character of public life.

The issue, put simply, is this: Habermas's conception of the public sphere – whether in the form of the bourgeois public sphere which emerged in the eighteenth century or in the form of his own, philosophically more elaborate model of practical discourse – is essentially a *dialogical* conception. That is, it is based on the idea that individuals come together in a shared locale and engage in dialogue with one another, as equal participants in a face-to-face conversation. The problem, however, is that this conception bears little resemblance to the kinds of communication established by and sustained through the media, and hence bears little resemblance to the kind of public sphere which the media have helped to create. Let us consider this problem further by returning for a moment to the arguments of *Structural Transformation*.

Many commentators have noted that, in accounting for the formation of the bourgeois public sphere, Habermas attributes a significant role to print. But if we reread *Structural Transformation* carefully, we will find, I think, that Habermas was not interested in print as such, in the distinctive characteristics of this communication medium and in the kinds of social relations established by it. His way of thinking about print was shaped by a model of communication based on the spoken word: the periodical press was part of a conversation begun and continued in the shared locales of bourgeois sociability. The press was interwoven so closely with the life of clubs and coffee-houses that it was inseparable from it: 'One and the same discussion transposed into a different medium was continued in order to re-enter, via reading, the original conversational medium.'[6] So while the press played a crucial role in the formation of the bourgeois public sphere, the latter was conceptualized by Habermas not in relation to print, but in relation to the face-to-face conversation stimulated by it. In this respect, Habermas's account of the bourgeois public sphere bears the imprint of the classical Greek conception of public life: the salons, clubs and coffee-houses of Paris and London were the equivalent, in the context of early modern Europe, of the assemblies and marketplaces of Ancient Greece. As in Ancient Greece, so too in early modern Europe, the public sphere was constituted above all in speech, in the weighing up of different arguments, opinions and points of view in the dialogical exchange of spoken words in a shared locale.

It is not difficult to see why, with this conception of the public sphere in mind, Habermas was inclined to interpret the impact of newer communication media, like radio and television, in largely negative terms. It was not only because the media industries had become more commercialized and harnessed to particular interestes; it was also because the kind of communication situation they created, in which the reception of media products had become a form of privatized appropriation, was a far cry from the dialogical exchange that took place among individuals who gathered together in the clubs and coffee-houses of early modern Europe. Habermas recognizes, of course, that radio and television create new forms of conversation – the TV chat shows, panel discussions and so on. But these new forms of conversation, he argues, are in no way comparable with the critical–rational debate that was constitutive of the bourgeois public sphere. 'Today the conversation itself is administered',[7] and active debate among informed citizens has been replaced by the privatized appropriation of a conversation carried out in their name.

However, we shall not arrive at a satisfactory understanding of the nature of public life in the modern world if we remain wedded to a conception of publicness which is essentially dialogical in character, and which obliges us to interpret the ever-growing role of mediated communication as a historical fall from grace. We should, instead, recognize from the outset that the development of communication media – beginning with print, but including the more recent forms of electronic communication – has created a new kind of publicness which cannot be accommodated within the traditional model. With the development of communication media, the phenomenon of publicness has become detached from the sharing of a common locale. It has become *de-spatialized* and *non-dialogical,* and it is increasingly linked to the distinctive kind of visibility produced by, and achievable through, the media (especially television).

This is not the place to examine in detail the characteristics of this new form of mediated publicness and to assess its social and political implications. Such an inquiry would require us to attend much more carefully than Habermas has done to the nature of communication media and their development over time; it would require us to look systematically at the social organization of the media industries on a global scale, and at the complex processes involved in the reception of media products; and, in general, it would require us to think again about what 'publicness' means in a world permeated by new forms of communication, a world in which information and symbolic content circulate through global networks at high speeds and in which individuals are able to interact with others, and observe persons and events, without ever encountering them in the same spatial–temporal locale. It is unlikely that this inquiry, in its more constructive dimension, would be greatly aided by Habermas's work – either his early work, which remained too closely tied to the traditional notion of publicness, or his more recent writings, which have, for the most part, become preoccupied with other themes. But there can be no doubt that, when Habermas outlined the arguments of *Structural Transformation* some thirty years ago, he set the terms of a debate which retains its urgency today and which deserves to be taken up, renewed and, indeed, resituated at the centre of social and political theory.

Notes and references

1 See Geoff Eley, 'Nations, publics and political cultures', in *Habermas and the Public Sphere,* ed. Craig Calhoun (MIT Press, Cambridge, Mass., 1992), pp. 289–339.
2 See Jürgen Habermas, 'Further Reflections on the Public Sphere', in *Habermas and the Public Sphere*, pp. 421–61.
3 Joan B. Landes, *Women and the Public Sphere in the Age of the French Revolution* (Cornell University Press, Ithaca, N.Y., 1988).
4 See Nancy Fraser, 'What's critical about Critical Theory? The case of Habermas and Gender', in her *Unruly Practices: Power, Discourse and Gender in Contemporary Social Theory* (Polity, Cambridge, 1989), pp. 113–43.
5 See Jürgen Habermas, *The Theory of Communicative Action,* vol. 2, *Lifeworld and System: A Critique of Functionalist Reason,* tr. Thomas McCarthy (Polity, Cambridge, 1987).
6 Jürgen Habermas, *The Structural Transformation of the Public Sphere: An Inquiry into a Category of Bourgeois Society*, tr. Thomas Burger with Frederick Lawrence (Polity, Cambridge, 1989), p. 42.
7 Ibid., p. 164.

8

The Dynamics of Electronic Networks

G.J. Mulgan

Sophisticated communications networks long preceded the development of electricity and electronics. The early Chinese Chou dynasty operated meassage services. The Mongol Yuan dynasty in the fourteenth century operated five routes with 1,600 post stations staffed by 70,000 men and 40,000 horses. One of the most extensive pre-electric networks was the French optical telegraph network, developed by Claude Chappe in the 1790s and based on the use of telescopes and visual signalling devices. By 1842 the War Department was responsible for a network with links totalling 3,000 miles and 534 stations. In eighteenth-century Russia semaphore messages could reputedly travel 1,000 miles in two hours.

It was electricity which transformed the potential scale and capacity of communication. Electricity, and later electronics, could deliver messages at speeds far higher than any previous delivery medium, while also controlling their flow. Electricity freed communication from the constraints of space and from the limits of physical transport. The telegraph was in this sense the decisive invention from which all other communications networks flowed. It was 'the first product – really the foundation – of the electrical goods industry and thus the first of the science and engineering based industries'.[1]

Numerous telegraphic devices using electricity were experimented with in the early nineteenth century, usually sponsored by armies. The first to gain widespread use was Edward Cooke and Charles Wheatstone's system, patented in Britain in 1837. The British telegraph used first five and later two lines to transmit any message. The United States adopted what came to be the standard solution after Samuel Morse's invention of a code which enabled messages to be sent along a single wire. In this way the telegraph focused attention for the first time on what has become a predominant concern of communications engineering: the economy of signals, that is to say, the economy of using bandwidth to convey information.

Since the first telegraph systems spread alongside railway tracks after 1844, an apparently endless succession of new electric and electronic networks formed on top of each other, rarely displacing old ones and always increasing the volume and number of communications. The telegraph systems soon set a pattern for future developments. They established the precedent of communications networks growing up around spectacular events: telegraphy linked Washington to the 1844 Democratic National Convention in Baltimore; later radio would be boosted by its ability to cover the Americas Cup, television by its coverage of the 1936 Olympics and the coronation of Queen Elizabeth II. Satellite communication would benefit from its association with later Olympics, the Moon landing and, more recently, fund-raising events such as Live Aid. Great events were one side of the coin. The other was the communication of an endless stream of news about financial and commodity markets. Telegraphy established the tradition of an intimate relationship between communications networks and finance: the earliest large-scale commercial use of the telegraph was by stockbrokers serving the New York and Philadelphia stock exchanges.

Telegraphy also set a pattern in other ways: 'virtually all subsequent developments in telecommunications can be seen, in latent form, in the conversion of telegraphic technology into a commodity bought and sold for profit and saved from the "wastes of competition" by collective actions that preserved monopoly prerogatives within the industry and shielded their beneficiaries from public accountability.'[2]

The very high fixed costs and low variable costs of cable networks like the telegraph have tended to make competition unstable. Competition threatens to reduce prices to variable costs, thus undermining revenues and the prospect of new investment. Monopoly, cartels and tight forms of regulation have all been used to limit this tendency. The US telegraph industry was a near monopoly by 1866, swallowed into the Western union conglomerate, which was one of the largest companies in US history and arguably the world's first great industrial monopoly. Two years later the British Telegraph Act authorized the Post Office to buy and run all the private telegraph companies in Britain, which had in any case already formed themselves into various market-sharing arrangements, just as the independent telephone companies had formed themselves into a near monopoly by the time of nationalization in 1912. Transoceanic cables were dominated by a group of British companies, providing a model which Marconi tried to replicate in cable's competitor technology, radio. Telegraphy set precedents in other ways too:

Morse's first line between Washington and Baltimore was financed by a $30,000 Congressional appropriation in 1843. Morse offered the United States Government his telegraph patent, although it was refused because of the apparent unprofitability of the new industry. Later, companies like Western Union depended heavily on railway rights of way which were in turn dependent on the federal land grant policy. Ever since, communications networks have depended on government aid, either direct or indirect. Whether under a rhetoric of regulation or deregulation, governments have consistently acted to sponsor stable monopoly, duopoly or oligopoly structures in communication, and to subsidize the leading edge of research, usually through military budgets.

The telegraph companies, like the telephone companies, immediately broke records. Along with the railway companies they were the largest of their time, needing unprecedented sums of money to sink in the ground or string in the air. American Telegraph and Telephones (AT&T) became the world's largest company in the twentieth century, and Japan's Nippon Telegraph and Telephone Corporation (NTT) became the world's most highly capitalized company in the 1980s. In Europe Siemens is the largest private sector employer, the Deutsches Bundespost (DBP) the largest public sector employer. In the early days of the networks huge workforces were needed to lay lines and to operate exchanges. These were also among the first genuinely transnational enterprises; the British cable companies and others like the Danish Great Northern company which laid cables across Siberia and Japan had to devise new ways of working and deploying resources. In their pyramidal structure, their precise division of labour and responsibility, and their production of a wholly standardized service they were quintessential examples of the new era of corporate capitalism, held up as models of efficiency.

Telephony was originally developed as a means of multiplexing telegraph and in some cases developed as an adjunct to the telegraph. Telephone networks were introduced into the United States in the late 1870s, and spread there much faster than in Europe. By 1914, 70 per cent of the world's telephones were in the United States. In Germany telephone services were in use in the early 1880s, not only in Berlin and the large cities but also to link villages too small to support a telegraph office. It was soon clear that the technology could be used in many different ways. Some were used to broadcast news, concerts and religious services before the use of the telephone as a point-to-point medium displaced all alternatives. The most famous example of broadcasting on the telephone was the Telefon Hirmondo (the 'telephonic town crier') in Budapest, created by Tivadar Puskas (who had earlier helped to invent the telephone switchboard) as a medium for the Magyar elite. Telephony in the United States was quickly consolidated into AT&T's near-monopoly, while in other countries it was generally run by government departments. In Britain, private companies operated under Post Office licence with little or no government support (though long-distance routes were taken over in 1892), before being fully nationalized in 1912. Sweden soon established a tradition of wide availability of communications networks, helped by intense competition between a Bell subsidiary and its local counterpart, and by 1895 had a telephone penetration rate nearly double that of the United States. In most countries the telephone made a slow but steady progress towards becoming a universal good: household penetration rates were by the late 1980s well over 90 per cent in the United States, over 100 per cent in much of Sweden, and between 70 and 100 per cent in most of Western Europe.

Unlike the electricity industry, which was riven by the conflict between AC and DC technologies, telephone networks all across the world used the same basic principles that had been established in Bell's patents. Radio, too, was initially developed under the tight control of its inventor, Marconi. Radio links for military and shipping uses emerged in the 1900s, and offered a means to bypass British cables. Not until Westinghouse's 'KDKA' in Pittsburgh began broadcasting in 1920 as a promotional gimmick to sell sets was it fully realized that radio is also effective as a medium for communication from one point to many. Radio broadcasting networks under commercial or state control, which generally used telephone land lines to connect their transmitters, sprang up in the 1920s. In the Soviet Union, more audio receivers were linked by wire than by radio until as late as 1964. Television networks were launched in most Western countries in the 1940s after a false start in the 1930s. Some attempts were made to broadcast to large communal screens (as in Germany in the 1930s and rural France in the 1940s). Television and radio have now reached almost 100 per cent penetration in most of the industrialized countries. Cable networks built first for the improved delivery of broadcast signals, and later providing their own material, became widespread in the 1960s and 1970s, reaching 60 per cent penetration in the United States by the late 1980s and 80–90 per cent in some of the smaller European countries.

Computer networks originally linked terminals to mainframes for timesharing, but gradually evolved into distributed structures during the 1970s and 1980s. Microwave networks for computer data and telephony have been available since the 1950s. Local area networks (LANs) providing high-speed data communication within a site, company or institution spread rapidly in the 1980s and have been developed into metropolitan area networks (MANs) covering part of a city (and often associated with a 'teleport' of satellite dishes) and wide area networks (WANs) which may cover several continents. Satellite networks first emerged in the 1960s in the wake of Sputnik, and have been used for broadcasting, for military espionage (two-thirds of all satellites launched have had a military function), for observing minerals or crop patterns, and for transmitting long-distance data and telephone conversations. Very small aperture terminals (VSATs) and mobile receivers are now beginning to extend the scope of satellite-based networks. Mobile and cellular radio networks have begun to transform the principle of communicating from one building to another into that of communicating from one person to another, unconstrained by location. Videotex networks like Prestel and Minitel, Lexis, Compuserve and The Source overlie the telephone network to provide information and messages on screens.

Amidst this burgeoning chaos of new, overlapping networks, technologies continued to be developed at great speed, often beyond the capacities of industry or regulators to respond. Each brings predictions that it will bring untold wonders, that it will render all existing technologies obsolete, and that it will irreparably destroy all existing industry and regulatory structures. Optical fibres, optical storage systems and switches and new transmission techniques are the 1990s prime candidates, expected to replace the electron with the photon as the raw material of communications. Ranged against them are a set of radio technologies, using various cellular and microcellular techniques, and advanced satellite technologies. Fast packet techniques based on self-routing electronic information that can turn voices and images into bursts of information have suggested entirely new models for organizing and linking networks. Advances in superconductive materials for use in switches and aerials point the way to rapid advances in the capacities and speeds of communication, while the supercomputer, neural networks and parallel processing techniques are dramatically increasing the range and depth of expertise and intelligence that can be made available over networks.

During the 1970s and 1980s new electronic networks spread, interconnected, overlapped and competed with a ferocious dynamism. Telegraph and telephone networks, FM, medium- and long-wave radio, VHF and UHF, cable and satellite television, cellular and cordless telephones and mobile radio, computer local area networks, 'neural networks' that mimic the workings of the human brain, videotex networks like Prestel and Minitel, payment networks for cash dispensers or international banks and retailer ordering networks continue to pile up on top of each other without apparent limit. New kinds of terminal, whether personal computers or fax machines, use older networks in new ways. Just as the invention of writing complemented rather than displaced the spoken word, so has each new form of communication accumulated on top of the old, bringing with it a new logical structure of connection, dependence and control.

Beneath the apparently expanding diversity of new networks, most new technologies have been incorporated within traditional structures. Older corporations and regulatory structures have proved proficient at adapting to new technologies. As Raymond Williams argued in relation to broadcasting, their history 'shows very clearly that the institutions and social policies which get established in a formative, innovative stage – often *ad hoc* and piecemeal in a confused and seemingly marginal area – have extraordinary persistence into late periods, if only because they accumulate techniques, experience, capital of what come to seem prescriptive rights'.[3] In telecommunications most of the dominant companies of the 1980s were also dominant in the 1920s; AT&T, IBM, Siemens, Philips and Ericsson are obvious examples. There is also a continuity in terms of control structures. Probably the most important are those of licensed common carriage whose origins date back to the sixteenth century and beyond and which are now being redefined to set conditions for the interconnection of networks. A common carrier is given rights to run a communications system, using a monopoly, on the condition that access is open to all and that communications are not interfered with. The most famous early common carrier was the Tassis (later Taxis) family which organized a postal system for the fifteenth-century Emperor Frederick III. Telegraphy, telephony and more recent services like videotex and the ISDN (Integrated Services Digital Network) have been dominated by common-carrier Postal, Telegraph and Telephone administrations, collectively known as the PTTs, whether as government departments, as public corporations, as state-owned private corporations (such as NTT in Japan after 1949) or, as in the case of AT&T in the United States, in the form of a regulated private corporation. In Britain state control was organized through the Post Office, bringing with it relatively weak accounting systems and annual parliamentary approval of budgets. In the communist countries telecommunication was run directly by ministries (often alongside transport and construction), a large proportion of profits being siphoned off for other areas of state spending. Broadcasting, too, was soon organized in state or quasi-state monopolies, based originally in Britain on a consortium of equipment manufacturers. Most satellite communication has been run by Intelsat, the strange phenomenon of a US-sponsored international nationalized industry, jointly owned by 112 of the world's state telephone monopolies, alongside its regional counterparts such as Eutelsat and Arabsat, and Intersputnik, which used Soviet space technology to provide satellite communication for the communist world.

This history of close links between states and networks, symbolized by the fact that the military networks of both East and West are more advanced than their civilian counterparts, shapes much of the politics of communications and control. In practice, the exercise of control over networks has taken many forms. Influence over cable networks depended on physical control. The British global network would have been impossible without Britain's dominion over innumerable islands, ports and islets such as Ascension or Gibraltar. Radio by contrast was more flexible, allowing competing empires such as that of the French to construct their own short-wave networks, no longer reliant on British cables. Control also depends on terms of interconnection. When the Pacific Cable Board (a consortium of governments in the British Empire) built a cable between Australia and Canada it ensured that it did not pass any non-British islands. Within the United States, AT&T dominated telephony by owning the long-distance network and using its control over interconnection as a lever on local telephone companies.

In competitive communications markets a number of generic control strategies have been pursued since the early days of telegraphy. Though all firms are different in detail, the patterns are remarkably consistent throughout the history of the communications industries. For large firms the ability to control the development of networks and ultimate profits has depended on three elements: interconnection strategies, patents strategies and vertical integration. Their aim is to restrict entry and to maximize market share. The means is the maintenance of control over a system of communication, rather as transport and energy companies have often sought control over a system in which they retain discretion over pricing and the lines of technical change. Since communication depends on the interworking of a system of receivers and transmitters, shared formats and the languages, some degree of systemic control is essential.

For smaller companies and entrants, success often depends on an opposite strategy, the ability to 'disintermediate', through bypassing established networks and creating a direct link to users. Where the systemic strategy offers a complete packaged service (such as the provision of a telephone set, access to local and long distance, maintenance and specialized services), the counterstrategy offers either a specialized service or a module or component. Alternatively the smaller company can offer a gateway between two systems: a physical link between different networks, or a means of converting from one computer language to another. In both cases systemic control is undermined.

AT&T, which until its 1983 divestiture was the world's largest corporation, provides a classic example. Initially AT&T licensed local telephone companies to operate their own networks, while using its long-distance network and control of interconnection to guarantee position and profits, which were consistently higher than those of the local companies. Later regulation was used to legitimize the monopoly and bar entry. Regulation shored up systemic control by banning unauthorized attachments to the network. At the same time the company made strategic use of patents and standards to control the terms on which networks and equipment could be interconnected: when its telephone patents ran out in the 1890s, the company actively accumulated other patents and inventions and sought to 'occupy the field' through the researches of Bell Labs and the systematic purchase of others' inventions. Later, patent pools were the key to the monopoly agreements on broadcasting made between RCA, Westinghouse, General Electric and AT&T. IBM, too, has used its domination of computing standards to limit the scope for interconnection of machines, to limit entry to the industry and thus control pricing.

The third element of AT&T's strategy involved vertically integrating to incorporate manufacturing so as to increase costs of entry and exercise full control over standards. Again this route has also been followed by many other companies, ranging from IBM to the Japanese electronics giants such as NEC, Fujitsu and Toshiba, which operate in a vertically integrated fashion from components manufacture to computers, communications and consumer electronics.

The alternative, disintermediating, route has been consistently used to weaken the systemic grip of companies like AT&T. Competing companies have sought to sell telephone handsets; they have built microwave networks that bypass long-distance routes; they have used satellites directly to reach large business customers and they have offered gateways (such as the modem) that allow the network to be used for other purposes. IBM has faced a similar series of inroads: PC clones, IBM compatible software and conversion devices to aid communication with other manufacturers' machines. All seek to make the system more modular and thus less amenable to central control.

The battles between these strategies have been echoed in technology. The technologies and architectures used in networks have been organized in structures which reflect pre-existing patterns of power. Telephone networks were traditionally organized in switching hierarchies, reaching from the home through local to central switches and organized in the form of a pyramid or tree and branch structure under the central control of the PTT. The first international radio networks were built on the same, star-shaped model, until it was understood that they could support many more horizontal links. The earliest computer networks were also hierarchical, tying relatively dumb terminals to a centrally controlled mainframe in star-shaped networks. Broadcasting has traditionally branched downwards from sources of central control and programming in the major cities.

With more recent generations of technology the incorporation of the new within old structures has become more turbulent and unpredictable. Disintermediation strategies have become more prevalent and more successful, taking advantage of the blurring of industry boundaries. Monopolies have faced competition within their traditional markets from competitors using substitute technologies and from erstwhile customers operating their own networks. During the 1980s AT&T entered computing (accumulating losses of $3 bn), IBM entered telecommunications (through its interests in Rolm, SBS and MCI), British Telecom, France Telecom and the DBP all invested in satellite and cable broadcasting, and the BBC began a data transmission service. In the cultural industries distribution technologies proliferated with ever greater speed: cable and satellite appeared alongside telephone networks, in competition with videos, CD-videos and digital tapes. Turbulence has been accentuated by the properties of open technologies (like the compact or personal computer) able to carry and control a wide range of types of communication. In telecommunications, competition has been deliberately introduced by governments (primarily the US, UK and Japanese) in the provision of services, in long distance and, indirectly, through the spread of private corporate networks. By the late 1980s the United States had half a dozen major long-distance companies, Britain two and Japan three. In addition the UK had two cellular radio operators and seven holders of licences for new mobile services, while Japan had over thirty new local public network operators in competition with NTT. All had highly competitive value added sectors, offering services over the public network. Where previously a single telephone network carried all voice or data signals, most advanced countries moved to a complex web of overlapping networks, ranging from videoconferencing to packet-switching, only some of which are open to the public. The history of ISDN exemplified the change. Initially conceived as a universal, standardized service, ISDN was instead marketed to target groups as one of a number of specialized services.

The fragmentation of the unitary network was aided both by trends in technology and by changes in the structure of regulation. Microwave and satellite technologies made it much cheaper to create long-distance networks to duplicate older, cable-based ones. More intelligent switching permits specialized logical networks to be created and reconfigured, and tailored to special needs even where the physical network remains under monopoly control. Packet switched networks based on the 'X.25' standard sustain transactional networks and VANs for such things as automated teller machines and hospital ordering systems. Private leased lines with ever higher transmission rates can be used by companies to link their own private exchanges, aggregating and circulating information about such things as stock turnover, physical output, fault levels and cashflow.

As the replacement of analogue techniques by digital ones gives networks a new degree of freedom, they have also become more important to the smooth working of other economic sectors. Financial institutions, car manufacturers and traders have taken on some of the characteristics of communications companies. As much as 50 per cent of the cost of a car and 60 per cent of the cost of a jet are accounted for by electronics. Each industry now has heavy fixed investments in communications technologies, and an almost total dependence on rapid and transparent communication. In this, they reflect fundamental pressures towards greater flexibility which arise from the changing nature of capitalist economy, the rapid growth of an intermediate service economy, and the move away from standardized mass production towards greater specialization, customization and shorter product cycles. Communication between different stages in the production process is under pressure to become as transparent as possible so as to speed up the circulation of goods, money and ideas, and to eliminate waste and downtimes.

While communication becomes central to the workings of economic life, the growing significance of communications costs and needs has raised the political profile of communications, prompting large corporate users such as General Motors, Mitsubishi, Hitachi, General Electric and Citicorp to lobby for lower costs and more suitable services, to develop their own systems, and to use communications as a tool of competitive strategy and positional advantage. Public networks are now overlaid with a myriad of private and exclusive networks, mainly built out of lines leased from PTTs. General Motors, in collaboration with Electronic Data Systems (EDS), is constructing what is probably the largest private network linking 500,000 terminals (roughly half voice and half data) in a private global network that will reputedly cost over $500m. Half of all international information flows now take place within transnational corporations.

Notes and references

1   John Carey, 'Technology and ideology', in *Communication as Culture*, ed. John Carey (Unwin Hyman, London, 1989), p. 202.
2   Richard B. Du Roff, 'The rise of communications regulation: the telegraph industry 1844–80', *Journal of Communications*, Summer (1984).
3   Raymond Williams, *Television Technology and Cultural Form* (Fontana/ Collins, Glasgow, 1974), p. 147.

9

The Masses: The Implosion of the Social in the Media

Jean Baudrillard

Up to now there have been two great versions of the analysis of the media (as indeed that of the masses), one optimistic and one pessimistic. The optimistic one has assumed two major tonalities, very different from one another. There is the technological optimism of Marshall McLuhan: for him the electronic media inaugurate a generalized planetary communication and should conduct us, by the mental effect alone of new technologies, beyond the atomizing rationality of the Gutenberg galaxy to the global village, to the new electronic tribalism – an achieved transparency of information and communication. The other version, more traditional, is that of dialectical optimism inspired by progressivist and Marxist thought: the media constitute a new, gigantic productive force and obey the dialectic of productive forces. Momentarily alienated and submitted to the law of capitalism, their intensive development can only eventually explode this monopoly. "For the first time in history," writes Hans Enzensberger, "the media make possible a mass participation in a productive process at once social and socialized, a participation whose practical means are in the hands of the masses themselves."[1] These two positions more or less, the one technological, the other ideological, inspire the whole analysis and the present practice of the media.

It is more particularly to the optimism of Enzensberger that I formerly opposed a resolutely pessimist vision in "Requiem for the media." In that I described the mass media as a "speech without response." What characterizes the mass media is that they are opposed to mediation, intransitive, that they fabricate noncommunication – if one accepts the definition of communication as an exchange, as the reciprocal space of speech and response, and thus of *responsibility*; in other words, if one defines it as anything other than the simple emission/reception of information. Now the whole present architecture of the media is founded on this last definition: they are what finally forbids response, what renders impossible any process of exchange (except in the shape of a simulation of a response, which is itself integrated into the process of emission, and this changes nothing in the unilaterality of communication). That is their true abstraction. And it is in this abstraction that is founded the system of social control and power. To understand properly the term *response*, one must appreciate it in a meaning at once strong, symbolic, and primitive: power belongs to him who gives and to whom no return can be made. To give, and to do it in such a way that no return can be made, is to break exchange to one's own profit and to institute a monopoly: the social process is out of balance. To make a return, on the contrary, is to break this power relationship and to restore on the basis of an antagonistic reciprocity the circuit of symbolic exchange. The same applies in the sphere of the media: there speech occurs in such a way that there is no possibility of a return. The restitution of this possibility of response entails upsetting the whole present structure; even better, it entails an "antimedia" struggle.

In reality, even if I did not share the technological optimism of McLuhan, I always recognized and considered as a gain the true revolution which he brought about in media analysis. On the other hand, though I also did not share the dialectical hopes of Enzensberger, I was not truly pessimistic, since I believed in a possible subversion of the code of the media and in the possibility of an alternate speech and a radical reciprocity of symbolic exchange.

Today all that has changed. I would no longer interpret in the same way the forced silence of the masses in the mass media. I would no longer see in it a sign of passivity and of alienation, but to the contrary an original strategy, an original response in the form of a challenge; and on the basis of this reversal I suggest to you a vision of things which is no longer optimistic or pessimistic, but ironic and antagonistic.

I will take the example of opinion polls, which are themselves a mass medium. It is said that opinion polls constitute a manipulation of democracy. This is certainly no more the case than that publicity is a manipulation of need and of consumption. It too produces demand (or so it claims) and invokes needs just as opinion polls produce answers and induce future behavior. All this would be serious if there were an objective truth of needs, an objective truth of public opinion. It is obvious that here we need to exercise extreme care. The influence of publicity, of opinion polls, of all the media, and of information in general would be dramatic if we were certain that there exists in opposition to it an authentic human nature, an authentic essence of the social, with its needs, its own will, its own values, its finalities. For this would set up the problem of its radical alienation. And indeed it is in this form that traditional critiques are expressed.

Now the matter is at once less serious and more serious than this. The uncertainty which surrounds the social and political effect of opinion polls (do they or do they not manipulate opinion?), like that which surrounds the real economic efficacy of publicity, will never be completely relieved – and it is just as well! This results from the fact that there is a compound, a mixture of two heterogeneous systems whose data cannot be transferred from one to the other. An operational system which is statistical, information-based, and simulational is projected onto a traditional values system, onto a system of representation, will, and opinion. This collage, this collusion between the two, gives rise to an indefinite and useless polemic. We should agree neither with those who praise the beneficial use of the media, nor with those who scream about manipulation, for the simple reason that there is no relationship between a system of meaning and a system of simulation. Publicity and opinion polls would be incapable, even if they wished and claimed to do so, of alienating the will or the opinion of anybody at all, for the reason that they do not act in the time–space of will and of representation where judgment is formed. For the same reason, though reversed, it is quite impossible for them to throw any light at all on public opinion or individual will, since they do not act in a public space, on the stage of a public space. They are strangers to it, and indeed they wish to dismantle it. Publicity and opinion polls and the media in general can only be imagined; they only exist on the basis of a disappearance, the disappearance from the public space, from the scene of politics, of public opinion in a form at once theatrical and representative as it was enacted in earlier epochs. Thus we can be reassured: they cannot destroy it. But we should not have any illusions: they cannot restore it either.

It is this lack of relationship between the two systems which today plunges us into a state of stupor. That is what I said: stupor. To be more objective one would have to say: a radical uncertainty as to our own desire, our own choice, our own opinion, our own will. This is the clearest result of the whole media environment, of the information which makes demands on us from all sides and which is as good as blackmail.

We will never know if an advertisement or opinion poll has had a real influence on individual or collective wills, but we will never know either what would have happened if there had been no opinion poll or advertisement.

The situation no longer permits us to isolate reality or human nature as a fundamental variable. The result is therefore not to provide any additional information or to shed any light on reality, but on the contrary, because we will never in future be able to separate reality from its statistical, simulative projection in the media, a state of suspense and of definitive uncertainty about reality. And I repeat: it is a question here of a completely new species of uncertainty, which results not from the *lack* of information but from information itself and even from an *excess* of information. It is information itself which produces uncertainty, and so this uncertainty, unlike the traditional uncertainty which could always be resolved, is irreparable.

This is our destiny: subject to opinion polls, information, publicity, statistics; constantly confronted with the anticipated statistical verification of our behavior, and absorbed by this permanent refraction of our least movements, we are no longer confronted with our own will. We are no longer even alienated, because for that it is necessary for the subject to be divided in itself, confronted with the other, to be contradictory. Now, where there is no other, the scene of the other, like that of politics and of society, has disappeared. Each individual is forced despite himself or herself into the undivided coherency of statistics. There is in this a positive absorption into the transparency of computers, which is something worse than alienation.

There is an obscenity in the functioning and the omnipresence of opinion polls as in that of publicity. Not because they might betray the secret of an opinion, the intimacy of a will, or because they might violate some unwritten law of the private being, but because they exhibit this redundancy of the social, this sort of continual voyeurism of the group in relation to itself: it must at all times know what it wants, know what it thinks, be told about its least needs, its least quivers, *see* itself continually on the videoscreen of statistics, constantly watch its own temperature chart, in a sort of hypochondriacal madness. The social becomes obsessed with itself; through this auto-information, this permanent auto-intoxication, it becomes its own vice, its own perversion. This is the real obscenity. Through this feedback, this incessant anticipated accounting, the social loses its own scene. It no longer enacts itself; it has no more time to enact itself; it no longer occupies a particular space, public or political; it becomes confused with its own control screen. Overinformed, it develops ingrowing obesity. For everything which loses its *scene* (like the obese body) becomes for that very reason *ob-scene*.

The silence of the masses is also in a sense obscene. For the masses are also made of this useless hyperinformation which claims to enlighten them, when all it does is clutter up the space of the representable and annul itself in a silent equivalence. And we cannot do much against this obscene circularity of the masses and of information. The two phenomena fit one another: the masses have no opinion and information does not inform them. Both of them, lacking a scene where the meaning of the social can be enacted, continue to feed one another monstrously – as the speed with which information revolves increases continually the weight of the masses as such, and not their self-awareness.

So if one takes opinion polls, and the uncertainty which they induce about the principle of social reality, and the type of obscenity, of statistical pornography to which they attract us – if we take all that seriously, if we confront all that with the claimed finalities of information and of the social itself, then it all seems very dramatic. But there is another way of taking things. It does not shed much more credit on opinion polls, but it restores a sort of status to them, in terms of derision and of play. In effect we can consider the indecisiveness of their results, the uncertainty of their effects, and their unconscious humor, which is rather similar to that of meteorology (for example, the possibility of verifying at the same time contradictory facts or tendencies); or again the casual way in which everybody uses them, disagreeing with them privately and especially if they verify exactly one's own behavior (no one accepts a perfect statistical evaluation of his chances). That is the real problem of the credibility accorded to them.

Statistics, as an objective computation of probabilities, obviously eliminate any elective chance and any personal destiny. That is why, deep down, none of us believes in them, any more than the gambler believes in chance, but only in Luck (with a capital, the equivalent of Grace, not with lower case, which is the equivalent of probability). An amusing example of this obstinate denial of statistical chance is given by this news item: "If this will reassure you, we have calculated that, of every 50 people who catch the metro twice a day for 60 years, only one is in danger of being attacked. Now there is no reason why it should be you!" The beauty of statistics is never in their objectivity but in their involuntary humor.

So if one takes opinion polls in this way, one can conceive that they could work for the masses themselves as a game, as a spectacle, as a means of deriding both the social and the political. The fact that opinion polls do their best to destroy the political as will and representation, the political as meaning, precisely through the effect of simulation and uncertainty – this fact can only give pleasure to the ironic unconscious of the masses (and to our individual political unconscious, if I may use this expression), whose deepest drive remains the symbolic murder of the political class, the symbolic murder of political *reality*, and this murder is produced by opinion polls in their own way. That is why I wrote in *Silent Majorities* that the masses, which have always provided an alibi for political representation, take their revenge by allowing themselves the theatrical representation of the political scene. The people have become *public*. They even allow themselves the luxury of enjoying day by day, as in a home cinema, the fluctuations of their own opinion in the daily reading of the opinion polls.

It is only to this extent that they believe in them, that we all believe in them, as we believe in a game of malicious foretelling, a double or quits on the green baize of the political scene. It is, paradoxically, as a game that the opinion polls recover a sort of legitimacy. A game of the undecidable; a game of chance; a game of the undecidability of the political scene, of the equifinality of all tendencies; a game of truth effects in the circularity of questions and answers. Perhaps we can see here the apparition of one of these collective forms of game which Caillois called *aléa* – an irruption into the polls themselves of a ludic, aleatory process, an ironic mirror for the use of the masses (and we all belong to the masses) of a political scene which is caught in its own trap (for the politicians are the only ones to believe in the polls, along with the pollsters obviously, as the only ones to believe in publicity are the publicity agents).

In this regard, one may restore to them a sort of positive meaning: they would be part of a contemporary cultural mutation, part of the era of simulation.

In view of this type of consequence, we are forced to congratulate ourselves on the very failure of polls, and on the distortions which make them undecidable and chancy. Far from regretting this, we must consider that there is a sort of fate or evil genius (the evil genius of the social itself?) which throws this too beautiful machine out of gear and prevents it from achieving the objectives which it claims. We must also ask if these distortions, far from being the consequence of a bad angle of refraction of information onto an inert and opaque matter, are not rather the consequence of an offensive resistance of the social itself to its investigation, the shape taken by an occult duel between the pollsters and the object polled, between information and the people who receive it.

This is fundamental: people are always supposed to be willing partners in the game of truth, in the game of information. It is agreed that the object can always be persuaded of its truth; it is inconceivable that the object of the investigation, the object of the poll, should not adopt, generally speaking, the strategy of the subject of the analysis, of the pollster. There may certainly be some difficulties (for instance, the object does not understand the question; it's not its business; it's undecided; it replies in terms of the interviewer and not of the question, and so on), but it is admitted that the poll analyst is capable of rectifying what is basically only a lack of adaptation to the analytic apparatus. The hypothesis is never suggested that all this, far from being a marginal, archaic residue, is the effect of an offensive (not defensive) counter-strategy by the object; that, all in all, there exists somewhere an original, positive, possibly victorious strategy of the object opposed to the strategy of the subject (in this case, the pollster or any other producer of messages).

This is what one could call the evil genius of the object, the evil genius of the masses, the evil genius of the social itself, constantly producing failure in the truth of the social and in its analysis, and for that reason unacceptable, and even unimaginable, to the tenants of this analysis.

To reflect the other's desire, to reflect its demand like a mirror, even to anticipate it: it is hard to imagine what powers of deception, of absorption, of deviation – in a word, of subtle revenge – there is in this type of response. This is the way the masses escape as reality, in this very mirror, in those simulative devices which are designed to capture them. Or again, the way in which events themselves disappear behind the television screen, or the more general screen of information (for it is true that events have no probable existence except on this deflective screen, which is no longer a mirror). While the mirror and screen of alienation was a mode of production (the imaginary subject), this new screen is simply its mode of disappearance. But disappearance is a very complex mode: the object, the individual, is not only condemned to disappearance, but *disappearance is also its strategy*; it is its way of response to this device for capture, for networking, and for forced identification. To this *cathodic* surface of recording, the individual or the mass reply by a *parodic* behavior of disappearance. What are they; what do they do; what do they become behind this screen? They turn themselves into an impenetrable and meaningless surface, which is a method of disappearing. They eclipse themselves; they melt into the superficial screen in such a way that their reality and that of their movement, just like that of particles of matter, may be radically questioned without making any fundamental change to the probabilistic analysis of their behavior. In fact, behind this "objective" fortification of networks and models which believe they can capture them, and where the whole population of analysts and expert observers believe that they capture them, there passes a wave of derision, of reversal, and of parody which is the active exploitation, the parodic enactment by the object itself of its mode of disappearance.

[···]

About the media you can sustain two opposing hypotheses: they are the strategy of power, which finds in them the means of mystifying the masses and of imposing its own truth. Or else they are the strategic territory of the ruse of the masses, who exercise in them their concrete power of the refusal of truth, of the denial of reality. Now the media are nothing else than a marvelous instrument for destabilizing the real and the true, all historical or political truth (there is thus no possible political strategy of the media: it is a contradiction in terms). And the addiction that we have for the media, the impossibility of doing without them, is a deep result of this phenomenon: it is not a result of a desire for culture, communication, and information, but of this perversion of truth and falsehood, of this destruction of meaning in the operation of the medium. The desire for a show, the desire for simulation, which is at the same time a desire for dissimulation. This is a vital reaction. It is a spontaneous, total resistance to the ultimatum of historical and political reason.

Note

1   Hans Magnus Enzensberger, 'Constituents of a theory of the media', *New Left Review*, 64 (1970), pp. 13–36.

10

The Question of Cultural Identity

Stuart Hall

It is now a commonplace that the modern age gave rise to a new and decisive form of *individualism*, at the centre of which stood a new conception of the individual subject and its identity. This does not mean that people were not individuals in pre-modern times, but that individuality was both 'lived', 'experienced' and 'conceptualized' differently. The transformations which ushered in modernity tore the individual free from its stable moorings in traditions and structures. Since these were believed to be divinely ordained, they were held not to be subject to fundamental change. One's status, rank and position in the 'great chain of being' – the secular and divine order of things – overshadowed any sense that one was a sovereign individual. The birth of the 'sovereign individual' between the Renaissance humanism of the sixteenth century and the Enlightenment of the eighteenth century represented a significant break with the past. Some argue that it was the engine which set the whole social system of 'modernity' in motion.

Raymond Williams notes that the modern history of the individual subject brings together two distinct meanings: on the one hand, the subject is 'indivisible' – an entity which is unified within itself and cannot be further divided; on the other, it is also an entity which is 'singular, distinctive, unique'.[1] Many major movements in Western thought and culture contributed to the emergence of this new conception: the Reformation and Protestantism, which set the individual conscience free from the religious institutions of the Church and exposed it directly to the eye of God; Renaissance humanism, which placed Man (*sic*) at the centre of the universe; the scientific revolutions, which endowed Man with the faculty and capacities to inquire into, investigate and unravel the mysteries of Nature; and the Enlightenment, centred on the image of rational, scientific Man, freed from dogma and intolerance, before whom the whole of human history was laid out for understanding and mastery.

[· · ·]

Those who hold that modern identities are being fragmented argue that what has happened in late-modernity to the conception of the modern subject is not simply its estrangement but its dislocation. They trace this dislocation through a series of ruptures in the discourses of modern knowledge. In this section, I shall offer a brief sketch of five great advances in social theory and the human sciences which have occurred in, or had their major impact upon, thought in the period of late-modernity (the second half of the twentieth century), and whose main effect, it is argued, has been the final de-centring of the Cartesian subject.

The first major de-centring concerns the traditions of Marxist thinking. Marx's writing belongs, of course, to the nineteenth and not the twentieth century. But one of the ways in which his work was recovered and re-read in the 1960s was in the light of his argument that 'men (sic) make history, but only on the basis of conditions which are not of their own making'. His re-readers interpreted this to mean that individuals could not in any true sense be the 'authors' or agents of history since they could only act on the basis of the historical conditions made by others into which they were born, and using the resources (material and culture) provided to them from previous generations.

Marxism, properly understood, they argued, displaced any notion of individual agency. The Marxist structuralist, Louis Althusser (1918–89) argued that, by putting social relations (modes of production, exploitation of labour power, the circuits of capital) rather than an abstract notion of Man at the centre of his theoretical system, Marx displaced two key propositions of modern philosophy: '(1) that there is a universal essence of man; (2) that this essence is the attribute of "each single individual" who is its real subject':

> These two postulates are complementary and indissoluble. But their existence and their unity presuppose a whole empiricist–idealist world outlook. By rejecting the essence of man as his theoretical basis, Marx rejected the whole of this organic system of postulates. He drove the philosophical category of *the subject*, of *empiricism*, of the *ideal essence* from all the domains in which they had been supreme. Not only from political economy (rejection of the myth of *homo economicus*, that is, of the individual with definite faculties and needs as the subject of the classical economy); not just from history; . . . not just from ethics (rejection of the Kantian ethical idea); but also from philosophy itself.[2]

This 'total theoretical revolution' was, of course, fiercely contested by many humanistic theorists who give greater weight in historical explanation to human agency. We need not argue here about whether Althusser was wholly or partly right, or entirely wrong. The fact is that, though his work has been extensively criticized, his 'theoretical anti-humanism' (that is, a way of thinking opposed to theories which derive their argument from some notion of a universal essence of Man lodged in each individual subject) has had considerable impact on many branches of modern thought.

The second of the great 'de-centrings' in twentieth-century Western thought comes from Freud's 'discovery' of the unconscious. Freud's theory that our identities, our sexuality, and the structure of our desires are formed on the basis of the psychic and symbolic processes of the unconscious, which function according to a 'logic' very different from that of Reason, plays havoc with the concept of the knowing and rational subject with a fixed and unified identity – the subject of Descartes's 'I think, therefore I am'. This aspect of Freud's work has also had a profound impact on modern thought in the last three decades. Psychoanalytic thinkers like Jacques Lacan, for example, read Freud as saying that the image of the self as 'whole' and unified is something which the infant only gradually, partially, and with great difficulty, *learns*. It does not grow naturally from inside the core of the infant's being, but is formed in relation to others; especially in the complex unconscious psychic negotiations in early childhood between the child and the powerful fantasies which it has of its parental figures. In what Lacan calls the 'mirror phase' of development, the infant who is not yet co-ordinated, and possesses no self image as a 'whole' person, sees or 'imagines' itself reflected – either literally in the mirror, or figuratively, in the 'mirror' of the other's look – as a 'whole person'. This is close in some ways to Mead's and Cooley's 'looking glass' conception of the interactive self; except that for them socialization was a matter of conscious learning, whereas for Freud subjectivity was the product of unconscious psychic processes.

This formation of the self in the 'look' of the Other, according to Lacan, opens the child's relation with symbolic systems outside itself, and is thus the moment of the child's entry into the various systems of symbolic representation – including language, culture and sexual difference. The contradictory and unresolved feelings which accompany this difficult entry – the splitting of love and hate for the father, the conflict between the wish to please and the impulse to reject the mother, the division of the self into its 'good' and 'bad' parts, the disavowal of the masculine/feminine parts of oneself, and so on – which are key aspects of this 'unconscious formation of the subject', and which leave the subject 'divided', remain with one for life. However, though the subject is always split or divided it experiences its own identity as being held together and 'resolved', or unified, as a result of the fantasy of itself as a unified 'person' which it formed in the mirror phase. This, according to this kind of psychoanalytic thinking, is the contradictory origin of 'identity'.

Thus, identity is actually something formed through unconscious processes over time, rather than being innate in consciousness at birth. There is always something 'imaginary' or fantasized about its unity. It always remains incomplete, is always 'in process', always 'being formed'. The 'feminine' parts of the male self, for example, which are disavowed, remain with him and find unconscious expressions in many unacknowledged ways in adult life. Thus, rather than speaking of identity as a finished thing, we should speak of *identification*, and see it as an ongoing process. Identity arises, not so much from the fullness of identity which is already inside us as individuals, but from a *lack* of wholeness which is 'filled' from *outside us*, by the ways we imagine ourselves to be seen by *others*. Psychoanalytically, the reason why we continually search for 'identity', constructing biographies which knit together the different parts of our divided selves into a unity, is to recapture this fantasized pleasure of fullness (plenitude).

Again, Freud's work, and that of the psychoanalytic thinkers like Lacan who read him in this way, has been widely contested. By definition, unconscious processes cannot be easily seen or examined. They have to be inferred by the elaborate psychoanalytic techniques of reconstruction and interpretation and are not easily amenable to 'proof'. Nevertheless, their general impact on modern ways of thought has been very considerable. Much modern thinking about subjective and psychic life is 'post-Freudian', in the sense that it takes Freud's work on the unconscious for granted, even when it rejects some of his specific hypotheses. Again, you can appreciate the damage which this way of thinking does to notions of the rational subject and identity as fixed and stable.

The third de-centring I shall examine is associated with the work of the structural linguist Ferdinand de Saussure. Saussure argued that we are not in any absolute sense the 'authors' of the statements we make or of the meanings we express in language. We can only use language to produce meanings by positioning ourselves within the rules of language and the systems of meaning of our culture. Language is a social, not an individual system. It pre-exists us. We cannot in any simple sense be its authors. To speak a language is not only to express our innermost, original thoughts, it is also to activate the vast range of meanings which are already embedded in our language and cultural systems.

Further, the meanings of words are not fixed in a one-to-one relation to objects or events in the world outside language. Meaning arises in the relations of similarity and difference which words have to other words within the language code. We know what 'night' is because it is *not* 'day'. Notice the analogy here between language and identity. I know who 'I' am in relation to 'the other' (e.g. my mother) whom I cannot be. As Lacan would say, identity, like the unconscious, 'is structured like language'. What modern philosophers of language, like Jacques Derrida, who have been influenced by Saussure and the 'linguistic turn', argue is that, despite his/her best efforts the individual speaker can never finally fix meaning – including the meaning of his or her identity. Words are 'multi-accentual'. They always carry echoes of other meanings which they trigger off, despite one's best efforts to close meaning down. Our statements are underpinned by propositions and premises of which we are not aware, but which are, so to speak, carried along in the blood-stream of our language. Everything we say has a 'before' and an 'after' – a 'margin' in which others may write. Meaning is inherently unstable: it aims for closure (identity), but is constantly disrupted (by difference). It is constantly sliding away from us. There are always supplementary meanings over which we have no control, which will arise and subvert our attempts to create fixed and stable worlds.

The fourth major de-centring of identity and the subject occurs in the work of the French philosopher and historian Michel Foucault. In a series of studies Foucault has produced a sort of 'genealogy of the modern subject'. Foucault isolates a new type of power, evolving through the nineteenth century and coming to full flower at the beginning of this century, which he calls 'disciplinary power'. Disciplinary power is concerned with the regulation, surveillance and government of, first, the human species or whole populations, and second, the individual and the body. Its sites are those new institutions which developed throughout the nineteenth century and which 'police' and discipline modern populations – in workshops, barracks, schools, prisons, hospitals, clinics and so on.

The aim of 'disciplinary power' is to bring 'the lives, deaths, activities, work, miseries and joys of the individual', as well as his/her moral and physical health, sexual practices and family life, under stricter discipline and control; bringing to bear on them the power of administrative re-gimes, the expertise of the professional, and the knowledge provided by the 'disciplines' of the social sciences. Its basic object is to produce 'a human being who can be treated as a "docile body" '.

What is particularly interesting from the point of view of the history of the modern subject is that, though Foucault's disciplinary power is the product of the new large-scale regulating *collective* institutions of late-modernity, its techniques involve an application of power and knowledge which further 'individualizes' the subject and bears down more intensely on his/her body:

> In a disciplinary regime, individualization is descending. Through surveillance, constant observation, all those subject to control are individualized. . . . Not only has power now brought individuality into the field of observation, but power fixes that objective individuality in the field of writing. A vast, meticulous documentary apparatus becomes an essential component of the growth of power [in modern societies]. This accumulation of individual documentation in a systematic ordering makes 'possible the measurement of overall phenomena, the description of groups, the characterization of collective facts, the calculation of gaps between individuals, their distribution in a given population'.[3]

It is not necessary to accept every detail of Foucault's picture of the all-encompassing character of the 'disciplinary regimes' of modern administrative power to understand the paradox that, the more collective and organized is the nature of the institutions of late-modernity, the greater the isolation, surveillance and individuation of the individual subject.

The fifth de-centring which proponents of this position cite is the impact of feminism, both as theoretical critique and as a social movement. Feminism belongs with that company of 'new social movements', all of which surfaced during the 1960s – the great watershed of late-modernity – alongside the student upheavals, the anti-war and counter-cultural youth movements, the civil rights struggles, the Third World revolutionary movements, the peace movements, and the rest associated with '1968'. What is important about this historical moment is that:

1   these movements were opposed to the corporate liberal politics of the West as well as the 'Stalinist' politics of the East;
2   they affirmed the 'subjective' as well as the 'objective' dimensions of politics;
3   they were suspicious of all bureaucratic forms of organization and favoured spontaneity and acts of political will;
4   as argued earlier, all these movements had a powerful *cultural* emphasis and form – they espoused the 'theatre' of revolution;
5   they reflected the weakening or break-up of class politics, and the mass political organizations associated with it and their fragmentation into various and separate social movements;
6   each movement appealed to the social *identity* of its supporters. Thus feminism appealed to women, sexual politics to gays and lesbians,

racial struggles to blacks, anti-war to peaceniks, and so on. This is the historical birth of what came to be known as *identity politics* – one identity per movement.

But feminism also had a more direct relation to the conceptual de-centring of the Cartesian and the sociological subject:

1   It questioned the classic distinction between 'inside' and 'outside', 'private' and 'public'. Feminism's slogan was 'the personal is political'.
2   It therefore opened up to political contestation whole new arenas of social life – the family, sexuality, housework, the domestic division of labour, child-rearing, etc.
3   It also exposed, as a political and social question, the issue of how we are formed and produced as gendered subjects. That is to say, it politicized subjectivity, identity and the process of identification (as men/women, mothers/fathers, sons/daughters).
4   What began as a movement directed at challenging the social *position* of women expanded to include the *formation* of sexual and gendered identities.
5   Feminism challenged the notion that men and women were part of the same identity – 'Mankind' – replacing it with *the question of sexual difference*.

In this Reading, then, I have tried to map the conceptual shifts by which, according to some theorists, the Enlightenment 'subject', with a fixed and stable identity, was de-centred into the open, contradictory, unfinished, fragmented identities of the postmodern subject. I have traced this through *five* great de-centrings. Let me remind you again that a great many social scientists and intellectuals do not accept the conceptual or intellectual implications (as outlined above) of these developments in modern thought. However, few would now deny their deeply unsettling effects on late-modern ideas and, particularly, on how the subject and the issue of identity have come to be conceptualized.

Notes and references

1   R. Williams, *Keywords* (Fontana, London, 1976), pp. 133–5.
2   L. Althusser, *For Marx* (Verso, London, 1966), p. 228.
3   H. Dreyfus and P. Rabinow, *Michel Foucault: Beyond Structuralism and Hermeneutics* (Harvester, Brighton, 1982).

11

Baudrillard and TV Ads

Mark Poster

Normally a sign is composed of a word and a mental image and is associated with a referent, a thing in the real world. When signs are exchanged between individuals they become symbolic; their meaning floats ambiguously between the individuals, associated as it necessarily is with their relationship to each other. The word does not simply have a "meaning"; it is also shared between the speakers, exchanged like gifts that enrich or diminish the social tie. Such at any rate is Baudrillard's linguistic utopia, his ideal speech situation.

The advertised consumer object changes all of that. The ad takes a signifier, a word that has no traditional relation with the object being promoted, and attaches it to that object. The ad constitutes a new linguistic and communications reality. These floating signifiers derive their effects precisely from their recontextualization in the ad. Extracted from an actual relation between lovers, romance or sexiness increases in linguistic power. In the ad, the sexy floor wax is more romantic than a man or woman in an actual relationship. This surplus meaning, to repeat, derives from the unique linguistic structure of the ad. Romance in the floor-wax ad is constituted by words and images that are *not found* in daily life. An attractive man abruptly appears in (penetrates into) an ordinary kitchen while an average woman futilely scrubs away using the wrong product. The very impossibility of the sexy man making his appearance in the kitchen as he does (he *pops* into the picture, for example, by virtue of a careful splice of the videotape) sets the ad apart from representational and scientific logic. The cartoon-like appearance of the man registers the image as fantasy, a fantasy of Prince Charming, but a Prince Charming who exists not in books of fiction, not in remote fairy tales, but in an image of a kitchen very much like one's own. Johnson's floor wax now equals romantic rescue. The commodity has been given a semiotic value that is distinct from, indeed out of phase with, its use-value and its exchange-value. The very "senselessness" of the relation romance = floor wax is a condition of its communications meaning.

Baudrillard's argument is not that people "believe" the ad; that itself would assume a representational logic, one subject to cause–effect analysis (how many people bought the product because they saw the ad). Nor is his argument based on irrational manipulation; the ad works on the unconscious of the viewer, subliminally hypnotizing the viewer to buy the product. This would be a Freudian-like reversal of the logic of representation. Instead Baudrillard sets his argument in linguistic terms: the ad shapes a new language, a new set of meanings (floor wax/romance) which everyone speaks or better which speaks everyone. Baudrillard calls the collective language of commodity ads "the code," a term which he has not adequately defined or elaborated.

The code may be understood as a language or sign system unique to the mode of information, to electronically mediated communication systems. The code speaks individuals in the same way that all language may be understood to speak individuals, as a sign system. As Saussure demonstrated long ago, the binary structure of signs, the set of semantic differences through which meaning is constituted, requires for its intelligibility that one situate the subject of speech not as an agent but as an effect of the structure of language. When a speaker utters the word "I" he or she *is spoken* by English, a language in which the words I and you are differentiated to indicate distinct linguistic positions. The social effect of the ad (floor wax/romance) is not economic or psychological but linguistic: the TV viewer participates in a communication, is part of a new language system. That is all. But that is also enough to constitute a social formation. Without comprehending this language effect of ads, critical social theory cannot grasp the new structural dimensions introduced by the mode of information. The temptation must be resisted to interpret the ad by the hermeneutics of suspicion within the representational logic of Marxism which sees the ad as a "corruption" of values, an "abuse" of language. Such a strategy will miss the point, will obscure the language of the code, and will reduce its effects to those of the logic of capital.

[···]

The historical constitution of language concerns the restructuring of the sign and the system of signs so that reality is configured differently in the communicative action of each mode of signification. With Baudrillard we can say that the mode of signification of the classical capitalist period was the representational sign. The social world was constituted in the figure of "realism" through signs whose stable referents were material objects. The medium of exchange that held together signifier and signified was reason. The communicative act that best exemplified the representational sign was reading the written word. The stability and linearity of the written word help to constitute the subject in reason, a confident, coherent subject who spoke the language of realism through signs whose highest ideal was the discourse of natural science. Modes of signification are certainly not exclusive or uniform in any epoch; but an argument could be made that in the epoch preceding our own, this representation form was dominant.

In the modern period the signifier held an abstract relation to the signified. For many words were the tools of reason, having no inherent connection with the meanings they evoked or with the things to which those meanings pointed, yet still secure enough. The metanarrative of reason underlay this mode of signification, certified for each individual repeatedly through acts of reading, through continuously following in the mind's eye the unidirectional flow of printed words. The bourgeoisie lived and many continue to live unselfconsciously in the cloud of the representational mode of signification. The construction of the great industrial empires was directed by those who had no doubt that words and things cohered and represented objects, just as bricks and mortar combine to form walls. Confronted by the morning newspaper or the ledger book, works constituted the subject in the mode of reason, as the instrumental subject. This adult, white, male subject surveyed the social world from a place of transcendental freedom only to the extent that he had already been constituted by the representational mode of signification.

In the informational mode of signification (the mode of information) things go differently. The abstract conventionality in the internal relation of the components of the sign characteristic of the earlier period is carried a giant step farther. The all-important link between sign and referent is shattered in what Henri Lefebvre, Baudrillard's mentor, called "the decline of the referentials." The new mode of signification is characteristic of the mass media. In Richard Terdiman's analysis, newspapers were the first to change from the mode of representation to the mode of information, from contextualized, linear analysis to a montage of isolated data giving an appearance of objectivity. But what else is so-called objectivity than this depoliticized simulation of truth. In Paris as elsewhere newspapers changed from being organs of particular points of view to purveyors of "all the truth that's fit to print" in the second half of the nineteenth century at a time when circulation soared to mass proportions. The more newspapers moved away from distinct communities, the more disjoint they were from their reference group, the more their discourse left the model of representation in favor of that of information.

In TV ads, where the new mode of signification is most clearly seen, floating signifiers are attached to commodities only in the virtuoso communication of the ad. The ability of language to signify, to present meaning is not simply acknowledged by recognition of its conventionality; it becomes the subject and structure of the communication. Each TV ad replicates in its structure the ultimate facility of language: language is remade, new connections are established in the TV ad through which new meanings emerge. If the TV ad is read through the representational mode of signification, it is interpreted as an offense, a manipulation, a set of falsehoods, deeply disgusting and even morally dangerous. And so it is as if the world is constituted with reference to the adult, white, male metanarrative of reason.

But it is difficult day after day to sustain such a reading of the TV ad and it is important to investigate why it is so difficult. As ad after ad is viewed, the representational critic gradually loses interest, becomes lulled into a noncritical stance, is bored and gradually receives the communication differently. My argument is that the ads constitute the viewer in a nonrepresentational, noninstrumental communications mode, one different from reading print. Surely the TV ad is designed to sell the product but in doing so it remakes language. The instrumental function is denegated by the TV ad; the ad only works to the extent that it is not understood to be an ad, not understood instrumentally. Through its linguistic structure the TV ad communicates at a level other than the instrumental which is placed in brackets. Floating signifiers, which have no relation to the product, are set in play; images and words that convey desirable or undesirable states of being are portrayed in a manner that optimizes the viewer's attention without arousing critical awareness.

A communication is enacted, in the TV ad, which is not found in any context of daily life. An unreal is made real, a set of meanings is communicated that have no meaning. In Baudrillard's terms a simulation of a communication is communicated which is more real than reality. The commodity-object in the TV ad is not the same as the one taken home from the store and consumed. The latter is useful but prosaic, efficient but forgettable, operational but ordinary. The object in the ad and in the store display is magical, fulfilling, desirable, exciting. The difference between the two is produced by the TV ad in its communication which constitutes the subject within the code. The hyperreal is linguistically created in the TV ad; it vanishes when the consumer becomes a user, when the subject constituted by the communication becomes a subject constituted in the everyday relation to the commodity-object.

Or perhaps not, perhaps the simulation effect continues. Baudrillard contends that the hyperreal is our "reality," not just in TV ads but as the way in which late twentieth-century culture mobilizes subjects. "*It is reality itself today that is hyperrealist....* Today it is quotidian reality in its entirety – political, social, historical and economic – that from now on incorporates the simulatory dimension of hyperrealism. We live everywhere already in an 'esthetic' hallucination of reality."[1] The generalization of the concept of the hyperreal from specific communications practices to the social totality is the problematic element in Baudrillard's discourse, the aspect of his position that the critical theory of the mode of information must reject. At this point in Baudrillard's position a differential analysis of a set of discourses/practices recedes in favor of global statements. Such statements as "We live everywhere already ..." make claims that are beyond the limit of the situated finitude of their author.

As one Marxist critic, Gerry Gill, has pointed out, "Baudrillard grants to the 'code' an almost total sway across economy, politics, ideology and culture ...."[2] He favorably compares Althusser's position to that of Baudrillard: "Where, for Althusser, ideology constitutes persons as subjects, for Baudrillard signs and the code assign subjects to their places in an hierarchical social order and locks them into a discourse which allows only commodity and sign exchange."[3] Gill's Marxism permits him to condone Baudrillard's early critique of commodities as a valuable supplement to historical materialism, but to reject the more recent work as the "ideology" of poststructuralism. Like the poststructuralists, Gill complains, Baudrillard abstracts from the "intersubjective moment" and then "revels in the experience of active de-centered subjectivity."[4] The Althusserian Marxist critique of poststructuralism contextualizes this "active de-centered subjectivity."

Poststructuralists practice a reading of texts in which meaning is actively constituted by the reader. The practice of the intellectual by which the self is constituted in isolated readings, Gill argues, has been extended by capitalism to all of mass society by the generalization of higher education. Mass education means "training in thinking hypothetically and systematically about the world [and] requires that the ego separate itself from identification with particular pre-given roles and norms of closed group life."[5] The poststructuralists thus theorize a new social practice, but their mistake, he claims, is that they omit the self-reflexive moment whereby their own practice is contextualized. Gill critically concludes that the "poststructuralist and deconstructionist project is a commitment to the social conditions which generate and maintain its distinctive mode of subjectivity . . . while masking its constitutive conditions. . . ."[6]

While this critique of poststructuralism may apply in some degree to Derrida, Barthes, Lacan and perhaps others, it is not germane to the position of Baudrillard. The theorist of the hyperreal is constantly at pains to capture those practices through which his position is generated. Few theorists are more self-reflexive than Baudrillard. His writing is bathed in a sense of the social reality around him and betrays a continuing effort to clarify his own experience in relation to that social present. Baudrillard's is not a case of the world being confined to the edges of the book. In fact, by implying that the mode of information is structured by the practice of reading, the Marxist critic is off target. The TV ad is not like reading, does not follow the linear logic of representation. One could argue the opposite: the spread of the hyperreal in TV ads and the like creates a practice of self-constitution that becomes translated by poststructuralists like Derrida, Foucault and Barthes into a new practice of reading, one that violates the traditional mode of signification associated with reading, one that breaks with the literalness and stability, the monolithic univocality of the printed word. If anything poststructuralists translate reading practices through the language of the mode of information. Precisely this may explain the violent opposition they arouse in so many quarters: they have transgressed the rules of representational discourse associated with the book, bringing to reading the vertiginous multivocality of the TV ad. Gill may be right that Derrida is not reflexive about the sociolinguistic context of his discourse, but he is wrong to define that discourse as one of reading. Deconstruction may better be defined as TV viewing applied to books. It takes the substanceless unreality of the TV ad as the metanarrative of writing.

The Marxist critique of the hyperreal is an ambiguous one. On one side the hyperreal is recognized as an increasingly dominant ideological moment; on the other it is condemned as an ideological misconstruction. One cannot have it both ways: either Baudrillard has got it wrong and the hyperreal does not correspond to practices of self-constitution in contemporary society, or something is at play in Baudrillard's position that uncovers an important feature of society, one that cannot be accounted for from within the categories of the mode of production, one whose articulated complexity requires discursive strategies that are antithetical to Marxism. The Marxist's ambivalence is revealed when he both condemns the self-absorption of poststructuralists and also affirms that they extend the freedom of the individual beyond "all prior limits of human existence."[7] The "peak experience" of reading in which the individual constitutes himself or herself by defining the meaning of the text also applies, Gill laments, to acts of consumption. But that is the "contradiction" of the mode of information: it promises a new level of self-constitution, one beyond the rigidities and restraints of fixed identities, but also makes possible the subordination of the individual to manipulative communications practices. The alternative is not to defend a collective subject (such as the Proletariat) whose time may be passed but to explore the lines of a new politics that open the existing forms of self-constitution to democratic reordering.

Baudrillard speaks of the end of the social and the end of history, a new situation in which Whig and Marxist perspectives have lost their resonance. By "the social" and "history" he means a culture in which subjects orient their practice around a sense of collective direction, in which public events are interpreted in relation to a "rational" metanarrative, in which a significant proportion of the population senses a connection between their petty affairs and the destiny of mankind.

> The masses are impervious to the workings of liberation, revolution, or historicity, but that is their method of self-defense, their riposte. They are a simulation model, an alibi at the service of a phantom political class which no longer knows the nature of the political power it exerts over the masses, and at the same time, the death of that very political process which is supposed to govern them. The masses swallow up the political, insofar as it implies will and representation.[8]

Conflict is thus displaced from party politics or class structure. The rules of the game have changed, if Baudrillard is right, so the Jacobin and Whig models of change no longer apply. Baudrillard's mistake is to assume that because the old models are gone, none will replace them.

The old models were male and white; one could argue that feminism and minority movements are new forms of change, forms that do not derive from the older mode of signification. Even if such is not the case Baudrillard's totalizing position forecloses the possibility of new movements. Sunk in a depressing hyperbole of the hyperreal, he transgresses the line of critical discourse in sweeping, gloomy pronouncements as if he knows the outcome to a story that has not yet been imagined, much less written. The concept of the mode of information is perhaps a small step in the critical comprehension of a drastically altered, deeply unrecognizable social field. Misrecognition stems as much from the dogged application of inappropriate theory and from limitations in the social context of the critical theorist as it does from an emerging social formation.

Notes and references

1   Jean Baudrillard, *Simulations*, tr. Paul Foss et al. (Semiotext(e), New York, 1983), pp. 147–8, emphasis in original.
2   Gerry Gill, 'Post-structuralism as ideology', *Arena*, 69 (1984), p. 70.
3   Ibid., p. 73.
4   Ibid., p. 75.
5   Ibid., p. 90.
6   Ibid., p. 93.
7   Ibid., p. 94.
8   Jean Baudrillard, 'The implosion of meaning in the media and the implosion of the social in the masses', in *The Mythos of Information: Technology and Post Industrial Culture*, ed. Kathleen Woodward (Coda, Madison, Wis., 1980), p. 145.

12

Postmodernist Sensibility

Scott Lash and John Urry

What social conditions specific to an era of disorganizing capitalism are conducive to the creation of an audience which is predisposed towards the reception of postmodernist culture? Before we outline these conditions, we will briefly delineate what we mean by postmodernist culture.

Postmodernist culture may be distinguished from, on the one hand, 'classic realist' and, on the other, 'modernist' cultural forms. Classic realism on this account is grounded in the quattrocento perspective in Renaissance painting in which a three-dimensional object is painted onto a two-dimensional canvas as if the latter were literally a window on the former; and in the narrative assumptions of the nineteenth-century novel. The birth of modernist culture which breaks with these assumptions takes place around the turn of the twentieth century. Modernist culture (Adorno's exemplars here were Picasso and Schönberg) is 'auratic' in Walter Benjamin's sense of the term. 'Aura' according to Benjamin assumed the radical separation of the cultural forms from the social: aura entails that a cultural object proclaim its own originality, uniqueness and singularity; it assumed finally that the cultural object is based in a discourse of formal organic unity and artistic creativity. Modernism is thus confined to high culture, while classic realism – in the popular novel, popular urban theatres, in cinema – comes also to pervade popular culture in the early twentieth century.

Postmodernist culture, for its part, like modernism departs from the visual and narrative assumptions of classic realism. But at the same time it, unlike modernism, is emphatically *anti*-auratic. Postmodernism signals the demise of aesthetic 'aura' in a number of ways.

1 It proclaims not its uniqueness but is positioned in a context of mechanical, if not electronic, reproduction.

2   It denies the high-modernist separation of the aesthetic from the social and any other hierarchical dualisms; and in particular it disputes the contention that art is of a different order from life.
3   It disputes the high-modernist valuation of such unity through pastiche, collage, allegory and so on.
4   ...gh-modernist cultural forms are received by audiences in ...nin called a state of 'contemplation', postmodernist forms ...y consumed in a state of distraction.
5   ...gh-modernist art is to be appreciated for the coherent ...formal properties of the aesthetic material, postmodernist ...cts the audience via its immediate impact, via an 'economy ...
6   ...ism in its challenge to aesthetic aura does not assume a ...igh-modernist diremption of high and popular culture.

Given this definition, the first flourishings of postmodern culture appeared in the historical avant-garde of the 1920s, in the critique of high modernism launched by, among others, the dada and surrealist movements. One major reason why the postmodern 1920s avant-gardes did not penetrate into popular culture was because a sufficient audience with the relevant predispositions was not present. In recent decades such a popular-culture audience has begun to take shape, however. Thus there has been the pervasion of postmodern forms in popular cinema, in which in the largest moneyspinning films postmodern 'impact' and 'spectacle' has progressively displaced the privacy of classic-realist narratives. Likewise in advertising and video, pictoral realism has been progressively replaced by dadaist and surrealist techniques of collage and montage. And also, there is to be found an intentional dissonance and shock value in punk and performance art.

Let us turn now to the social conditions for the creation of an audience for each cultural form.

The semiotics of everyday life

Postmodern cultural forms, we just noted, refuse the distinction between art and life, between the cultural and the real. We shall argue that an audience is sensitized to the reception of such cultural objects because of a 'semiotics of everyday life' in which the boundary between the cultural and life, between the image and the real, is more than ever transgressed. Or because of a semiotics in which already cultural images, that is, what are already representations in television, advertisements, billboards, pop music, video, home computers and so on, themselves constitute a significant and increasingly growing portion of the 'natural' social reality that surrounds people.

[···]

Jean Baudrillard is perhaps the foremost figure to discuss the relation of post-industrialism to the sphere of culture. He gives an account of the transition from 'industrial capitalism' to 'consumer capitalism' and consumer capitalism is for him very much as disorganized capitalism is for us. Baudrillard analyses how this transition brings about what might be called a transformed 'semiotics of everyday life' which predisposes audience reception of postmodernist culture. Baudrillard uses the conventional semiotic 'triangle', where the signifier is an image, a sound, a word, or an utterance; the signified is a meaning, usually a thought or a concept; and the referent is the object in the real world to which both signifier and signified point. In industrial capitalism in this context, domination is effected through the referent which for Baudrillard is capital, both as means of production and as the commodities produced. In industrial capitalism then the 'social bond' is through the exchange of exchange-values; and the centrality of exchange-value itself is legitimated through use-value, or a set of arguments based around the maximization of utility.

What is then most important for Baudrillard about contemporary *consumer* capitalism is that we consume, no longer products, but signs: that we consume the signs of advertisements, of television; and that objects of consumption themselves have value for us as signs. It is the image, then, in contemporary capitalism, that is consumed, the image in which we have libidinal investment. The exchange-value of commodities thus has been transformed into a 'sign-value'. Signs – which comprise both signifier and signified – 'float free from the referent' or product, and domination and the 'social bond' are no longer through the referent but the sign. Moreover, our identities are constructed through the exchange of sign-values, and the means of legitimation of the signifier (or the image) is the signified. Baudrillard's consumer capitalism has become a fully fledged 'political economy of the sign'.

Domination through the sign takes place through the arbitrary assignments by established power of signifieds, or meanings, to signifiers. The type of signifieds in which Baudrillard is interested are not ordinary denotations or connotations, but fundamental ideologies or ultimate values. Domination through the sign or at least through discourse would characterize not just consumption but the sphere of production in today's service and information-based economies in which employer–employee relations are no longer so often mediated by means of production. Domination here is through the assignment of a single and univocal meaning or signified to the signifiers.

Resistance, by contrast, contends Baudrillard, takes place through the refusal of the 'masses' in contemporary consumer society to accept this connection of signifier to signified. Baudrillard's argument is that the masses reject the signifieds attached to media images, both by established power, as well as the signifieds which the left has promoted (such as 'the people', the proletariat). Instead, he contends, the masses accept *all* images in the spirit of *spectacle*; that is, they refuse to attach meaning to images which have been intended to carry meaning. Baudrillardian spectacle is no longer a universe of referent, signified or even signifiers, but of the 'model', of 'simulation' and of 'hyperreality'. What television broadcasts for example is not reality, but – through choice of subject matter, editing and so on – a *model*. The masses of viewers, he observes, are no more taken in by the putative reality of television images than they are by its meanings. They *know* that it is a simulation; they are cognizant of the hyperreality of the image; and they thrive on its 'fascination'. In their turn the masses simulate the models of media images, and in their conformity to media 'hyperreality' the masses become models themselves. Everyday life and reality itself then become 'imploded' into the hyperreality of the spectacle. Baudrillard's world of spectacle is a world of 'simulacra', that is, where there is no original and everything is a copy. The masses simulate the media which in turn hypersimulate the masses. It is a depthless world of networks of information and communication in which 'the sender' (television, computers) is the receiver, and in which the subject like the media is a 'control screen', a 'switching centre'. It is a universe of communication networks in which information is purely instrumental in that it 'has no end purpose in meaning'.

We agree with much in Baudrillard's analysis: with the importance of the sphere of consumption for the constitution of individual and collective identity; with the idea of post-industrial domination through communications in the sphere of production; with the idea that in contemporary capitalism what is largely produced – in the media, a large part of the service sector, in parts of the public sector – consists of communications and information. We agree also with his contention – and this is of course a hallowed idea whose lineage stretches from Veblen to Bourdieu – that images rather than products have become the central objects of consumption. This point is borne out in research carried out by William Leiss on changes in advertising practices. Leiss examined national (as distinct from specialist) product advertising in two Canadian general circulation magazines from 1911 to 1980. He found over this period and in particular after the Second World War a decline in printed text and a concomitant rise in visual imagery. He also found a decline in 'propositional content', that is, of (often specious) arguments regarding the utility of the product to an 'almost purely iconic representation' of images put into juxtaposition with the product. In the early decades of Leiss's sample advertisements were intended to convince consumers to purchase manufactured products. With this aim they contained detailed descriptions of products, focusing on values of efficiency, durability, reliability and cleanliness. Women were cast in functional if traditional roles, as they were instructed how to use the products in the household. In recent decades utility and functionality are increasingly dispensed with. Appeal is no longer to practical rationality, as a Watsonian behaviourist (or Freudian) conception of an irrationalist human nature is assumed. Instead of being cast in functional roles, women become sex objects and images which are helter-skelter attached to products like adjectives. Instead of being told how to use products, women are directed to use the product in order to be like the sex object associated with it; men to use the product in order to *have* her.

The main problem, however, with Baudrillard's argument is that what he understands as the principle of cultural resistance in contemporary consumer society is in fact more often than not its principle of *domination*. That is, that domination in the semiotics of contemporary everyday life is not through the attachment of signifieds, of meanings to images by culture producers, but by the particular strategies of dominant social groups to *refuse* to attach any meanings to such images. That is, the implosion of meaning, subjectivity and the real world or the social is not primarily a way for Baudrillard's 'silent majorities' to resist domination, but instead a way that 'masses' are indeed dominated. It is plausible that the overload of sounds and images that we experience in everyday life, over the television, radio, walkman, billboards and bright lights, has helped create a sensibility to postmodern cultural objects in which meaning is devalued. But surely cultural producers in, for example, today's cinema of the spectacle are aware of this change in the audience and produce films that cater to it. So our first point against Baudrillard is that dominant culture often operates itself through the delinkage of meaning from images. Our second point is that there is not anything necessarily disruptive, much less subversive, about masses who implode meaning and their subjectivities into flat hyperreality. In explanations of social movements, resistance is conditional upon coherent forms of identity, or more precisely collective identity. And by most accounts collective identities are constituted around ultimate sets of meanings. Finally, if subjectivity is imploded into the unfortunately too lifelike Baudrillardian networks of communication and information, there is little place left from which to launch any type of substantive critique.

Simon Frith's recent work on popular music gives an excellent illustration of how cultural products which feature the primacy of image and spectacle can at one moment be disruptive of the conditions of consumer capitalism and at another moment function to reproduce just such conditions. Frith distinguishes 'rock' from 'pop' critiques of consumer society. The 'rock' critique, dominant until the 1970s, is an effectively 'modernist' critique of consumer capitalism in its preference for an auratic culture of authenticity, the natural, and live performance. The 'pop' critique by contrast is effectively postmodernist and grew out of the late 1970s and especially from punk.

Punk challenged the modernist and auratic dispositions of rock in a number of ways. It mocked the rock cult of the LP (long-playing record), whose original and auratic pretentions bore careful listening the first time through. Punk instead foregrounded the single; instead of originality, repetition was thematized, and to listen to a punk recording for the first time was like already having listened to it before. Whereas rock was essentially to be listened to, and thus consistent with modernist aurality, punk was a matter of the visual, the image; it was to be seen. Whereas rock propounded the modernist thematic of the creative artist, punk only entailed the learning of a few chords (and at that, badly), and at least some kids on any block were capable of that. While rock featured a modernist aesthetics of beauty, punk foregrounded an anti-aesthetic of discordant and intentionally nerve-jangling cacophony. Where rock promoted, especially in the LP, at least some notion of the (modernist) integral work of art, pop's avant-garde critique promotes the heterogeneous, in pastiches such as Malcolm McClaren's *Duck Rock*, which mixes together a number of previously recorded sound sequences. Whereas (typically American) rock artists had or seemed to have genuine connections with the popular communities from which they sprang, the (typically British) pop artist was from an art school background, and self-consciously differentiated himself or herself from the masses in the audience. Thus a number of pop performers promoted an avant-garde and 'camp' (in Sontag's sense) consciousness of the image, sang in detached and ironic tones, and laid open sexual (and also racial) ambiguity. They expressed contempt for the mass audience they intended to shock, and self-referentially mocked their own popularity.

The pop (and postmodern) critique of consumer capitalism through spectacle was, as Frith observes, but a short step from the celebration of music's commodity status. This has taken place via a pop music, quite disconnected with avant-gardes, whose rise to fame has been most of all dependent on the video. The replacement of the critical avant-garde by video-pop is partly explicable in terms of the late 1970s slump in record sales, itself explicable by the rise in youth unemployment but also by the new competition for youth leisure time via home computers and video recorders. The record companies' response to this, notes Frith, was swift: they shifted to a younger market and promoted singles at the expense of LPs; they built on what had always been a visual orientation of this early-teens market and thus focused on promoting stars; and these now became 'multimedia performers' with heavy record company investment in videos. The response, though inconclusive, has been an increase in sales in the mid-1980s. But the new video-based music has meant 'the incorporation of pop into the aesthetics (and, we would add, the politics) of advertising'.

We have then, partly via a critical analysis of Baudrillard's work, given an account of how the semiotics of everyday life in consumer (disorganized) capitalism predisposes an audience to the reception of postmodern cultural forms. The most important features of such a semiotics which bear affinities with characteristics of postmodern culture that we outlined are: the consumption of images instead of products; the new importance of spectacle at the expense of meaning; and a situation in which the boundaries between the realm of culture and everyday life itself are continually transgressed and blurred. Here the 'masses' not only 'simulate' the media, but popular culture, the media and pop music are themselves inseparable from the semiotics of everyday life, a phenomenon emphasized by Andy Warhol's photorealism in which paintings are not windows out onto the world but windows out onto the media, the advert, the image. It is an everyday experience of a reality which itself – through the walkman, video, television, adverts, styles – is already cultural and hence a hyperreality that creates an audience attuned to the anti-auratic and figural or spectacular nature of postmodernist culture.

13

The Decline of Modernism

Peter Bürger

For some time sociologists and philosophers have tended to label present-day society 'post-industrial' or 'postmodern'. Understandable as the wish is to set off the present from the age of advanced capitalism, the terms selected are no less problematic. A new epoch is introduced before the question is even asked, let alone answered, as to how decisive current social changes are, and whether they require that a new epochal boundary be set. The term 'postmodern', moreover, has the additional disadvantage of only naming the new period abstractly. There is an even more drastic disadvantage. Of course, deep economic, technical and social changes can be observed when compared with the second half of the nineteenth century, but the dominant mode of production has remained the same: private appropriation of collectively produced surplus value. Social democratic governments in Western Europe have learned only too clearly that, despite the increasing significance of governmental intervention in economic matters, the maximization of profit remains the driving force of social reproduction. We should therefore be cautious about interpreting the current changes and not evaluate them prematurely as signs of an epoch-making transformation.

Even in art, talk of the 'postmodern' shares the defects of the sociological concept of the 'postmodern'. From a few quite accurate observations, it prematurely postulates an epochal threshold which, however, can be indicated only abstractly, since a concrete definition obviously fails. Despite this general objection to the concept of the 'postmodern', it is difficult to deny that in the last twenty years changes have taken place in the aesthetic sensitivity of those strata which were and are the carriers of high culture: a positive stance towards the architecture of the *fin de siècle* and hence an essentially more critical judgement of modern architecture; the softening of the rigid dichotomy between higher and lower art, which Adorno still considered to be irreconcilably opposed; a re-evaluation of the figurative painting of the 1920s (e.g. in the great Berlin exposition of 1977); a return to the traditional novel even by representatives of the experimental novel. These examples (they could be multiplied) indicate changes that must be dealt with. Is it a question of cultural phenomena that accompany political neo-conservatism and therefore should be criticized from a consistent modern standpoint? Or can so unambiguous a political classification not be ascertained, and do the aforementioned changes compel us to draw a more complex picture of artistic modernity than even Adorno did?

If, starting from the postmodern problematic, one returns to Adorno's writings on aesthetics, and especially music, one discovers, not without surprise, that he was very much preoccupied with the problem of the decline of the modern age at least since the Second World War. Adorno first encountered this problem in the early 1920s in his first composition teacher who, as an opponent of atonal music, sought to lead his pupils back to tonality by portraying the former as old-fashioned. Adorno tells of this in his *Minima Moralia*: 'The ultra-modern, so his argument went, is already no longer modern, the stimuli which I was seeking had already become dull, the expressive figures which excited me belonged to an old-fashioned sentimentality, and the new youth had more red blood corpuscles, to use his favorite phrase.'

[···]

Adorno's thoughts on the waning of modernism are formulated from the perspective of production; they should therefore be complemented by a remark on changes in the area of reception. Among younger persons today one can often notice a way of dealing with literary works that can only be characterized as low-brow from Adorno's standpoint. I mean the widespread renunciation of any discussion of aesthetic form in favour of a discussion of the norms and patterns of behaviour which are the basis of the actions of the characters portrayed. The questions which are asked of the work then do not read: How are the aesthetic form and content of the work communicated? but: Did this or that character act correctly in this situation? How would I have behaved in a comparable situation? Such an attitude of reception can be dismissed as inadequate to works of art and can be judged as a sign of a cultural decline. But one can also ask whether the reading of a realistic novel that is interested mainly in procedures of narrative technique does not miss precisely its specific achievement. One can even go further and ask whether the novel does not become primarily an autonomous work of art detached from the living practice of individuals by the fact that a particular discourse marks it as such. What first seemed to be only a lack of culture could prove to be the starting point of a new way of dealing with works of art that overcomes the one-sided fixation on form and at the same time places the work back in relation to the experiences of the recipients.

Do these observations justify the characterization of the art of the present as one of postmodernism, and what implications does this have? To answer these questions, I would like to distinguish three different readings.

1   *The anti-modern reading.* It could use Adorno's theorem that there is in every epoch just *one* advanced stock of material, and turn it against Adorno. The signs of a waning of the new music which he noted turned, it could be argued, away from twelve-tone music and returned to tonality. Since comparable processes of decline can be seen in abstract painting and modern literature, a return to objectivity or to realistic forms of narration is suggested here too. Of course, metaphysical validity could no longer be attributed to the traditionally normative genres, but they had their place as artistic means. As Valéry repeatedly showed, artificially posed difficulties (for instance, the fulfilment of a complicated verse scheme) acted as stimulants to artistic achievement. In brief, one could formulate a theory of postmodernism as a pleading for the new academicism and in so doing appeal once again to Adorno who has regretted the loss of the 'pedagogical virtues of academicism'.

That Adorno was as far from thinking of a return to academicism as he was from any call for moderation (he calls 'the ideal of moderate modernism' disgusting) is not adequate to refute the above argument. Its strength consists precisely in that it – rightly, it would seem – raises the claim of drawing from Adorno's reflections the conclusions which he evaded. Also the argument drawn from Adorno's critique of Lukács that realistic forms are *as such* affirmative has become unconvincing, since non-objective paintings have become the decor of managerial suites and are used as montages for magazine covers. If one does not want to settle for a political critique of aesthetic restoration, then one will have to try to show its weakness by way of immanent critique. It lies in an *aporia* that is otherwise typical of neo-conservatism. For it can attain its own standpoint (here: the return to tonality, to objectivity and to traditional literary forms) only by the abstract negation of modernism. But this approach contradicts its own conservative self-understanding, which values not new beginnings, but preservation and development. Since the anti-modern version of the postmodern theorem can preserve nothing of modernism, it comes to contradict its conservative self-understanding. That unmasks it as a badly secured polemical position which has nothing to contribute to the comprehension of the possibility of art today.

2   *The pluralistic reading*. It could be formulated approximately as follows: theorists of modernism have held the objectively illegitimate thesis that only modern art has attained the heights of the epoch. They thereby devalued implicitly or explicitly all rival artistic movements. The decline of modernism shows the one-sidedness of a concept of tradition which recognizes in music only the Schönberg school, and in narrative literature only a few authors such as Proust, Kafka, Joyce and Beckett. The music and literature of the twentieth century, however, were much richer. The consequence of this position for the present reads: there is no advanced material, all historical stocks of material are equally available to the artist. What counts is the individual work.

This position has a series of arguments in its favour. There can be no doubt that a construction of tradition such as Adorno's is one-sided. We should not forget, however, that it owes to this one-sidedness its capacity for making connections recognizable. That today, however, no particular material can still be regarded as historically the most progressive is indicated not only by the motley array of different things, so confusing for the outsider, which every local fine arts exhibit documents. It is demonstrated mainly by the intensity with which some of the most conscious artists explore the use of the most varied stocks of materials. A few of Pit Morell's etchings contain reminiscences of Renaissance drawings along with the expressive directness of the paintings of children and the insane. And Werner Hilsing paints at the same time surrealist, expressionist and cubist miniatures, thus reflecting the possibility of a multiplicity of material. If one wanted to try to draw any conclusions from this, it would be that aesthetic valuation today must detach itself from any link with a particular material. Less than ever does the material guarantee in advance the success of the work. The fascination which correctly emanates from periods of consistent development of material (say, in early cubism) must not mislead one into making it the supratemporal criterion of aesthetic valuation.

The insight into the free availability of different stocks of material which exists today must blind us neither to the resulting artistic difficulties nor to the problematic of the position which is here called pluralist. Whereas Adorno would single out almost all of current artistic production as worthless, the 'pluralist' runs the danger of recognizing everything equally and falling prey to an eclecticism which likes everything indiscriminately. Art thus threatens to become an insipid complement to everyday life, i.e. what it always was to the popularizations of idealist aesthetics.

Instead of drawing from the questioning of the theorem of the most advanced material the false conclusion that today everything is possible, one would have to insist on the difficulties which confront works today. If reliance on the correspondence between the artistic material and the epoch has vanished, a reliance which is the historico-philosophical basis of Adorno's aesthetics, then for the productive artist too the abundance of possibilities can appear as arbitrariness. He cannot counter it by surrendering to it, but only by reflecting upon it. That can be done in many different ways: by radical restriction to *one* material, but also by the attempt to use the multiplicity of possibilities. The decision is always legitimized only afterwards, in the product.

3 *Towards a contemporary aesthetic.* I would explicitly not like to place this third reading under the auspices of postmodernism, because the concept suggests an end to the modern era, which there is no reason whatever to assume. One could instead claim that all relevant art today defines itself in relation to modernism. If this is so, then a theory of contemporary aesthetics has the task of conceptualizing a dialectical continuation of modernism. It will strive to affirm essential categories of modernism, but at the same time to free them from their modernist rigidity and bring them back to life.

The category of artistic modernism *par excellence* is form. Subcategories such as artistic means, procedures and techniques converge in that category. In modernism, form is not something pre-given which the artist must fulfil and whose fulfilment the critics and the educated public could check more or less closely against a canon of fixed rules. It is always an individual result, which the work represents. And form is not something external to the content; it stands in relation to it (this is the basis of interpretation). This modern conception of artistic form, which originates in the modern age with the victory of nominalism, ought to be irreplaceable for us. Though we can imagine a work of art in which individual elements are interchangeable (from a picture of Pollock's one can cut off a part without essentially changing it, and in a paratactically constructed narrative individual parts arranged in succession can be interchanged or even left out); but we cannot imagine a work in which the form as such would be arbitrary. Irreplaceability means that in the act of reception we apply a concept of form that grasps the form of the work as particular, necessary within certain limits, and semantically interpretable.

But irreplaceability must not be confused with unchangeability. The aesthetics of idealism grasps the work of art as a form/content unity. 'True works of art are such, precisely by the fact that their content and form prove to be completely identical,' says Hegel.[2] But in this positing of a unity of subject (form) and object (content) history did not come to a stop. Rather, the development of art in bourgeois society bursts asunder the idealistically fused elements of the classical type of work. The concept of the work held by idealistic aesthetics was itself already an answer to the modern phenomenon of the alienation of individuals from themselves and the world. In the organic work of art, the really unresolved contradictions are supposed to appear as reconciled. Hence the demand of a form–content unity that alone can generate the appearance of reconciliation. Now, to the extent that bourgeois society develops into a system that is subject to crises, but none the less closed, the individual increasingly feels impotent *vis-à-vis* the social whole. The artist reacts to this by attempting to prove, at least in his own field, the primacy of the subject over the given. This means the primacy of the subjectively set form, the primacy of material development. The result is achieved first in aestheticist poetry: the striving for purity of form, which has characterized the idealist conception of art since its earliest formulations, threatens to annihilate that which makes producing a work worthwhile, i.e. the content. The novel, which can absorb the fullness of reality, for a long time proves to be resistant to the coercion to formalization. Only with Robbe-Grillet's *nouveau roman* is the aestheticist project of a 'book about nothing' realized also in this genre. Here too the emancipation from the matter as something given and withdrawn from the control of the subject leads to emptiness.

The earliest answer – unmatched to this day despite all contradictions – to the developmental tendencies of art in bourgeois society is given by the historical avant-garde movements. The demand for a return of art to life, the abolition of the autonomy of art, marks the counterpole to that tendency which extrapolated the status of autonomy right into the work. The aestheticizing primacy of form is now replaced by the primacy of expression. The artist-subject revolts against form, which now confronts him as something alien. What should master the facticity of the given proves to be a coercion which the subject inflicts on himself. He rebels against it.

And where do we stand, we who are the heirs both of aestheticist formalism and of the avant-garde protest against it? The answer to the question is made more difficult by the fact that we have had to confirm both the decline of the modern (in Adorno's sense) and the failure of the avant-garde attack on the institution of art. Neither anti-modernism nor historical eclecticism can be considered adequate designs for the aesthetic theory of the present. But merely clinging to the theory of aesthetic modernity, as Adorno has formulated it, also fails to see relevant phenomena of contemporary artistic production, e.g. the *Aesthetic of Resistance*, in which Peter Weiss uses the narrative techniques of the realistic novel throughout. Instead of propagating a break with modernism under the banner of the postmodern, I count on its dialectical continuity. That means that aesthetic modernism must also recognize as its own much that it has until now rejected. That is, no more tabooing of tonality, representation, and traditional literary forms; but at the same time distrust of this material and of the appearance of substantiality which emanates from it. The recourse to past stocks of material must be recognized as a modern procedure, but also as an extremely precarious one. The modern is richer, more varied, more contradictory than Adorno depicts it in the parts of his work where he sets up boundaries out of fear of regression, as in the Stravinsky chapter of *Philosophy of Modern Music*. The artist can rely on what seems to him to be immediacy of expression which yet is always mediated. Since the expressive strength of the painting of children and of the insane is recognized, there can no longer be any taboo against regression. But it would be mistaken to believe that it is enough to imitate the clumsy drawings of first-formers to produce good paintings. The dialectics of form and expression must be executed as something irreducibly particular, whereby the latter no longer means individual situation but social experience refracted through the subject.

Already Hegel prognosticated the free disposition over forms and objects for art after the 'end of art'. This prospect becomes cogent at the moment when there is no longer any generally binding system of symbols. To the question of a criterion for putting a stop to the bad wealth of historical eclecticism, first a distinction would have to be made between an arbitrary toying with past forms and their necessary actualization. Second, after the attack of the historical avant-garde movements on the autonomy of art, the reflection on this status ought to be an important trait of important art. To the extent that this reflection is translated into artistic conduct, it encounters the historico-philosophical place of art in the present. If this is plausible, then Brecht's work should have a place within the literature of our century which Adorno does not concede to it.

On the side of reception, the dialectical continuation of modernity means the striving to combine the above-mentioned reception stance oriented to living practice with sensitivity for the specific achievement of forms, which modern art has taught us since impressionism and aestheticism. With the risk of being misunderstood, what is meant can be characterized as the re-semanticization of art. This term is misleading because it does not appeal to the formal *a priori* of art. What Adorno criticizes as 'material fetishism' in a modernism consistent in its rational tendencies has its complement on the side of reception – the readiness to celebrate even the monochromatically painted canvas as an extraordinary artistic event. Against this, the semantic dimension of the work of art must be emphasized.

In closing, let me return to the concept of 'postmodernism'. Perhaps the problematic of the concept can be most readily delineated if one says that it is both too broad and too narrow. Too broad, because it relegates to the past the modern concept of form, which is irreplaceable for us. Too narrow, because it restricts the question of contemporary art to the question of a material decision. But that is not permissible because the changes which are currently taking shape are also precisely changes in the way of dealing with art. If the claim formulated by avant-garde movements to abolish the separation of art and life, although it failed, continues as before to define the situation of today's art, then this is paradoxical in the strictest sense of the word: if the avant-gardist demand for abolition turns out to be realizable, that is the end of art. If it is erased, i.e. if the separation of art and life is accepted as matter of course, that is also the end of art.

Notes and references

1   T.W. Adorno, *Minima Moralia. Reflexionen aus dem Beschädigten Leben* (Suhrkamp, Berlin, 1951), p. 291.
2   G.W.F. Hegel, *Encyclopedia of the Philosophical Sciences* (Heidelberg, 1817).

PART II

Media Representation

THIS PART GROUPS together a variety of cultural forms and in so doing captures the experience of contemporary culture. John Hargreaves (Reading 14) considers the interconnections between the media and sporting events. Once again one can say that what is at issue here is not just the media representation of pre-given events, but the reconstruction of those events through the media. Sport has enormous significance in contemporary popular culture, Hargreaves points out. The circulations of the tabloid dailies are vitally dependent upon their sports sections, while television sport has grown more and more important over recent years.

Media sport, like other cultural products, is considerably influenced by political and economic considerations; but its content can in no way be reduced to such influences. The media representation of sport is not what the spectator at the event experiences. It is a re-formed and re-presented world, organized in terms of its own frames of meaning. The media, indeed, play a central role in treating sport as autonomous and 'outside politics'. The interpretative frames which media sport creates depend upon very much the sorts of phenomena Baudrillard analyses – involvement in sequences of signifiers and images to which the actual sports event itself is almost irrelevant. Hargreaves' analysis does not follow Baudrillard's view strictly, however, because he stresses that the images and frames of media sport react back upon, and shape, external systems of power and ideology.

If the mass media essentially produced passivity in their audiences, we might expect such passivity to be most pronounced among the young, who have had less time than adults to form critical reactions and alternative opinions. In their discussion Bob Hodge and David Tripp (Reading 15), analysing the impact of television, argue that even young children in fact approach television in a creative and selective way. Children, as they put it, are 'active and powerful decoders of television'. Any television programme can be 'read' in a diversity of ways and children bring a distinct input to what they watch. As against Baudrillard, Hodge and Tripp claim that children can and do distinguish between television imagery and outside reality, although they do also gain meanings from television programmes in terms of which they renegotiate their activities in the wider world.

In Reading 16 Robert Bocock discusses the development of consumerism in modern societies. Consumerism was directly associated with the growth of cities, which provided central sites for the development of industries as well as leisure facilities. Urbanism, as George Simmel and others have remarked, is closely involved with the basic traits of modernity itself. The metropolis is internally diverse, bustling and anonymous. Many urban contacts are fleeting and ephemeral, while modes of consumption become signifiers of styles of life. The city epitomizes the contrasting influences of standardization and individualism in modern culture. It promotes a 'massifying' of social life, accommodating large aggregates of people; at the same time it makes possible forms of diversity and consumer taste for which the traditional village community allowed no place.

The widespread disappearance of the traditional local community is surely one of the factors underlying the popularity of soap operas. As Christine Geraghty (Reading 17) points out, the soaps provide narratives and familiar characters which allow the viewer to discover a continuity lacking in the kaleidoscope of mediated experience today. Soaps tend to have an underlying predictability which to the uninitiated merely seems tedious. For the person who has got 'into' the story, however, there is a sense of comfort and 'being at home' within a familiar framework of events. Agreeing with Hodge and Tripp, Geraghty stresses that this is an active process on the part of the viewer, who brings to each episode a richness of past viewing and interpretation that allows what seems to be thin and superficial material to gain great solidity. Yet it would be a mistake, Geraghty shows, to exaggerate the internal coherence of soaps. They combine a variety of aesthetic elements and conventions, including realism, entertainment and melodrama. For this reason they are often condemned by cultural critics; but in fact the tension between these components generates much of their dramatic power and emotional appeal.

Women form a high proportion of the audience for soaps, in which romantic themes are often prominent. They are also by far the dominant consumers of popular romantic novels and magazines. Like soaps, romantic literature tends to be characterized by a number of repetitive themes. These have similarities to works recognized to belong to genres of high culture as well as making up an authentic domain of popular romances. Anne Cranny-Francis (Reading 18) finds antecedents of contemporary romances in the works of the Brontë sisters. In their books, as in most popular romances, there is ordinarily a strong male hero and the plot revolves around the romance between him and the heroine. Love is quite often portrayed as elemental force which sweeps both individuals away; yet the love of the woman also tends to 'humanize' and domesticate the forceful male. Some texts, Cranny-Francis says, represent women and men in satisfying relationships of equal power; but for the most part romantic stories tend to reproduce patriarchal structures in the wider society.

In Reading 19 Janet Wolff discusses a different aspect of the influence of patriarchy upon cultural production. Pursuing similar themes to those raised by Bocock, she points out that the connection between modernity and metropolis was explored among others by Charles Baudelaire in his version of the *flâneur*. The *flâneur* is an individual who saunters through the city, scrutinizing the diversity of goods in the shops and the hurrying crowds. He seems to be only an observer, but in fact his aimless behaviour expresses some basic traits of modern social life. For he is a participant in that very language of signifiers of which Baudrillard and others speak.

The *flâneur* is male: as Wolff says, the literature of modernity (and postmodernity) tends primarily to describe the experience of men. Modernity, as well as modernism, are centred in the public worlds of political, economic and city life; these were worlds in which women, until relatively recently, had little or no place. Baudelaire's *flâneur* points up the 'fugitive' and fleeting nature of the encounters which characterize the life of the city; but women could not stroll the streets in the mode of the *flâneur*. There is no equivalent *flâneuse*. The development of modernity went along with the formation of new sorts of 'private' domain which associated women specifically with domesticity. Women were made invisible by the very world which created modern institutions.

In the final reading in this part (Reading 20) the discussion shifts to a woman who became very visible indeed: Marilyn Monroe. Graham McCann focuses his discussion upon Monroe as an example of the Hollywood star system yet also exploited by it. To be a 'star' is to be commodified, turned into a standardized product available for a mass audience; it is also to become inserted into that chain of signifiers of which we have spoken above.

The star system was in some part encouraged by the Hollywood studios for purely business purposes. The star has certain easily marketable characteristics: her face, legs or figure. Stardom is thus carried through a sequence of films; the star is recognized to be 'the same' even though the parts she is playing and the plots of the films differ. Yet the sequence of films also permits the development of a different narrative, one which shares a good deal with the soap opera motif. The films become seen as events in the narrative of the star's life, with its triumphs and tribulations.

14

Media Sport

John Hargreaves

Of all the apparatuses involved in the achievement of hegemony none is more implicated in sports than the mass media. Of the media's different facets we need to concentrate on the press and broadcasting, since it is these institutions, rather than the cinema, book publishing, etc., that are in more or less instantaneous, continuous touch with the majority of the population. Most work on the media and power has concentrated on the character of news and current affairs, while the significance of other aspects of the media's output in this respect has tended to be overlooked. Media sport is ostensibly nothing to do whatever with power, politics and ideology, and is everything to do with skilled, exciting and above all entertaining leisure activity. The importance of testing this claim can be seen when we recall that more people are involved in sport through the press and broadcasting than in any other way. Furthermore, the heavier reliance of working-class people on the media in their leisure-time activity makes it fairly safe to assume that media sport has gained the allegiance of a large proportion.

Today, the sports section of the mass-circulation newspaper is crucial in maintaining its market position. As Hall points out, the tabloid is a reversible newspaper: it can be opened and started at either end and even bigger headlines at the sports end stimulate the reader to start there. We find the more working-class the readership (*Daily Star*, *The Sun*, *Mirror*) the greater the proportion of the paper devoted to sport, with the *Daily Star* giving 55 per cent more space to sport than the *Daily Mail*, the tabloid with the lowest working-class readership.

Although a fairly large number of different sports are covered, one of the most striking features is the virtual saturation of the available space by the coverage of football and horse-racing, two sports which have traditionally enjoyed a large working-class following. At times, horse-racing gets more actual space than football, but in terms of the main sports stories the vast majority concern football. The policy is quite clearly to attract working-class readers with coverage of the sports to which they are most attached. The fact that sport is classified in the trade as a 'revenue goal' rather than an 'advertising goal', that is, it increases circulation as opposed to attracting advertising directly, supports this interpretation. It is not possible to ascertain the proportion of the readership which is motivated to buy papers because of their sporting content, but we know for example that, once purchased, more than half the men and a third of the women read the sports pages of the Sunday newspapers.

The advent of televised sport from the 1950s onwards marked a crucial step in the development of a mass audience for sport. The ease of accessibility, its immediacy and apparent authenticity, made TV the major competitor of the popular press. It is possible to estimate the size of the audience for sports programmes, as well as the proportion of the total output devoted to sport. Near the end of the 1970s 12.2 per cent of BBC TV programme time was taken up with sport, putting it in fourth place behind current affairs/features/ documentaries, the Open University and films, while BBC Radio devoted only 3.45 per cent to sport, which places it in sixth position out of twelve categories. IBA (Independent Broadcasting Authority) figures for televised sport are roughly similar at about 11.5 per cent of viewing time. Sport is probably more central than these figures suggest, since it is often programmed for prime-time transmission and because the categories with which it is compared cover, in some cases, a fairly heterogeneous output. In the 1970s the BBC sports programmes 'Grandstand' and 'Sportsnight' regularly attracted audiences of 3 million and 7 million respectively; and particular sports events attracted even larger audiences – of the magnitude of 10 million for the Commonwealth Games and professional boxing, 13 million for the Wimbledon Final, 14 million for the Grand National, and as many as 29 million, or over half the population, for the World Cup Final. Such figures compare very favourably with those for the most popular programmes in other categories on both public and independent channels. It is plain that sports coverage is a major weapon in the ratings war between BBC and ITV, and the undoubtedly high ratings for sports include large numbers of working-class people. Sport not only attracts large audiences, it does so relatively cheaply. Expensive as it may be in terms of absolute costs (satellite charges, rights, etc.), the high unit costs per hour for the very high ratings gained compare favourably with drama and light entertainment: in these terms an hour of drama is three times as expensive as an hour of the World Cup.

The argument that the nature of the media's output is determined by market forces and the social background and experience of their personnel, and that the media ultimately serve the interests of dominant groups, does have merit. It cannot be entirely insignificant that virtually all the top sports commentators, presenters and management in both commercial and public broadcasting graduated via the commercial press, many of them from Fleet Street itself. Nor is the fact that the structure of ownership and control of the media as a whole, which is remarkably concentrated in Britain, gives owners in the private sector, and governments where public-sector broadcasting is concerned, the power to appoint and dismiss management. The relationship between media sport professionals and the sports community off whom they live is structurally and culturally close: a considerable proportion of sports journalists and management are former outstanding sports performers, coaches, administrators or erstwhile sportsmen themselves. Jimmy Hill, former professional footballer and secretary of the Professional Footballers' Association, now chairman of Coventry City Football Club and BBC sports presenter, epitomizes the phenomenon and there are plenty of others who do so, although perhaps not so spectacularly. Sports reporting and commentary, like critical appreciation of the arts in the media, tends to be merged with and positively oriented towards, the community upon which it reports and comments. Also, with regard to the evident success that media sport has registered with a working-class audience, it may be significant that football journalism and perhaps some other branches of sports journalism attracts proportionally more recruits from a working-class background than any other field of journalism. Their status as a group among their colleagues is low – with crime reporters, they are the lowest-paid journalists. As such, sports journalists are closer than others to working-class culture, a fact that is likely to enable them to trade off it in their work in a way that resonates with familiar modes of expression and structures of feeling, rendering it both more intelligible and more appealing to the working-class audience.

A perspective stressing the exogenous structural and cultural constraints on the media can be a useful corrective to attempts to tackle the problem of the media and power purely in terms of a content analysis of news and current affairs. As Golding and Murdock point out, the determining pressures underlying the construction of what is finally presented to audiences cannot be simply read off the content. But neither, on the other hand, is the character of media sport reducible to the economic and political context and the social background of the personnel. To treat it as such is to neglect what it is about the media themselves as institutions that enables media sport to involve a mass audience so successfully. Like all cultural production, media sport requires elucidation in terms of the specific character of the institutions concerned, the technology that is employed and, above all, the occupational culture of media-sport professionals. It is on the latter aspect we wish to concentrate from now on, in particular on media-sport news values.

Media professionals claim to be reporting impartially on reality, or merely conveying to the audience 'what actually happened'; but this doctrine of epistemological naturalism will not hold up to an examination of how the media treat sport. Alternatively, it is now a commonplace in media sociology that news is constructed in terms of professionals' values and the routine practices to which they give rise. Sporting events undergo a transformation when they are presented in the media: what appears on the screen and in the press and comes across on radio is not what the spectator or performer at the event experiences. Media sport does not just present the world as it is, already constructed – it re-presents the world in terms of its own inferential framework and thus creates events with their own features – media events. Sports journalists and editorial staff select from, rank, classify and elaborate the world of sport in terms of a 'stock of knowledge' as to what constitutes sports news. An interpretive framework is thus encoded in the flow of communication to the audience – in the items selected, the language, the visual imagery, the stylistics of the presentation, which constitutes an inducement to the audience to interpret the world reported on in preferred ways. It is as if, when readers, listeners and viewers are presented with sport in the media, they are simultaneously issued with a set of instructions or maxims as to how the communication should be read, heard and seen. In order to accomplish this successfully, this inferential framework must be related to the culture of the majority of the audience. The transformation of sport into a media spectacle draws not only on professional values – through the latter it draws on the audience's knowledge, values and expectations, as well as the sports community's.

That media sport intervenes in what it reports on, rather than reporting it as it is, is already clear from the fact that sports have actually been changed to make them more amenable for media coverage. The process of constructing media sport that we are analysing here, however, is of a different order altogether from this aspect.

At the simplest level what is selected for reporting and commentary is often a function of the distribution of information-gathering resources. For economic reasons these tend to be concentrated in areas previously defined by professionals as 'news-worthy', so sports-news gathering tends to be a self-fulfilling prophecy: we receive lots of news about sport in elite nations, and the media professional is constantly surprised by 'upsets', 'shock results', when 'unknowns', notably from Third World countries, defeat the elite. It is perhaps, in many cases, only surprising precisely because of the failure to attend to them earlier.

Media sport operates a preferred view of the social world by natural-izing it. It is because sport is so 'obviously' physical, i.e. concerned with the body, governed by natural laws, which function irrespective of what the observer thinks or feels about them, that it can be claimed to have nothing to do with politics or society and that values can be encoded in reporting on sport. Yet sport is no more or no less 'natural' than any other activity in which we indulge collectively – it is socially structured. The main way that sport and social order are naturalized in media sport is through the fiction that sports constitute a separate reality. The separate reality of sport is signified by the routine practice of separating out sport from other news and confining it to a separate sector – the sports section of the newspaper, the sports programme, the sports news. The occasions when sport escapes from its status as separate reality are relatively rare, and they occur when there is an angle present that justifies redefining the item as falling outside this separate reality. In our analysis of a week's popular daily newspapers, out of several hundred sporting stories, on only fourteen occasions did a story involving sport appear outside the confines of the sports section, and in only two out of these was sport the real focus of attention. Half of them were in fact related to sex, politics and crime, and the rest fell into the 'bizarre' and 'per-sonality' categories. Only one of the fourteen managed to achieve front-page status and predictably this concerned the attempted suicide of a married woman with whom an England international footballer was alleged to be having an affair. In this particular week none of the inter-national-status events managed to reach the front pages, although there were, in fact, three that were theoretically eligible – a world boxing championship fight, the Wightman Cup and the Wales–All Blacks rugby match.

The most usual way sport breaks out to the front page, or becomes a major news item on radio or TV, is when Britain triumphs in an international event. During the Moscow Olympics in 1980, for example, the only time sporting events, as opposed to the boycott, broke through to the front page was when a British performer's fortunes were at stake and when Britain won medals. Otherwise, sport achieves prominence in the main news when it gets pulled into issues over which political forces are mobilized already, such as South Africa and the Moscow Olympics boycott, or football violence and law and order. The institutionalized separation of sport from the rest of 'reality' in the media encodes that notion with which we are all familiar, and which begs the question of the relation between sport and power, namely, that sport has nothing to do with politics. Under the auspices of the 'no politics in sport' rule, media sport, as we shall see, can accomplish much ideological work.

The claim to be merely reproducing reality is most tenaciously held and appears to be most persuasive where TV is concerned, which indeed shows the event 'as it is actually happening'. But even here the technology of TV and the preferred practices of the professionals construct sport differently from how the spectator sees it. For example, when football is televised, the positioning of the main camera at the half-way position, on one side of the ground, in the stand, gives a view of the game that is quite different from the view of it from behind the goal. The former approximates more to the perspective of the middle-class spectator, with the cameras taking up an 'impartial' location, giving an equal view of both teams and with the commentator supporting neither team; whereas the latter corresponds to that of the working-class supporter, who has traditionally stood on the terraces in all weathers, behind his team, urging it on in a thoroughly partisan manner. The relatively poor picture quality of TV means the camera can only cover a maximum of an eighth of the pitch in long-shot, if the players are to be at all distinguishable. In face of this technological limitation, English professionals, when compared to others, such as the West Germans, have been found to prefer frequent alternate long-shots with close-ups of individual players, or small groups of players, and it has been calculated that the ratio of time spent on close-ups of this kind to time spent on long-shots is much greater in British televised football. The viewer's attention tends to be thereby directed away from team strategy towards the game's more individualistic aspects. The greater proportion of the game that occurs off-camera then has to be filled in for the audience by the commentator, giving him more latitude to interpret the action. What occurs on-camera is also interpreted for the viewer by the commentary ('that was a good goal' etc.). Unlike the spectator at the event the TV viewer's observation is interrupted by 'action replays', which again, typically, close in on the individual performer at what are interpreted as key dramatic, entertaining moments – the tackle and confrontation, the goal, the shot, the save, moments of successful achievement or failure, with individuals' facial expressions and gestures highlighted. More often than not nowadays, the average viewer sees a heavily edited recording of the highlights, a multiple construction of reality, a truncated, action-packed spectacle, injected with pace, which omits the build-ups and the 'dull patches'. The crucial point here is that British TV coverage plainly gives primacy to entertainment when compared with other styles of coverage. The BBC, for example, explicitly acknowledges that action replays are put in for the benefit of the 'mums and daughters' watching, rather than for the connoisseurs, a practice in keeping with TV producers' perceived need to hurry on the pace to keep the audience with the programme. The concurrence of the British press in such practices provides additional evidence of their cultural specificity. West German TV coverage of the World Cup in 1974, which eschewed close-ups for a more 'neutral' coverage, focusing on team play in long-shots, was criticized by columnists like Brian Glanville of *The Sunday Times* and by Derek Dougan for its 'lack of professional skills'(!).

Further confirmation that the media do not merely report on events or show them as they actually happen is provided by the fact that a good deal of work beforehand is put into preparing their audiences for how they should be seen and interpreted, that is, in building up the event. For example, the TV and *Radio Times* and *TV Times Magazine*, with their enormous circulations, built up the 1974 World Cup by nominating several stars beforehand as representatives of their countries' playing styles and national characteristics. The opening sequences of TV sports programmes set the scene immediately prior to the event to be shown. The graphics draw attention to selected aspects and themes, like the Scottish bagpiper symbol at the beginning of ITV's coverage of the 1978 World Cup in Argentina, which signalled the nation's importance *vis-à-vis* others in the competition. The montage of insets, packed with champions in action, at the beginning of BBC TV's 'Grandstand', prepares us for non-stop action and excitement. The use of 'atmospheric' music in the signature tunes (quasi-military, or with an ethnic trace) connotates entertainment, excitement and visits to exotic places.

Impartiality and objectivity is signalled by the practice of analysing performances with the help of accredited experts. Structured access is a fundamental feature of the organization of the media, and the use of the accredited expert in broadcasting is now a time-worn device, which developed originally in BBC news and current affairs programmes as a solution to the problem of establishing objectivity and achieving 'balance' over politically controversial matters. In the press the equivalent of the accredited expert enters through the use of the attributed quotation and the sports-personality-as-writer. Expertise, in signifying objective, factual treatment and knowledgeable opinion, functions to authorize preferred interpretations. Since experts are used as primary definers of reality in the media, who is defined as an expert, which experts are selected from those available, and what kind of questions are put to them by reporters, presenters and anchormen, is crucial in the definition of reality. 'Recognized experts' are selected by professionals, and they are almost invariably former sportsmen or practising performers, or coaches and officials – but these are not necessarily the most expert among those in the field. An additional qualification is that they should be celebrities or stars with entertaining personalities or 'characters' who are good on TV. Little-known or relatively unsuccessful figures, say a Fourth Division footballer, never appear as experts; it is the elite who are so identified, that is, what is considered relevant is not only what is said, but also who is saying it. A framework of values necessarily underpins the selection and definition of issues in the ensuing analysis, and what the audience is presented with is therefore a summing up reflecting the values of media professionals and their expert advisers. On this basis performances are assessed and achievement or failure is recorded, praise and blame are allocated, stars are nominated, the level of entertainment rated, whether the rules were adhered to and properly enforced is ascertained and whether nations and representatives conformed to the consensus stereotypes of them. The sports spectacle is thus used, not only to exemplify and judge technical skill, but to prescribe moral values and to comment prescriptively on social relationships.

We wish to focus from now on, on those aspects of media sports discourse and routine practice which are most important in this respect and which articulate on key processes whereby hegemony is achieved. We will examine how order and control, competitive individualism and civil privatism, sex and gender, the primacy of the nation and ethnocentricity tinged with racism, are constructed in media sport. Before doing so, it should be clear that there are differences in the ways individual media sports are constructed and more work needs to be done on elucidating these differences. We do not claim there is a uniform input to the power network from media sport, but what we do claim is that it makes a significant input in certain identifiable ways.

Media sport often reads like a handbook of conventional wisdom on social order and control. There are homilies on good firm management, justice, the nature of law, duty and obligation, correct attitudes to authority, the handling of disputes, what constitutes reasonable and civilized behaviour, on law and order and on the state of society generally. Media sport encodes an ideology of order and control, in the way the conduct of participants in sports events and that of spectators is depicted.

The main news values that structure order and control as a theme are the notion that news should be placed within a familiar framework to make it intelligible to the audience (conventionality); that sport should be presented as dramatic, sensational and full of suspense; that sport is about structured competition and the orderly resolution of conflict; and that unpredictable, deviant, rare and violent aspects are newsworthy, since they threaten change and change for the worse. Consequently, routine practices draw our attention to whether participants are conducting themselves in the prescribed manner. The media-sports professional treats the rules and procedures governing the behaviour of participants as 'constitutional' or sacrosanct. Participants are therefore expected to abide by the rules, and crucially they are expected to submit without question to decisions made by those in authority over the proceedings. One does not argue with the officials in charge – one gets on with the game and leaves the officiating to them. When rules are infringed, the guilty parties are expected, as a matter of course, to be punished by those in charge, and the officials, unless they are foreign, are seen as administering the rules impartially. When rules are broken persistently, the situation is presented as problematic, as a threat and a challenge to authority, which has to be dealt with firmly and the situation brought back under control. Instances of rule infringement and confrontations with figures of authority consequently figure among the most dramatic moments in media sport. It is this framework that determines the media's routine practice of focusing on whether 'what happened' was within the rules or not: was the ball in or out?, did the player foul the opponent?, was there dissent with an official? and so on, and crucially, whether the decision of the official in charge was correct, or in other words, was justice done? TV technology supports a very powerful claim to infallibility here, through the device of the sloweddown action replay, which is now used standardly to analyse decisions, and media professionals and accredited experts devote a good deal of their time to discussing their correctness. On the whole, unless the officials are foreign, in which case chauvinism tends to creep into reportage, their authority is vindicated by the media, and mistakes by officials are, with a few exceptions, treated with sympathetic understanding. Indeed, more and more frequently officials are criticized in media sport for not 'stamping their authority' on the proceedings, or on the conduct of sports generally. The logic dictates that infringements and how they are dealt with – arguments between players and officials, 'incidents' between participants and especially infringements involving violence – are selected and highlighted, not only because they are dramatic, but also as occasions for demonstrating the correct resolution of conflict, that is, it encodes a reassurance that the rule of law and not anarchy and chaos prevails. Stories of confrontations, shots of players, or players and officials eyeball-to-eyeball, fouls, temper tantrums and so on, are all at a premium. At the same time the standard practice is to strongly denounce and disapprove of such behaviour as 'childish', 'unsporting', 'gratuitous violence', etc. The routine practice dictates that justice must also be seen to be done, so punishment rituals are accorded a very special place in this construction – players being shown the card, individuals being publicly warned by officials, dismissals from the scene of action, players emerging from disciplinary hearings, etc. Exemplary punishments are singled out for detailed attention and lengthy discussion, and universally now, 'violent' and 'undisciplined play' is condemned as a 'bad example' with calls for severer punishments and firmer handling.

A common device used to bring off the moralizing is the practice of depicting actors in stereotypical terms as heroes and villains. Heroic status accrues to those participants in the drama whose conduct exemplifies the conventions, and these are the figures who are more usually singled out for praise. In fact, where the media give their own annual awards for sportsman and sportswoman of the year, one of the main criteria of selection is the 'example' set by the individual. Rebels and nonconformists on the other hand tend to be cast as the villains. One sees examples of this kind of stereotyping in the media's treatment of individuals like George Best, Ilie Nastase, John McEnroe and others who have been subjected to a stream of adverse publicity and criticism bordering on vilification for being 'undisciplined', 'playboys', 'unsportsmanlike', etc. But in its portrayal of the villain, media sport again achieves a form of accommodation with British working-class culture, which traditionally has shown a certain tolerance of, and even covert support for, the deviant. The subtext of media condemnation is often a sneaking admiration for the villain and rule-breaker, who cocks a snook at authority, but this relatively safe form of accommodation comes down eventually mostly on the side of authority. As they have always done, while supporting the powers that be, the media, especially the popular press, exploit the attractions deviance possesses for the audience. The language of the football reports and stories is just as violent, if not more so, than the very phenomenon it is at such pains to condemn, and in this sense it is all part of the same phenomenon.

Although the problem of 'indiscipline' and bad behaviour applies increasingly across the board, often now in more middle-class sports like tennis as well, it is the working-class game of football that receives by far the majority of the media's attention, and it is with respect to this sport that the media's presentation most directly and explicitly articulates with the political debate concerning the present 'state of society'. Football hooliganism began to be reported regularly in the 1960s and it has been a regular main news item throughout the 1970s and 1980s providing one of the most consistent examples of sport getting mixed up with what are social and, more lately, political issues in the media. Its treatment is completely at one with the way deviance, crime and law and order are constructed in the media from the consensual viewpoint. 'Football hooliganism' is a gift to the media, to the press especially, driven by competition from within its own ranks and particularly from TV to search out the 'big bang' story; and the way football hooliganism has come to be treated has important consequences for the phenom-enon itself and for the treatment of law and order issues. In constructing its account, the press relies typically a great deal on primary definers – football-club managers, the Football Association and the Football League, the police, judges and magistrates, politicians and the transport authorities. Reports of court proceedings, and especially the judge's pronouncements and details of the sentences meted out, are dwelt on. What the press adds on its own part, that is, apart from its principles of selection, is an account worked up in a stereotyped vocabulary which stigmatizes young working-class football supporters as animals and lunatics. This exaggerates the problem, oversimplifies the causes, draws attention away from the question of causation and concentrates instead on the 'threat to society' angle and how repressive the solution should be. The 1970s opened with headlines like: 'SAVAGES! ANIMALS!' (*Daily Mirror*); 'SMASH THESE THUGS!', 'MURDER ON SOCCER TRAIN', 'BIRCH 'EM!' and 'FANS GO MAD' (*The Sun*).

The mid-1980s has seen the media giving the maximum possible exposure, in graphic detail, to the lethal results of Liverpool supporters' assault on Juventus supporters at the Heysal Stadium in Brussels, and to the British Prime Minister's vehement (and metaphorically speaking, violent) denunciations of hooligans and her threats of punitive action against offenders. Press photos and video complete the theme of mind-less, frightening violence – police battling with sections of the crowd, the piles of bodies and the wreckage of the stadium and the agony of the bereaved. One type of press photo providing a particularly striking image of mindless violence is the 'dart photo', used repeatedly: a spec-tator's face is shown in close-up, with a dart (thrown during the match) embedded near the corner of one eye. Another shows a young policeman, in head and shoulders close-up, with a dart, again thrown by a spectator, embedded in the lower cheek. The thrust of this presentation is to suggest that conflict around football is so anti-social, irrational and threatening that the only way it can be dealt with effectively is by tougher disciplinary measures. When causes of the problem enter this discourse they figure merely as fillers between the drama. It is the solution that becomes the major focus of the media's attention. The absence of an account in terms of power and process and the attribution of cause solely to the irrationality and moral defectiveness of the deviants is typical of the media's construction of matters with a complex causation involving civil disorders and of social conflict in general.

TV is no exception in this respect, although it employs a less violent vocabulary than the press. In a BBC TV discussion in an edition of the 'Sportsnight' programme devoted to 'The State of Football', for example, Graham Taylor, the Manager of Watford United Football Club at the time, somewhat unpredictably departed from the programme's agenda by explaining the problem in terms of the commercialization of the game and how it had alienated the supporter. As soon as Taylor mentioned the viciousness of the game in this context, the presenter interpreted this as a reference to soccer hooliganism, which had not in fact been mentioned at all by Taylor, and immediately cued in the accredited experts, who had been lined up to define the game's problems as being due to hooliganism. Almost the entire focus of the programme thereafter was shifted to discussion of the need to find a solution to this and to calls for punitive sanctions. A similar programme on ITV during the same year (1980) was skewed even more heavily towards attributing the cause of 'football's decline' to hooliganism. Under continual prompting and questioning from the presenter, six of the ten accredited experts/spokesmen/primary definers blamed hooliganism and put forward heavier sentencing as the solution. Attempts to suggest other causes were made by some of the participants, but they were set aside by the presenter, who adhered closely to his agenda. It was concluded that football hooliganism was a reflection of the 'moral decline of the country'. In an ironic sense this was, indeed, the point: in an economically and politically declining Britain, as the social costs become increasingly evident, the football hooligan has been constructed in the media as one of a series of 'folk devils' (others are 'muggers', drugtakers and pushers, strikers, pickets and terrorists) who are somehow responsible for, and symbolic of, the 'decline in moral standards'. By stigmatizing one section of the population as the villains, and by recommending a hard stamping-down by authority as the solution, the media have played a major part in constructing politics in a law and order mood. The violence around football is not a media invention – it is a serious problem with political implications, not least for workingclass people. The point is that the media's intervention has ideological effects: it displaces the incipient conflict between dominant and subordinate groups over problems generated by the present crisis to the level of concern with law abiding, and helps to mobilize mass support for authoritarian solutions to the predicament of subordinate groups. One is sometimes tempted to think that if football violence had not existed it would have been necessary to invent it.

Individualism and civil privatism is constructed through the media-sport professionals' assumption that personalities constitute the core of the audience's interest, that interest is sustained by entertainment and that sport is basically about achievement through struggle. Media sport nowadays is largely built around the individual's attributes, the person's thoughts and feelings. Getting to the top is attributed to their talents, of course, but above all to their competitiveness and perseverance, the appropriate reward for which is seen as money in large amounts, prestige and glamour. We have seen that even in a game like football where team-work is so important, attention is nevertheless focused on the individual, through the routine practice in British TV coverage of making frequent close-ups of players, showing their problems, achievements and failures. The press's treatment is substantially the same, except that personalization and dramatization are carried further in competition with TV and rival newspapers. Paradoxically, the relatively large number of photos in the sports sections almost never depict action, despite the obsession with it in the written text. Instead they disclose personalities, posed for the camera outside the context of action, or taken from actual action shots, usually showing only head and shoulders, or just the single figure of the personality. The written text completes the personality angle: it is packed with details of individuals' achievements, successes and failures, their opinions and feelings, details of their private lives and most importantly of their salaries. It was typical, for example, that the coverage of the Wightman Cup focused on the question of whether Virginia Wade's career was over or not. The journalists themselves figure as personalities as well. Many of the columns in the sports sections are headed by photos or graphics of the writer, whose feelings, reactions and assessments are again conveyed through a highly personalized style.

The entertainment values that underpin media sport articulate with a shift in the historical development of individualism towards promoting the family as the individual's source of well-being, and away from the ideal that individuality is promoted by extending opportunities to participate in public life. The individualism–familism–civil privatism syndrome draws on the working-class ideal of respectability which entails, among other things, the injunction to be independent as an individual, to live up to decent standards, to be as good as others in this respect and to do as much as possible for one's family. But second, in working-class culture there is a strong traditional belief also that life is not just a matter of work and ambition, it is also to be enjoyed at the moment; so entertainment and the leisure in which to enjoy it are also valued highly. The message that 'keeping up with the Jones's' by maximizing consumption within the family unit is enjoyable, manages the tension between respectability and hedonism. At the same time it subsumes them, together with the competitive, egoistic dimensions of individualism, into a coherent whole, ultimately prescribing civil privatism and fulfilment in leisure as the good way of life. The tendency among media-sport professionals to perceive the audience as strictly limited in its capacity to attend to anything for more than a little while, and as therefore requiring constant stimulation with entertainment, is fully consonant with consumerist, civil privatist ideology. Media-sports professionals have been at the forefront of reform campaigns to transform sport as a whole into family-oriented entertainment on middle-class lines. One of the routine practices signalling this value loudly is literally to give marks for 'entertainment value' and continually to raise the question: was it entertaining enough? Entertainment is brought off with linguistic practices aimed at creating the impression of action, excitement and suspense – it is brought off with the language of the battlefield: tackles are 'bone-crunching', opponents are 'demolished', 'crushed' and 'humiliated', and terms like 'blitz', 'blast', 'charge' and so on, proliferate. Goals are 'slammed', athletes 'power' their way to the tape, opponents are 'annihilated'. No work has been carried out so far in this country comparing the linguistic structure of media sport with working-class linguistic usage. Some work in Britain analysing sports writing in the Sunday newspapers and the language used to report on football matches and football hooliganism points to its lexical and conceptual poverty. With some exceptions the language, even when compared with usage in the rest of the media, is notoriously stereotyped. The vocabulary is limited, reference is overwhelmingly to the concrete as opposed to the abstract and it contains relatively few qualifiers and modifiers. What in aesthetic terms could be categorized as repetitive, cliché-ridden, over-written prose, constitutes in socio-linguistic terms a restricted code. It is doubtful whether the restricted code can be attributed solely to the working-class nature of the audience: there is little reason to think 'sportugese' coincides with working-class usage and the extent to which working-class linguistic codes are 'restricted' is disputable anyway. Rather, what 'sportugese' seems to represent in socio-linguistic terms is an attempt on the part of the media-sports professionals to make sports entertaining for the working-class audience – an attempt which, on the whole, has been quite successful in terms of attracting and keeping that audience.

The media constitute one of the prime sites for the reproduction of gender divisions and sexism. Men figure far more than women as participants and even more so as media-sport professionals. Apart from crime reporting, sport is probably the most male-dominated sector of the media and it remains so, despite the rising number of women participants in sport, the greater amount of interest in sport among women in general and, above all, the existence of a significant number of women sports stars. The few women who have gained entry to this male media preserve tend to be restricted to reporting and commenting on 'women's sports'. The fact that it has proved harder for women to break into media sport as professionals than to break into sport itself is a good indication that media sport plays a strong conservative role in the reproduction of inequality between the sexes. Male commentators in male-dominated sports like cricket and football are, no doubt, what the majority of the audience expects, and in fulfilling this expectation the media accommodate to the prevailing pattern of gender division. But men also report and comment more frequently on women's sporting activity than vice versa, and even when sports are very popular with women, say, women's tennis, or gymnastics, as opposed to women's cricket, which is not popular, male commentators are far more prominent. The image of women in media sport is therefore predominantly constructed by men. Experience in other sectors of the media suggests that, if more women were employed in media sport, sexist stereotyping would not necessarily disappear, but what would be likely to change is the conservative rigidity with which it goes on.

[···]

Images of gender in media sport reproduce the current pattern of male hegemony by articulating firmly with the discourse and practice of familism–civil privatism, which naturalize the sexual division of labour – that is, the tendency of women to be more closely confined to their familial roles and to less rewarding jobs and their consequent unequal position in society. On the other hand, women's stronger anchorage within the family confers on them a major role in the construction of 'normal' family life. In fact it makes them the major relay through which consumer culture penetrates and pervades family life and through which men are induced under high pressure from women to achieve individual success on their behalf.

The sharp gender divisions constructed in the media are likely to resonate more strongly with conceptions of gender subscribed to by the more culturally and politically conservative sections of the population.

Among dominant groups these are the forces which resist further advance by women into top business and professional positions, political life, etc. Among the working class, where more widespread assent is given to rigid gender divisions and a subordinate role for women, working-class conservatives are likely to assent more strongly still. Media sport accommodates to this important aspect of working-class culture particularly closely.

A sense of unity conferred by the feeling of belonging to the nation, cutting across class, ethnic, gender and other loyalties, is perhaps the very linchpin of a hegemonic system, and the media are, arguably, the most important institution reproducing national identity today. Since the 1950s especially, with the expansion of TV coverage of international events, media sport has increasingly provided opportunities for people to identify with the nation through sport.

Coverage of the great annual sporting occasions, such as the Cup Final, the Derby, the Oxford and Cambridge Boat Race, etc., tends to convey a sense of a national way of life, but it is in coverage of international events in which 'we' compete against foreigners that 'Britishness' or 'Englishness' constitutes conventional reference points signifying membership of a unique community, sharing a common, valued and specific way of life, which supersedes or takes precedence over all other loyalties and identities. The notion of the 'national interest', frequently invoked in media discourse on political topics, is transposed into media-sports discourse when 'our' competitors and representatives are made the focus of the media's attention on international occasions: how are 'we' going to fare? and how have 'we' done? are the issues as, for example, the Olympic medal table is scrutinized to keep track of 'our' achievements, *vis-à-vis* the other elite nations. As we have noted already, when a gold medal or a major competition is won, that is precisely the occasion when the episode breaks out of its separate reality and achieves the status of 'national' news. The ceremonial and ritual surrounding these occasions, prominently displaying the national symbols – the flags, the parades, the uniforms, the patriotic hymns and anthems, the participation of elite figures symbolic of national unity – especially members of the royal family, but also the Prime Minister and others – signal preferred conceptions of national unity which powerfully invoke feelings of identity. A particularly significant aspect of media-sport proceedings is the award ceremony which signifies not only individual or team achievement, but above all national achievement and glory. When media sport concentrates attention on these particular ceremonial and ritual aspects as opposed to other respects – the behaviour of the crowd, the action in progress, etc. – it invokes national unity in a manner more consistent with the dominant class's preferred view. For this aspect, compared with others on which the media focus, is more subject to control and influence by dominant groups. It is predominantly their cultural capital that is being put to work in the elaborately staged ceremonial, for example the Wimbledon Finals ceremony on the Centre Court when, immediately prior to presenting the trophy to the victor, the Duke and Duchess of Kent, having descended from the royal box, enter the court. Silence reigns, and while we all wait, literally in our millions all over the country, they pause casually on their way between the two ranks of ballboys to 'have a word' with one or two of them, as if there were no one else there, before proceeding to confer honour on the victor, on our behalf, to tumultuous applause. Dominant groups' symbolic work is not simply transmitted in pure unmediated form, but is merged in a construction of the nation which also embodies an accommodation to working-class and other groups' feelings of national identity. The latter aspect tends, on the whole, to be reproduced more in the way the action is depicted.

The construction of the nation in media sport is not unproblematic. A difficulty is presented, for example, by a degree of ambiguity about being British, which is not present in the conception of being English, and in some ways the consensus on what constitutes the nation is more firmly rooted in the latter than the former conception. In order to resolve the tension between what it means to be English, as opposed to being Welsh, Scottish or Irish, ideological work is required, for indigenous national identities are strongly represented in some sports. When, for example, Wales and England clash on the rugby field at Cardiff Arms Park, media coverage of royalty's attendance and the accompanying ritual and ceremony forms an integral part of the symbolic work carried out to ease tensions between these different nationalisms within the UK, which are expressed on this occasion. But the presence of more than one nation within a single political unit also has its advantages. Where there is no representative of England in major international competitions, the media's problem of finding a conventional reference point with which the audience can identify is solved by searching out the 'British connection'. For example, in the 1974 and 1978 World Cup competitions, from which the English team had been eliminated early on, the Scottish team was made to stand for Britain. The simultaneous necessity to construct 'Scottishness' was accomplished through the portrayal of Scots playing style – 'brilliant individualism', 'fighting spirit', 'tempestuousness' and 'inconsistency'. Consistent with this type of signification in the 1974 World Cup, it was the better-known Scottish players employed by English League clubs who were made the focus of attention for what was, after all, a predominantly English audience. However, when Scotland failed badly after a massive build-up in the media for the 1978 World Cup, this was widely interpreted in the media as a Scottish national disaster, rather than a British one.

Media sport strongly contrasts 'us' with other nations, peoples and races in the way that playing styles of other peoples and nations are depicted. Television coverage of the World Cup, for example, maps the world in a fashion that largely depicts North and Western Europe against Southern and Eastern Europe, and Europe versus Latin America, and unlike the Olympics it does not represent the conflict between the superpowers. Instead, other sorts of divisions are constructed: within Europe between the 'Nordic' and the 'Latin', and within Latin America, between Spanish-speaking and Portuguese-speaking multiracial Brazil. The major motivating signifiers here are hair and skin colour: 'Latin' connotes 'fiery' and also 'bad' (cynical, dishonest, dirty – the England football manager Alf Ramsey's celebrated castigation of the Argentinians as 'animals' partakes of this kind of discourse). 'Nordic' is 'cool' and 'good' (professional, open, disciplined). This division also corresponds very roughly with the distinction between the richer and poorer countries. The problem with forcing playing styles into such moulds is that in reality the 'Nordic', 'cool' and 'rich' Dutch, for example, have a good deal in common, in terms of playing style, with the 'Latin', 'fiery', 'poor' Brazilians, and similarly the 'Latin' Italians have much in common with the 'Nordic' Scots.

[···]

Contrary to working-class people's common perception of ethnic minorities as not forming part of the nation, media sport welcomes the presence of members of ethnic minorities in British teams, treating them equally as 'our' representatives. On the whole, South Africa does not get much sympathy in media sport and the activities of the National Front at football matches are usually deplored. Since sports are one of the few publicly recognized areas of achievement for black people, their depiction as representatives of Britain in international competition signals that progress is being made in achieving racial equality and racial harmony, whereas the facts on the position of black people and the state of race relations in general are quite the opposite. Notably, racism is widespread among the working class. On such a sensitive political issue media sport accommodates more to dominant discourse on race and not so much to its working-class audience. Nevertheless, it does follow the latter course in the sense that, by portraying blacks as being successful in sports and failing to portray them as being successful otherwise, it reproduces the myth – widespread in Britain – that blacks, being naturally better at physical pursuits and less so at intellectually demanding ones, are closer to nature and therefore less civilized than whites. The media practice that reinforces the myth is, of course, the absence of black people and, indeed, of ethnic minorities in general from the ranks of media-sports professionals. It is whites almost exclusively who construct images of non-whites in media sport, a reflection of a general tendency in the media to exclude ethnic minorities from the more prestigious influential controlling positions. Their absence suggests that media-sport management fears alienating its predominantly white audience and accommodates to it accordingly. The consequent ethnic stereotyping of black British as well as black non-British nationals that goes on is not very surprising. In cricket reporting, for example, West Indian and black British cricket supporters are typically depicted in terms of their 'exuberance', their 'excitability' and their 'colourfulness'. The connotations of immaturity and indiscipline that such labelling has are unlikely to be lost on a British audience, which has still not shaken off a good deal of its imperialist cultural heritage, as the camera pans around laughing black spectators, jumping up and down, gesticulating, shouting, playing drums, etc., all of which is accompanied by an attitude of good-natured, amused tolerance on the part of the commentator.

Media sport often gives voice to the view, also widespread in Britain, that sports bring people of different nations and peoples closer together; whereas it is extremely unlikely that media sport counteracts chauvinist, ethnocentric, and occasionally racist-tinged conceptions of national identity and of national differences held by the population at large – and by the working class in particular. Indeed since such sentiments tend to be encoded in media-sport discourse practice itself, the prevailing exclusionist sense of national identity, uniting indigenous subordinate groups behind dominant groups against 'outsiders' within an over-arching hegemony, is more likely to be reinforced from this direction. The code of media sport is but one aspect of a multi-layered process, whereby an exclusionist sense of national identity is reproduced by the media. In contrast to the public technology of an earlier era (the railways, streetlighting, etc.), the privatizing technology of broadcasting, whereby a centralized transmitter sends messages to scattered household receivers, strongly articulates with that aspect of the political culture which identifies a privatized life-style with being English – an identification succinctly expressed in the old adage 'an Englishman's home is his castle'.

The paucity of firm, well-grounded conclusions in research on the effects of mass communication so far dictates caution when interpreting the relation between media sport and working-class culture and the likely effects of media sport on the working-class audience. A process of selective accommodation to working-class culture certainly takes place, but it is selective in the sense that the accommodation is to those aspects of working-class culture which are compatible with media-sport professionals' values and which do not jeopardize their relationship with dominant groups. It is these elements that are more likely to be reinforced. Dominant groups are more likely to be accommodated to when sport becomes politicized, as in the case of football violence and the Moscow Olympics, and it is then that media sport is deployed in support of dominant groups' interests, and that it amplifies, rather than simply reinforces, social forces. Media sport, then, is likely to make an input to the more conservative aspects of working-class culture and in particular to exert an overall conservative effect on the relation between sport and working-class culture.

15

Ten Theses on Children and Television

Bob Hodge and David Tripp

Hodge and Tripp's discussion stems from research they carried out on children and television. They offer 'ten theses' about children and television.

1   Children typically have the capacity to be active and powerful decoders of television, and programmes watched by them are potentially rich in meaning and cultural value; though not all programmes and ways of viewing are of equal benefit for all children.

Children's semiotic powers and the complexity of the meanings they construct and consume make up the central premise of our whole argument. This premise is not a blanket excuse for anything on television that children watch. It is not the end of discrimination in this area, but the rational basis for a beginning. We do not see all children as equally active and adequate 'readers' under all circumstances; nor do we see all programmes as equally dense in meaning or culturally valuable. Media professionals should not underrate children's ability to handle great complexity, nor should they under-provide for that need of children for relevant complexity. Lobbyists are very important in maintaining high production standards. Children's television is notoriously given the smallest budgets and least attention, and economic reasons are too often justified by reductive assumptions about children's semiotic abilities. It seems better to give them good programmes made for adults than cheap, insubstantial programmes whose main claim to be tailored to children's needs appears to be the fact that adults would not watch them with enjoyment. Educationalists, parents and researchers alike should take this generally despised area of children's lives and development more seriously and with greater respect for its actual and potential value. However, there can be too much television watching by children. Though

television is functionally redundant up to a point, there will be a de-
creasing return from heavy viewing as more of the same kind of viewing
displaces other important activities. So it is generally more important
for adults to limit the total time spent viewing than to select the programmes viewed.

2   Children's cognitive and semiotic systems develop at least up till
the age of 12, so that they not only prefer different kinds of programmes
from adults, they also respond differently to programmes, and interpret
them differently: but from the age of 9 they are capable of their own
kind of understanding of most mainstream television.

It is impossible to capture in a few short sentences the nature, scope
and implications of children's growing powers of interpreting and
understanding television. For media producers the concept of multilevel
'family' programming, capable of being 'read' in different but appropriate ways by different age levels, is a valid one, better we would suggest
than an attempt to match specific levels of development with programming targeted to very specific age ranges. In general children enjoy and
can learn much from some programmes that are regarded by many
adults as 'too old' for them, though they will be responding in their own
distinctively 'childlike' way. We believe that there is a parallel in children's developing ability to handle complex television messages, with
the idea of young children not being imperfectly socialized miniature
adults but well adjusted to a social system which is different from that
of adults, not necessarily inferior. As with the development of language,
it seems that children's systems increasingly approximate to adult systems as they are exposed to, and allowed to operate in, adult systems.
This means that educationalists and parents need not be too concerned
at children watching the most popular adult shows.

3   Children's television typically carries dominant ideological forms,
but also a range of oppositional meanings.

This mixed content of children's television (and other television and
other media), and the typical contradictions of response to which it
gives rise, is, we believe, the crucial content issue for children's television. Media producers should be, and mostly are, well aware that an
excessive overbalance of the dominant ideology makes for dull and
unprofitable children's television: though producers sell programmes to
advertisers and networks, rather than to children, and these corporate
bodies tend to have a different attitude towards the dominant ideology.

Different programmes give different amounts of space to oppositional readings, and recuperate the dominant ideology with different degrees of effectiveness. However, since these components are so subtly inter-mixed, and since different ways of reading and conditions of reception can so radically alter the thrust of a programme, any attempt to use legislation to specify and control the ideological content of television programming is likely to be futile – and any such attempt would itself have to take sides on ideological issues. However, although tight leg-islative control of television content would prove ineffective, or else would remove much of the entertainment and stimulus value of children's television, there are other more constructive responses to the mixed ideological content of children's television. Parents and educators can recognize and use the contradictions of specific programmes to help to clarify some fundamental social issues, for children and for themselves. They should do this, not only by relying on children's active processing of the message, but also by making children more conscious and aware of what they are processing and how.

4   It has long been known that the reality factor – television's per-ceived relation to the real world – is variable, depending on age, experi-ence and social conditions. Indeed, it is a decisive factor determining the nature of media responses and media effects. But the ability to make subtle and adequate reality judgements about television is a major developmental outcome that can only be acquired from a child's experi-ence of television.

Differences in modality judgements account for most of the reactions by children that most surprise and trouble parents: their apparent over-reaction, their impressionability. Parents are right to protect their chil-dren from over-stimulation when they are young, but they should not worry unduly about occasional 'modality mistakes' or over-reactions to specific programmes. These are indicative that learning is taking place, as children try to make things fit their scheme of the world by ex-perimenting. Nor should parents be over-anxious at older children's seeming callousness, as if it were 'narcotization', when it is simply an accurate perception of the unreality of television.

The process of refining modality judgements – about television messages and other message systems – should be a major concern to educators, since it is of such obvious importance in equipping them to cope with the barrage of messages they will be confronted with as citizens in a mass-communications society. The processes of media production, as part of the necessary knowledge for a media modality system, should be part of everyone's school knowledge.

The pathological modality problems which do exist, for some children, should be seen as part of a more general social problem, and it is principally that problem, not merely its associated television symptoms, which should be the focus of attention by government agencies and other concerned bodies. Using television as a scapegoat is too often an excuse for inaction with regard to deeper causes.

5   All children need some fantasy programmes, such as cartoons for younger children. All children, particularly older ones, also need some programmes which touch more closely their reality.

Young children's liking for cartoons, so frequent a target for lobbyists and concern for parents, is a natural and healthy developmental phenomenon. Older children need programmes with the greater impact that comes from higher modality. Successful children's programmes utilize this, though they do not always seem to be explicitly and consistently aware of it. But people of all ages prefer a mix of modality types, to give the range of media effects, from relaxation to excitement. It is only by providing programmes with a range of modality values that children will experience a sufficiently rich modality environment to enable them to learn to distinguish one kind from another.

6   Media violence is qualitatively different from real violence: it is a natural signifier of conflict and difference, and without representations of conflict, art of the past and present would be seriously impoverished.

The issue of violent content cannot be considered apart from the modality value of media representations of violence. The strong move by lobbyists, especially overt in the United States but also effective in Britain and Australia, to limit the depictions of violence on television is therefore based on a radical misconception of how the media work. This said, it remains true that high-modality violence is likely to be disturbing to young children, who will neither enjoy nor learn well from such programmes. Furthermore the ideological meaning of some kinds of violence – as in some kinds of pornography or racism – must be sufficiently offensive to be banned on those grounds: not because of violence as such but because of the world-view they are proclaiming and legitimating.

7   Meanings gained from television are renegotiated and altered in the process of discourse, and in that form have social status and effect.

The activity of children in response to television does not stop with watching programmes, but continues with all sorts of other acts of meaning-making. Anyone concerned with the effects of television must follow up the sometimes tortuous course of this redefinition and appropriation. This is especially true for parents and teachers, if they want to engage constructively and directly with the real meanings at issue. That is, adults in their contact with children should take an active part in helping to mediate children's interaction with and ideas about television. Significant adults should be wary of blanket rejection of programmes which are avidly viewed by children, or which provoke strongly positive responses. They should also acknowledge the role of peer interaction, as vital for a child's normal development.

8   General ideological forms have an overall determining effect on interpretations of television.

Ideological forms in television can only confirm and replicate what is widely promulgated by other means. Television is often unjustly blamed for the breakdown of other ideological apparatuses by the Right, or attributed with the combined effectivity of all the rest by the Left. But television has too diffused and contradictory a content to have a single effect one way or another on its own: it has a social role to play, but only in conjunction with other forces and structures, and can never be singly and aberrantly determining.

9   The family is not simply a site for countering the meanings of television; it is also active in determining what the meanings will be.

The family remains a powerful agent of socialization in contemporary society. There are determinations of the family itself in a class society, and parental authority is contested by other sites of power, including school and peer groups. Whereas parents may feel powerless, or seek to exercise power by limiting their children's viewing, a more open and equal relationship over television could be an educative and bonding factor. Families need to think about and act upon the way in which they interact with their televisions, not simply try to control the quantity or kind of programmes viewed when and by whom. Such control will typically produce friction and struggle, as it usually combines arbitrary routines with *ad hoc* exceptions.

10   The school is a site where television should be thoroughly understood and drawn into the curriculum in a variety of positive ways.

The suspicion of television by educators, the barriers that are set up between television and schooling, are, we feel, unjustified and wasteful of a potentially valuable resource. The common argument is that one should keep television out of the school because 'children spend too much time in mindless television viewing anyway'. This is in fact as good a reason for bringing television into the school curriculum as it is for excluding it. The less one knows and understands about the medium, the less one engages with it in a discriminating fashion. Television literacy and appreciation are obvious school subjects which seem to be making too little progress. Overall, television is a factor which modern education cannot simply deplore or ignore but should come to terms with as part of its primary function of equipping students to be adequate citizens in the society in which they live.

16

The Emergence of the Consumer Society

Robert Bocock

In the late nineteenth and early twentieth centuries new patterns of consumption began to develop among the urban middle and working classes. These patterns centred especially around the new department stores in city centres. The new department stores were sites for the purchase *and* display of a variety of commodities – groceries, furniture, clothing, crockery, kitchen utensils, and new electrical equipment as these were developed and mass produced in the course of the twentieth century – all under one roof. Such city-centre shops offered more choice than local ones could do, although butchers, fishmongers, greengrocers and bakers remained in local high streets, and groceries in particular were obtainable in local corner shops. The city-centre department stores developed as trams, trolley buses and railways emerged to carry people into the centre from the outlying suburban areas during the late nineteenth and early twentieth centuries.

Cities such as London, Paris, Glasgow, New York, Chicago, and Berlin expanded their transport networks and developed large city-centre department stores from the 1890s up to the First World War in 1914. The sociologist George Simmel (1858–1918) observed Berlin during the late nineteenth century: a city bulging with new migrants, especially from eastern Europe, including Poland. In his essay *The Metropolis and Mental Life* (1903) Simmel argued that the modern city is 'not a spatial entity with sociological consequences, but a sociological entity that is formed spatially'.[1] Cities grew around centres of government as well as around particular industries, from steel to lace-making. The shops and leisure facilities such as theatres, music halls and sports stadia all grew up to satisfy the social and psychological desires of the new urban classes.

A new, distinctive urban culture, linked to consumption, thus emerged in these metropolises. The daily life of people who lived in a great metropolis, Simmel argued, is affected by the need to cultivate a 'blasé attitude' towards others, 'for it was only by screening out the complex stimuli that stemmed from the rush of modern life that we could tolerate its extremes. Our only outlet . . . is to cultivate a sham individualism through the pursuit of signs of status, fashion, or marks of individual eccentricity.'[2]

Some became 'dedicated followers of fashion'; others walked around just looking – providing an urban audience for others to parade before. The stress was on the individual: everyone tried to remain socially detached from one another, or blasé as Simmel noted. One modern sociologist, D. Frisby, has written of Simmel's work on metropolitan life as follows:

> In the opening passage of his essay on the metropolis, Simmel asserts that 'the deepest problems of modern life derive from the claim of the individual to preserve the autonomy and individuality of his existence in the face of overwhelming social forces' and are concentrated in the metropolis. The individual must 'resist being levelled down and worn out by a social–technological mechanism' such as the metropolis. Extreme subjectivism is the response to the extreme objectification of culture that is found there. Hence the individual's struggle for self-assertion, when confronted with the pervasive indifference of much metropolitan social interaction, may take the form of stimulating a sense of distinctiveness, even in an excessive form of adopting 'the most tendentious eccentricities, the specifically metropolitan excesses of aloofness, caprice and fastidiousness, whose significance no longer lies in the content of such behaviour, but rather in its form of being different, of making oneself stand out and thus attracting attention'. In part, this arises out of 'the brevity and infrequency of meetings' which necessitates coming to the point as quickly as possible and making a striking impression in the briefest possible time.[3]

Modern consumerism, therefore, in part results from this new way of life in the metropolis, the city and its suburbs, for this gives rise to a new kind of individual who is anxious, as Simmel expressed it in the above quotation, 'to preserve the autonomy and individuality of his existence in the face of overwhelming social forces', and thus to avoid 'being levelled down and worn out by a social–technological mechanism' – the metropolis.

The processes involved in living in the city increased the awareness of style, the need to consume within a repertory or code which is both distinctive to a specific social group and expressive of individual preference. The metropolitan individual is no longer the older type Max

Weber had analysed in his work on Calvinism, who would not spend 'foolishly' on relatively trivial items of clothing or adornment. Rather the person in the big city consumes in order to articulate a sense of identity, of who they wish to be taken to be.

The signs or symbols which a particular individual uses as a means of marking themselves from others have to be interpreted and understood by others. Someone can only mark themselves as being *different* from others if they also share some common cultural codes with others within which these signs of difference can be read and interpreted. This produces a ceaseless striving for the *distinctive*, with the higher social status groups continually having to change their patterns of consumption as the middle-middle, lower-middle and working-class strata copy their habits. For example, drinking champagne or malt whisky, once the preserve of the aristocracy, has moved down the social status ladder in this century, so that the upper echelons either cease to drink these drinks or consume more exclusive and expensive vintages.

This aspect of the consumption process was observed by the sociologist Thorstein Veblen in the United States during the late nineteenth century. He was concerned, particularly, with one specific social class, the *nouveaux riches* – the 'new rich' – of the late nineteenth century. These groups, whose wealth was recently acquired, aped the European aristocracy, or tried to do so in order to win social acceptance. The middle classes and the working classes, black and white, were not yet caught up in this process, which Veblen termed 'conspicuous *consumption*'.

[···]

Simmel and Veblen's work marked a shift of attention in sociology from economistic to social definitions of class. Classical Marxism operated within a broadly economistic set of assumptions, and emphasized the concepts of *economic class*, especially the bourgeoisie and proletariat. These were firmly located in terms of their respective relationship to the means of production, that is, the factories, the mines, the machinery and energy sources, and (to a lesser extent) the means of distribution (the shops, department stores and transport systems) of modern capitalism. According to Marx, the bourgeoisie, which owned these means of production and distribution, had a set of economic interests which were directly opposed to those they employed, for they sought to maximize profits and to minimize costs, including wage and salary costs. This economistic model remained of great intellectual and political importance in the first half of the twentieth century; but it did present problems in understanding, explaining and conceptualizing the broader processes of social change taking place in the United States, Britain and Western Europe in this period. Quite apart from the great events – the First World War, the Depression, the Wall Street Crash, the rise of Nazism and Fascism, and the Second World War – there were other changes, which may not have seemed so important at the time because they were less dramatic, but which were, in one sense, underlying some of the major historical events. These included the changes in the class and status systems of such capitalist societies, which were, in turn, related to the process of consumption rather than to that of production. In peace time, the members of the proletariat were preoccupied with building up and preserving, not only their wages and salaries, relative to others, but also their *social status*, that is, their own sense of who they were, of how socially worthy they were: worthy, that is, of prestige or esteem from others.

[⋯]

Social status groups use patterns of consumption as a means of establishing their rank or worth and demarcating themselves from others. It is not only Veblen's *nouveaux riches*, or the metropolitan individuals analysed by Simmel, but *all* status groups, which use some markers to differentiate themselves from others, in the Weberian view. The markers they use to do this include group values about consumption, although as Parkin points out any social or physical attribute may be used to effect social closure, to mark who belongs to a particular social group and who is excluded. The types of housing, furnishings and decorations; the types of music enjoyed; the kinds of clothing which are worn; the type of transport used; all these aspects of the process of consumption may be used as markers of difference between social status groups.

The existence, persistence and increasing growth of social status groups in the twentieth century has helped to generate a plethora of patterns of consumption. The growth of consumption in modern capitalist societies now affects, not only the upper and middle class, but the two-thirds of the population which made up what most sociologists called the 'working classes', i.e. those earning a wage for manual work of some kind. In other words, the twentieth century has witnessed the increasing growth of consumerism among most, if not all, major social status groups, including those who have the lowest incomes, from the state or from paid employment.

In North America the Depression of the 1930s and in Europe the two World Wars (1914–18 and 1939–45) delayed the development of 'mass consumerism', as the process of the incorporation of the broad working class into consumerism came to be called in the 1950s and 1960s. Since the end of the 1940s, however, the capitalist societies of North America, Western Europe, Britain, Japan and Australia have experienced a massive development of 'mass consumption'. This phrase encapsulates the processes whereby the majority of the working classes in these societies became 'consumers', not only, or even primarily, 'workers' in the production process.

[⋯]

As the majority (between two-thirds and three-quarters) of the populations of Western capitalist societies became more affluent, the mode of consumption changed from one concerned primarily with basic material provision (which many people still lack in the major capitalist societies as well as in the world as a whole) to a mode concerned more with the status value and symbolic meaning of the commodity purchased. As consumerism spreads and becomes a 'global' phenomenon, those in most societies in the world who live above subsistence level may find themselves caught up emotionally in desiring consumer goods and experiences (such as travel) which they cannot afford to buy for themselves. In this way 'consumerism' may influence even the symbolic life of the poor. More traditional religious, ethnic and political symbols still hold tremendous appeal to many groups in the world, but the symbols surrounding Western consumption often co-exist with these other forms of symbolism.

Notes and references

1   D. Frisby, *George Simmel* (Routledge, London, 1984), p. 131.
2   D. Harvey, *The Condition of Postmodernity* (Blackwell, Oxford), p. 26.
3   Frisby, *George Simmel*, pp. 131–2.

17

Women and Soap Opera

Christine Geraghty

Soaps like *Dallas* and *Dynasty* relish spectacle so that it becomes the object of comment, separate from the workings of the plot. The pleasure in lavishness and extravagance leads to an emphasis on glamour which underpins the use of locations and the presentation of the stars. *Dynasty,* for instance, makes use of exotic locations such as Hong Kong, and while the spectacle is limited by the constraints of a TV budget, the shots of scenery and the city, together with the use of luxurious hotel rooms, enormous offices and expensive shops, offer the audience a deliberately artificial world. Great emphasis is placed on the Carrington mansion with its imposing staircase, elaborately furnished rooms and luxuriant grounds. The milieu appears to be a parody of the myth of English country living with its servants, its cholesterol-laden breakfasts, its riding stables and formal gardens. *Dallas*, although deliberately more down-market, still rates a swimming pool, servants, candlesticks on the table and extensive land and, significantly, when its ratings were falling it looked to more spectacular locations in Europe and the USSR to redeem its position.

In both cases, the settings provide an exotic backdrop for the characters themselves who are the main source of the spectacle of conspicuous consumption. It is on the women, in particular, that this spectacle is focused. They provide that slightly out-of-date glamour which is the hallmark of the programmes. There is always a sense of excess about their clothes because the decorative emphasis is so strong that their functional purpose is dangerously neglected. Their dresses are deliberately stylized and uncomfortable, the colours garish, the glitter out of place. They teeter on their high heels, the hair falling over the eyes as their walk is restricted by tight skirts. Tears do not affect the eye shadow, the lip gloss gleams through a passionate denunciation, a true flush never ruins the effect of the carefully applied blusher. This is particularly true of Alexis in *Dynasty*. The dress in which she conducts an emotional scene is almost as important as the dramatic implications of the scene for the narrative. This emphasis on make-up and dress gives women viewers the licence to look on the female stars of soaps as model objects of desire but the style presented to us is not simply to be admired. The women of US prime-time soaps look and dress like light entertainment stars – Carol Channing, Shirley Bassey – even when down on the ranch, and their excess pushes the programmes towards a parody of their own glamorous expectations. The clothes and hairstyles are to be mocked by the female viewer as well as envied. Who would really want to look quite like that – and yet who would not?

[···]

If light entertainment aesthetics can be most clearly demonstrated in the US prime-time soaps, British soaps also have their elements of spectacle. Setting is not so important here and glamour is even more closely associated in the British programmes with certain women characters. This element can be seen most strongly in *Coronation Street* which has had a strong tradition of glamorous middle-aged women exemplified in the characters of Elsie Tanner, Rita Fairclough and Bet Lynch. Elsie began as a rather run-down and harassed mother but developed over the years her own style which aspired to a glamorous ideal well beyond *Coronation Street*. Unlike her US counterparts, Elsie's mascara did run but her bouffant hair-dos, stylish dresses and curvaceous figure referred back to a pre-1960s notion of glamour associated with stars such as Diana Dors. Other characters such as Rita Fairclough, who, appropriately in terms of the light entertainment analogy, was once a night club singer, followed this model, while the barmaid, Bet Lynch, took it to extremes of parody with the excesses of her hairstyles, earrings and tightly belted waist being subject to the same kind of comments as Alexis's ballgowns. Certain women in other British soaps carry the same kind of glamorous connotations – Angie, the publican's wife in *EastEnders,* was almost theatrically made up, while Nicola in *Crossroads* was specifically presented as the British version of the US female stars with her impeccable make-up and clothes which purport to be businesslike but which verge on the extravagant.

[···]

The visual characteristics of US and British soaps – the close-ups of faces, of important objects, the deliberate movement of a character

across a room, the lingering of the camera on a face at the end of a
scene, the exchange of meaningful glances – work to make every gesture
and action seem highly coded and significant, marking out emotional
relationships and enabling the audience to understand the significance
of every action. This is particularly important given the complicated
nature of the stories being told. Soap narratives, like those of film melodramas, are marked by what Steve Neale has described as 'chance happenings, coincidences, missed meetings, sudden conversions, last-minute
rescues and revelations, *deus ex machina* endings'.[1] These kinds of
stories can be seen in the whole range of TV soaps, *EastEnders* as well
as *Dallas*, but Neale takes us further by commenting on the effect of
such dramatic organization. The 'course of events', he argues, 'is unmoti-
ated (or under-motivated) from a realist point of view, such preparation
and motivation as does exist is always "insufficient." There is an *excess*
of effect over cause, of the extraordinary over the ordinary.'[2]

It is this excess of meaning over motivation which lies at the heart of
soaps' adoption of the melodramatic aesthetic as a way of drawing the
audience into the programmes. On first examination, it would seem that
TV soaps leave the audience too little work to do. They lack the satisfying sense of achievement of working out the ramifications of *Tinker
Tailor Soldier Spy* or even *Miami Vice*. If the *mise en scène* is over-
expressive, if the acting gives us signposts to the meaning and if (in the
US prime-time soaps at least) music underlines it even for the slowest
viewer, what is there left for members of the audience to do? It is this
sense that soaps are too easy to understand, predictable and facile,
which is the source of many a critic's dissatisfaction. And yet Neale's
analysis indicates that there is a space for the reader at key moments to
provide an explanation for the excesses of the melodramatic aesthetics
which are inadequately explained by the cause and effect process of the
narrative. What is the reason for the welling up of music, the exchange
of glances, the slamming of a door? Such spaces are most characteristically signalled by a close-up on a character after a dramatic confrontation – on Sue Ellen, drunkenly staring at JR, on Angie Watts looking
unblinkingly into the camera as Den stalks away, on Sheila Grant,
hunched in the corner of the sofa as her son Barry leaves once more.
All these moments have narrative explanations but their intensity is
more than the events of a particular episode warrant. They have to
be filled in by the audience, those blank faces given a reason through
the viewer's knowledge of the programme's past and a recreation of
the feelings which the character must therefore be experiencing. It is
this identification with heightened emotion through the filling of the
space created by the excessive expressiveness of the *mise en scène* and

performance which is the most important element in TV soap opera's melodramatic aesthetic. It enables the most unlikely characters to take on a representative role for the viewer – 'It's everybody' – and dramatically engages those who only a moment before may have been detachedly commenting on Joan Collins's latest dress.

[···]

The pursuit of realism has been an impetus for change in British soaps but the bedrock of the appeal to realism has remained the same – a value placed on a specific setting, an 'authentic' regional experience and a particular class representation.

In their different ways, all four of the British soaps on which I am focusing work with these concepts. The settings are specific – a street, a motel, a square, a small housing development – and are defined geographically so that the audience builds up a precise sense of place. As importantly, each serial is able to call up and indeed help to create the connotations of a region – least successfully, perhaps, in *Crossroads'* attempts to speak for the Midlands, but crucially in *Coronation Street's* invocation of Manchester and the North, *EastEnders'* referencing of London's docklands and, most particularly, in *Brookside's* commitment to Liverpool. In all cases, this regional authority gives the soaps a sense of specificity crucial to realism and the ability to work with regional characteristics – cockney quick-wittedness, a scouse eye for the main chance, Northern straight talking and a Midlands aspiration to gentility. In themselves, such characteristics may be clichéd and sweeping but they form part of the way in which British culture absorbs, uses and contributes to regional differences. And finally, the setting and region give each soap the opportunity to present working-class characters, even in the Crossroads Motel where the working-class characters take on the 'servant' roles. The assumption, in British film history, that realism must take as its subject the working class can be traced back to the documentary movement of the 1920s and 1930s and their patronising approach can still be discerned in some of the British soaps, but the commitment to bring to the screen working-class accents, mores, problems and pleasures – still largely absent from much of British television – is an important element in the soaps' claim to realism.

By now it will be clear that soaps do not offer a coherent aesthetic experience and in particular that they do not work entirely in the realist tradition which is so valued in Britain. Instead, soaps deploy a range of aesthetic elements and offer a mix of generic conventions which confuses or makes them an object of scorn to those who seek to confine them to a particular format. Within a single episode, soaps can move from one set of conventions to another and back again and within an evening's viewing the soaps offer a surprisingly wide range of aesthetic experiences within a common narrative organization. This shifting between the different traditions contributes to the experience of engagement and distance which is so characteristic of soap viewing. But the values of light entertainment, melodrama and realism do not always fit smoothly together, for while the melodramatic mode might work to pull the audience into the drama, the conventions of light entertainment demand a more detached approach. I will close this discussion, therefore, by demonstrating how an analysis of this shifting between light entertainment, realism and melodrama helps us to understand particular aspects of the aesthetic experience of watching soaps.

Acting style and performance are frequently the subject of critical condemnation or amusement. The classic complaint about soaps is that of bad acting. Thus, commenting on the cliffhanger episode in which Kristen shot JR, Clive James wrote:

> With the possible exception of JR himself, everybody in the cast is working flat out to convey the full range of his or her, usually her, emotional commitment. Sue Ellen, in particular, was a study in passionate outrage. Her mouth practically took off. . . . It is even possible that Miss Ellie shot him, since she has been showing increasing signs of madness, singing her dialogue instead of saying it.[3]

What is not understood in this kind of criticism, however, is that acting in soaps is required to register in three different ways which are almost inevitably at odds with each other. First of all, in light entertainment terms, the performance is required to be that of a star. Light entertainment looks for an identity between star and character, and in that sense what is valued is not acting but being the character. Larry Hagman *is* JR and his appearances outside *Dallas* on chat shows, for instance, are used to reinforce that claim to identity. Within the programmes, there is a tendency to concentrate on the face as being the main focus of the star's uniqueness and there will be frequent repetition of the star's characteristic feature – Linda Gray's trembling mouth, Noele Gordon's understanding look, Leslie Grant's little boy grin, Joan Collins's mock-innocent gaze. To a certain extent, this emphasis on the face in close-up chimes in with the demands made by the conventions of TV melodrama in which the significance of every gesture needs to be underlined. For the purposes of melodrama, acting is required to be both expressive and mysterious. It needs to express clearly the significance of key words and gestures and to leave sufficient space for the audience to make its own deductions. The emphasis on eyes and mouth, the number of meaningful looks and thoughtful nods, can be explained by these requirements. But the aesthetics of realism demand that acting be 'in character' so that the particularities of each fictional individual are drawn on to give weight to the performance. This mode values an acting style which depends on a distance between performer and character. Unlike the star persona valued by the light entertainment aesthetic, the realist approach demands a fictional character very different in looks and speech from the actor. Thus the actress Jean Alexander, spruce, smartly dressed and middle class in speech, is in magazine articles set against the character of Hilda Ogden whom she played in *Coronation Street* as nagging, gossipy and down at heel, though capable of moments of dignified pathos. This space between actress and character can be understood as a guarantee of a realist performance but the detailed gestures required by such a style may be at odds with the melodramatic mode in which every gesture has a meaning in terms of the narrative and not just character. A major soap actor may be called on to work in three different modes: that of a star (light entertainment), an emotional representative (melodrama) and a character actor (realism).

[···]

The examples given here show that the different aesthetic modes at work in soap operas may sometimes be in conflict, as they often are when we analyse acting and performance, and sometimes work together, as they do in terms of camera movement and position. What is important is to move away from the blanket condemnation of the aesthetic experience offered by soaps and the defensive response which refuses to acknowledge the justification of any criticism. The tripartite framework outlined here should enable us to begin to analyse why soaps look as they do and to understand the sometimes contradictory aesthetic pleasures they offer.

Notes and references

1   Steve Neale, 'Melodrama and tears', *Screen,* 27 (6) (November–December 1986), p. 6.
2   Ibid., p. 7.
3   Clive James, *Glued to the Box* (Picador, London, 1983), p. 92.

18

Feminist Romance

Anne Cranny-Francis

In 1979 the distribution figure for Harlequin books, a leading publisher
of popular romances, stood at 168,000,000 copies, spread through ninety-
eight countries of the world. Given the popularity of this genre and its
predominantly female audience it is mandatory to include some analysis
of the romance in this study, even though, perhaps surprisingly, feminist
rewritings of the romance are not easy to find. This scarcity also characterizes several other genres I do not have space to consider here, but
which also promise interesting insights into the formation of subjectivity
and the ideological significance of generic conventions: westerns, the
spy/thriller subgenre of detective fiction, occult fiction. However, it is
romantic fiction which foregrounds the central problematic of many
feminist generic texts, the nature of female–male relationships in a
patriarchal society and the constitution of the gendered subject.

The romantic novel is structured by two central ideas or aims: the
characterization of a strong, male figure, the hero, and the romance and
marriage between him and the heroine. This is not an innovative plot,
having been used in many texts as the focus for a discussion of such
issues as social propriety, marriage arrangements and the nature of
fidelity. What is new is the fetishization of the romance plot; in these
contemporary romances the romantic plot itself is the focus of the text.

A novelistic antecedent of the contemporary romance is Samuel Richardson's epistolary novel *Pamela: or Virtue Rewarded* (1740) which deals
with the constant battle of the servant girl heroine, Pamela Andrews, to
protect her virginity from assault by her 'master'. Her success results in
her marriage to this same man; that is, he does eventually deflower
Pamela, but at a price. The tension in the novel arises from the fact that
Pamela is constantly under threat of rape from the man who will become

her husband and this rape fantasy remains a motivating force in romantic fiction. It also features in one of the two novels which seem to be the foundation of virtually all contemporary romance, *Wuthering Heights* and *Jane Eyre*.

In *Wuthering Heights* (1847) Emily Brontë constructs the archetypal romantic hero, Heathcliff, while in *Jane Eyre* (1847) Charlotte Brontë constructs the typical romantic plot, the romance and marriage of Jane Eyre and her wealthy suitor, Edward Rochester. The books feature two great loves, those of Heathcliff and Cathy, and of Jane Eyre and Edward Rochester, but the outcomes of these loves are very different. Heathcliff and Cathy do not marry, though their love continues undiminished. Jane and Rochester do marry, but only after he has been blinded and maimed, symbolically castrated. These different outcomes are a function of the representation of power in these texts and the way that this structures characterization.

Heathcliff is originally presented as *déclassé*, brought home from the Liverpool slums by Mr Earnshaw. Heathcliff may be Earnshaw's bastard, or a gipsy, or a member of some other marginalized group, but his origins are never explained. At the Heights he is raised as a member of the yeoman-farmer class of the Earnshaws, though Heathcliff will not inherit the land on which he works. This class of working farmers is dying out, superseded by the new class of capitalist farmers, who may live on their land but pay others to work it. Heathcliff goes on to learn and use the practices of the bourgeois class (when he returns to the Heights as a gentleman) against both his own adopted class (when he takes the Heights from Hindley) and later against the capitalist farmer (as he destroys the Linton family). In betraying his own class, constitutive of his own subjectivity, he too is destroyed. In a novel which describes in detail the changing social formation of rural England Heathcliff represents a transitional phase, from yeoman farmer to capitalist landholder; his violence is the violence of revolutionary social change.

In terms of race, also, Heathcliff is the outsider. He is tall, dark, passionate, violent, uncivilized, the stereotypical Celt who stands in marked contrast to the fair, rationalist, physically untried, 'civilized' Englishman. Heathcliff is a member of a marginalized race and culture in nineteenth-century Britain, one being driven to extinction by the 'civilizing' British.

The love of Heathcliff and Cathy is represented in the text as an elemental force, as basic and powerful as the windswept moors on which they live. Their love seems outside social law, non-ideological, because it is not dependent on economic circumstances. This is also the reason for its non-consummation in social terms, as marriage. Cathy and

Heathcliff do not marry, because they would not be able to survive in their society. So Cathy explains to Nelly Dean her decision to marry Edgar Linton:

> 'Nelly, I see now that you think me a selfish wretch; but did it never strike you that if Heathcliff and I married, we should be beggars? whereas, if I marry Linton I can aid Heathcliff to rise, and place him out of my brother's power.'[1]

Cathy deserts her own class to join Linton as a capitalist farmer, but, in so doing, she too is destroyed. By this means Emily Brontë signifies that love *without economic motive* cannot exist in a bourgeois society. It is a disruptive force which will inevitably be destroyed, or at least be denied any material reality. Accordingly, in representing this transgressive love, Brontë employs non-realist, fantastic elements (the ghostly apparition of Cathy, Heathcliff's increasingly bizarre appearance) which disrupt the (bourgeois) realist surface of her text.

In *Wuthering Heights* both Heathcliff and Cathy are strong characters, in the sense that they are both independent, autonomous, self-willed. This strong, female characterization is also transgressive, violating conventional representations of women. If the text is not to become totally fantastic or utopian, Cathy must be destroyed. It is therefore highly significant that she dies in childbirth; that is, that her defining (under patriarchy) gender identity, which she disrupts by her refusal of femininity, destroys her. Cathy is sacrificed to her biological determinants, and hence to her ideological definition.

In *Jane Eyre* both characterization and plot structure are very different, the relationship between Jane and Rochester hearkening back to that of Pamela and her 'master'. Rochester is established as a powerful figure within the text, not seemingly outside ideology like Heathcliff, but in terms of the dominant ideological positioning of his society. Rochester's power is a construct of class and race ideologies. His first wife, Bertha Mason, is of mixed blood which, given the white bias of his society, establishes him as the dominant partner even though she is very wealthy (the reason for their marriage). When Bertha Mason refuses to accept her subjugation, remaining an assertive, powerful woman, she suffers the fate of many Victorian women, fictional and real; she is declared mad. Jane Eyre, his second wife, is of a lower social status than he, from the respectable but impoverished lower middle class. Rochester has great economic power over Jane which he uses constantly to test her, much as Mr B. tested Pamela. Rochester's ugliness, which is almost fetishized in the text, cannot detract from his power and consequent attractiveness. In fact, this fetishization of Rochester's homely appearance is used by Charlotte Brontë to show that male attractiveness is not a physical attribute but a social (ideological) construction; a function of power, which is in turn a construct of the ideologies of class and race.

Jane and Rochester are able to marry because, in a patriarchal bourgeois society, a woman from a lower class position who assents to her own construction as a patriarchal subject – that is, who preserves her femininity at the cost of her own desires – can, supposedly, marry into a higher class. This is so because, in this (sexist) discourse, a woman's social status is identified with that of her father and then of her husband. She is essentially class-less, an object, a commodity, without any class positioning of her own. Rochester's blinding and maiming, his symbolic castration, is subsequently used by Brontë to demonstrate the consequences of this ideology for women, the denial of their desire. Jane's last minute inheritance of a fortune which makes her no longer dependent economically on Rochester signifies, by its very absurdity, the true nature of these fictional unions – not *grande passion*, but a socially sanctioned, economically viable marriage. In other words, Charlotte Brontë's text not only foregrounds the romance plot and the female fantasy of marrying an attractive (that is, powerful) man, but it also demonstrates both the consequences of this fantasy for women and its ideological – economic – determinants.

Contemporary romantic fiction combines the construction of a strong, male character, a combination of Rochester and Heathcliff, with the development of a romance between him and the heroine. The conventions used in the characterizations and the plot structure of the modern romance reveal its ideological function as did those of their nineteenth-century predecessors. In the modern romance the male hero is usually an established professional man, often from a wealthy family, and occasionally from an aristocratic background. He is often some ten to fifteen years older than the heroine, with the added experience – personal and professional – this entails. The assumptions are that he is white, middle or upper class and heterosexual. The heroine is correspondingly younger, less experienced, less established, less wealthy, and often from a poorer and less socially elevated background. The plot usually traces the subjugation of the heroine to the hero whom she initially dislikes because of his arrogance. In recent books this arrogance is often characterized as male chauvinist behaviour, which it usually is, but which the heroine eventually learns is the result of his true sensitivity. Accordingly the heroine learns that feminism is rather limited and immature, masking a fear of men. In the Harlequin romance *Public Affair*, for example, the heroine is a university secretary who rejects the advances of a presumptuous male academic. She belongs to a women's group and rejects his overt sexism. However, the main arguments for feminism in the book are presented not by other women, or by the heroine herself, but by another male academic, Jeffrey, a truly loathsome piece of work. Jeffrey's 'feminism' is clearly a strategy to deny women even the superficial courtesy of patriarchy.

> Jeffrey had never ever opened a door for her or held her chair. Instead he gave her high-sounding intellectual arguments on how such behavior was demeaning.
>   'When I do something for a woman that she could perfectly well do for herself, I'm transmitting an unspoken message to her. The message is, "You are incapable. Weaker. You must depend on me." It is an integral part of the reason women have never achieved equal status with their male counterparts. They unwittingly permit themselves to be demeaned by a cultural norm that, on the surface, is designed to display favoritism,' he told her in his typically wordy, arrogant manner. 'Never let a man do that to you,' he warned.
>   After her own bad experience Liza had taken his warning quite seriously.
>   Jeffrey had established another rule.[2]

Jeffrey is a bore and an exploiter, so it is highly significant that the 'feminist' discourse should be identified with this character. Of course, Jeffrey's feminism is as superficial and absurd as his character, but represents fairly accurately the reductionist view of feminism commonly propagated by its detractors. In other words, the reader is positioned by the text to identity feminism with an exploitative and dismissive attitude to women and, quite appropriately, to dismiss it. The fear of men to which this feminism is often attributed is also shown to be misguided, particularly by the association of feminism with a pathetic male character like Jeffrey. And yet this fear is constantly evoked by the text, by descriptions of the strength of the hero and by allusions to the barely suppressed violence suggested by his physique and often by his look, his 'penetrating' male gaze. Violence is associated so regularly with the hero that it is a major preoccupation of critics of the romance who, like Tania Modleski, consider that these novels 'perpetuate ideological confusion about male sexuality and male violence, while insisting that there is no problem (they are "very different")'.[3]

The powerful (brutal, violent) masculinity of the hero is fetishized in these texts; that is, he is fetishized in gender terms, his class and race characteristics apparently marginalized. The resolution of these narratives devolves upon a rape fantasy, with the hero's dangerous masculinity the source of the heroine's fear and admiration. The discursive practice she acts out in the text is that, so long as she is very feminine (like Pamela, like Jane Eyre), she will not be attacked, a common ideological (mis)conception. She and the hero are united when Heathcliff becomes Rochester, not through physical disability, but through revealing his disabling and endearing sensitivity. In *Wuthering Heights* Cathy disabuses her sister-in-law Isabella of any such interpretation of Heathcliff: 'Pray, don't imagine that he conceals depths of benevolence and affection beneath a stern exterior! He's not a rough diamond – a pearl-containing oyster of a rustic: he's a fierce, pitiless, wolfish man.'[4] The resolution of the narrative comes with the heroine's marriage to a man of elevated social status and wealth; his violence is revealed as healthy male sexuality and the rape fantasy vanquished by the legalization of their intimate relations. In these texts rape and marriage are antithetical concepts, precisely because marriage, the end-point of the romance, is primarily a legal and economic relationship, not an intimate or personal one. This interpretation of the patriarchal marriage is not new; Richardson wrote about marriage in these terms in 1740. Modern romances, however, do not deconstruct the patriarchal marriage or the erotic relationship which is its initial phase. Instead they fetishize it; the relationship itself is the focus of the narrative, displacing from reader attention its economic determinants. The erotic desire which motivates the narrative enacts, in displaced form, not only the erotic desires of the reader, but her or his economic desires – for wealth, security, status – from which the erotic is inseparable. Simultaneously these texts conceal or mystify the threat of violence, of rape, which sustains male dominance under patriarchy, and the essentialist patriarchal characterization of masculinity.

[···]

Some generic texts do represent women and men in fulfilling egalitarian relationships, with strong female characters who are not forced to accept either subjugation or a castrated partner as a result of their independence, and strong male characters whose power is not a function of their ability to subjugate others. However, these relationships usually appear in utopian and science fiction, in which non-realist conventions are used to displace the setting to another time and/or place. Strong female characters exist and are happy *because* they are represented in an entirely different social formation, non-patriarchal and non-bourgeois. Similarly strong male characters can be formulated without the threat of rape to sustain them *because* they no longer represent the dominance of a particular class and race. The nature of the social formation has been changed and so accordingly has the ideological significance of textual conventions. But do the egalitarian relationships represented in these texts constitute a romance? Or is the romance actually defined by an unequal power relationship and a dominant male?

In her novel *Lady Oracle* Margaret Atwood deals with the romance relationship in yet another way, by writing about the content of romantic fiction and the concept of reader position within her fictional text. Her main character, Joan Foster, is the writer of a best seller called *Lady Oracle* which critics describe as an interrogation of the problems and frustrations of contemporary relationships from a woman's point of view. Foster actually wrote the book during experiments in automatic writing, when she hypnotized herself and then allowed her subconscious to dictate her writing. She does not even understand the resultant manuscript which the publishers agree is a montage of contemporary popular writing. Foster also writes romantic fiction under the pen-name Louisa K. Delacourt and the implicit suggestion Atwood makes is that the same critical opinion might be applied to all of the same author's writing, so that her Regency romances are also an interrogation of contemporary relationships from a woman's point of view. Throughout the book Atwood has Foster experiment with the development of her latest novel, *Stalked by Love*. Tiring of her traditionally virtuous heroine, Charlotte, Foster decides to favour her tempestuous villainess, Felicia, who, like herself, has long red hair. But Foster's own life begins to intrude into the text and Felicia feels herself abandoned not by Redmond, her fictional rake/husband, but by Foster's own husband, Arthur. Then Foster has Felicia attempt to murder the nauseating Charlotte, only to have her saved by Redmond in typical male hero fashion. Finally Foster arrives at the most radical conclusion of all:

> [Felicia] took hold of the doorknob and turned it. The door unlocked and swung outward. . . . There, standing on the threshold, waiting for her, was Redmond. She was about to throw herself into his arms, weeping with relief, when she noticed an odd expression in his eyes. Then she knew. Redmond was the killer. He was a killer in disguise, he wanted to murder her as he had murdered his other wives. . . .
>   'Don't touch me,' she said, taking a step backward. She refused to be doomed. As long as she stayed on her side of the door she would be safe. Cunningly, he began his transformations, trying to lure her into his reach. His face grew a white gauze mask, then a pair of mauve-tinted spectacles, then a red beard and moustache, which faded giving way to burning eyes and icicle teeth. Then his cloak vanished and he stood looking at her sadly; he was wearing a turtle-neck sweater.
>   'Arthur?' she said. Could he ever forgive her?

Redmond resumed his opera cloak. His mouth was hard and rapacious, his eyes smouldered. 'Let me take you away,' he whispered. 'Let me rescue you. We will dance together forever, always.'

'Always,' she said, almost yielding. 'Forever.' Once she had wanted these words, she had waited all her life for someone to say them. . . . She pictured herself whirling slowly across a ballroom floor, a strong arm around her waist. . . .

'No,' she said. 'I know who you are.'

The flesh fell away from his face, revealing the skull behind it; he stepped towards her, reaching for her throat.[5]

Redmond is revealed as a composite of all the men in Foster's life, her husband, her lover and the fictional men who sustain the behaviour of the real ones. In deconstructing Redmond Atwood reveals the true nature of this character, the patriarchal male who appears in one guise as a fictional hero, in another as an eccentric artist, in yet another as an academic and husband. All are deadly to women in wanting to annihilate their individual subjectivity, to make the women the passive objects of their affection and abuse. In this way Atwood demonstrates to the reader the relationship between fictional representation and social practice, that these fictional heroes do not compensate for the inadequacies of reality but are constitutive of that reality. Which is perhaps the reason for the equivocal ending of the novel which has Joan Foster paying hospital visits to the reporter she mistakenly hit over the head with a bottle, a Jane Eyre ending for Joan Foster.

[· · ·]

To conclude, in feminist generic fiction the writer constructs a feminist reading position which involves a particular negotiation of the discourses inflected by the traditional text and those discursively indicated by the revision of traditional conventions. This (re)negotiation and (re) construction of an alternative, non-patriarchal and non-bourgeois reading position can operate as the basis for a renegotiated subject position; it is a negotiation which fundamentally challenges the discursive negotiation constitutive of the patriarchal, bourgeois subject. Feminist generic fiction constructs a reading position which (1) deconstructs femininity, revealing it as an ideological construct, (2) deconstructs the patriarchal narrative, showing it as a mechanism by which women are constructed in purely gender terms, and as subject to men who are constructed in terms of gender, class and race, (3) deconstructs the bourgeois narrative, showing it to be a mechanism by which the white, middle-class male is defined as the value position in relation to which those negotiating differently the discourses of gender, race and class are ranked.

Romantic fiction is the most difficult genre to subvert because it encodes the most coherent inflection of the discourses of gender, class and race constitutive of the contemporary social order; it encodes the bourgeois fairy-tale. It also encodes the anger and frustration of all those whose lives are devalued by that negotiation – goose-girls and goose-boys – and it sets them at each other's throats; the kings stand by to appropriate the spoils. But at least the goose-girls and goose-boys have a voice, and that voice is increasingly vocal; even Mills & Boon/ Harlequin heroines now have decent jobs. As Tania Modleski notes: 'An understanding of Harlequin Romances should lead one less to condemn the novels than the conditions which have made them necessary.' It is crucial to recognize that this condemnation must be directed not only at patriarchal, but also at bourgeois, white supremacist ideology.

Notes and references

1   Emily Brontë, *Wuthering Heights* (Heron, London, 1966), pp. 83–4.
2   Sarah James, *Public Affair* (Harlequin, Toronto, 1984), p. 28.
3   Tania Modleski, 'Feminism and the power of interpretation: some critical readings', in *Feminist Studies/Critical Studies*, ed. Teresa de Lauretis (Indiana University Press, Bloomington, Ind., 1986), pp. 42–3.
4   Brontë, *Wuthering Heights*, pp. 105–6.
5   Margaret Atwood, *Lady Oracle* (Virago, London, 1982), pp. 342–3.

19

The Invisible *Flâneuse*: Women and the Literature of Modernity

Janet Wolff

The literature of modernity describes the experience of men. It is essentially a literature about transformations in the public world and in its associated consciousness. The actual date of the advent of 'the modern' varies in different accounts, and so do the characteristics of 'modernity' identified by different writers. But what nearly all the accounts have in common is their concern with the public world of work, politics, and city life. And these are areas from which women were excluded, or in which they were practically invisible. For example, if the chief characteristic of modernity is the Weberian idea of increasing rationalization, then the major institutions affected by this process were the factory, the office, and the government department. There have, of course, always been women working in factories; the growth of bureaucracies was also to some extent dependent on the development of a new female workforce of clerks and secretaries. Nevertheless, it is appropriate to talk of this world as a 'male' world for two reasons. First, the institutions were run by men, for men (owners, industrialists, managers, financiers), and they were dominated by men in their operation and hierarchical structure. Second, the development of the factory and, later, the bureaucracy coincides with that process, by now well documented, of the 'separation of spheres', and the increasing restriction of women to the 'private' sphere of the home and the suburb. Although lower middle-class and working-class women continued to go out to work throughout the nineteenth century, the ideology of women's place in the domestic realm permeated the whole of society, at least in England, as evidenced by the working-class demand for a 'family wage' for men. The public sphere, then, despite the presence of some women in certain contained areas of it, was a masculine domain. And in so far as the experience of 'the modern' occurred mainly in the public sphere, it was primarily men's experience.

In this essay, however, I shall not pursue the more orthodox socio-logical analyses of modernity, which discuss the phenomenon in terms of the rationalization process (or perhaps the 'civilizing process' – this, of course, places the event at a much earlier date). I want to consider the more impressionistic and essayistic contributions of those writers who locate the specifically 'modern' in city life: in the fleeting, ephem-eral, impersonal nature of encounters in the urban environment, and in the particular world-view which the city-dweller develops. This focus is not foreign to sociology: the essays of George Simmel immediately come to mind as studies in the social psychology of city life, and the more recent sociology of Richard Sennett has revived interest in the diagnosis of the modern urban personality. But a particular concern for the ex-perience of modernity has also run through literary criticism; here its early prophet was Charles Baudelaire, the poet of mid-nineteenth-century Paris. Walter Benjamin's essays on Baudelaire, written in the 1930s, provide a fascinating (though typically cryptic and fragmentary) series of reflections on Baudelaire's views on 'the modern'. As a starting point for the investigation of this particular literature of modernity, I take Baudelaire's statement, in the essay written in 1859–60, *The Painter of Modern Life*: 'By "modernity" I mean the ephemeral, the fugitive, the contingent, the half of art whose other half is the eternal and the im-mutable.'[1] This is echoed in Marshall Berman's recent book on the experience of modernity, which describes the 'paradoxical unity' of modernity: 'A unity of disunity: it pours us all into a maelstrom of perpetual disintegration and renewal, of struggle and contradiction, of ambiguity and anguish. To be modern is to be part of a universe in which, as Marx said, "all that is solid melts into air".'[2] It also recalls Simmel's account of the metropolitan personality: 'The psychological basis of the metropolitan type of individuality consists in the *intensifi-cation of nervous stimulation* which results from the swift and unin-terrupted change of outer and inner stimuli' (italics in original).[3]

For Simmel, this is closely related to the money economy, dominant by the late nineteenth century. It is worth stressing that, although cities were not new in the nineteenth century, the critics (and defenders) of modernity believed that urban existence took on an entirely different character around the middle of the nineteenth century. Though any such dating is, to some extent, arbitrary (and will vary, anyway, from Paris to London to Berlin), I think it is useful to take this period of accelerated urbanization, coupled with the transformations in work, housing, and social relations brought about by the rise of industrial capitalism, as the crucial years of the birth of 'modernity'. Berman gives modernity a pre-history, in those elements of the modern which began to appear in the period before the French Revolution and which found their expression in Goethe's *Faust*. Bradbury and McFarlane, who focus on the later period of 1890 to 1930, credit Baudelaire as an 'initiator' of modernism. But they are writing about the rather different phenomenon of modern*ism* in the arts; although 'modernism' and 'modernity' are often conflated, I do not think anyone has claimed that Baudelaire was a modernist poet, in the sense of revolutionizing poetic language and form. There is no contradiction in locating the early experience of 'modernity' in the mid-nineteenth century, and its later expression in the arts at the end of the century.

The peculiar characteristics of modernity, then, consist in the transient and 'fugitive' nature of encounters and impressions made in the city. A sociology of modernity must, ultimately, be able to identify the origins of these new patterns of behaviour and experience, in the social and material aspects of the contemporary society. Simmel, as I have said, relates the metropolitan personality and what he calls the 'blasé attitude' to the money economy. Marshall Berman, beginning from Marx's account of the 'melting vision', seems to take over at the same time Marx's analysis of the basis of this vision in the radical changes wrought in society by the bourgeoisie and the capitalist mode of production. Baudelaire, on the other hand, considers the phenomenon itself, and not its causes. It is not my task here to provide a sociology of modernity, and so I shall not assess competing accounts of the social or economic base of the modern experience, nor even examine very closely the adequacy of the conceptions of 'modernity' I discuss. What I want to do is to take those accounts, which do describe, more or less sociologically, the modern urban experience, and consider them from the point of view of gender divisions in nineteenth-century society. To that extent, it does not really matter whether a particular account is adequately grounded in a social–historical understanding of the period, or even whether an account is internally consistent. (As Berman shows, Baudelaire employs several different conceptions of 'modernity', as well as changing evaluations of the phenomenon.)

Baudelaire's comments on modernity are most explicit in his writings on art criticism, though the same themes can be found in his poetry and in his prose poems. An early reference appears at the end of his review of 'The salon of 1845', appended almost as an afterthought in the final paragraph. Here he commends contemporary painting, but laments its lack of interest in the present.

No one is cocking his ear to tomorrow's wind; and yet the heroism of *modern life* surrounds and presses upon us. We are quite sufficiently choked by our true feelings for us to be able to recognize them. There is no lack of subjects, nor of colours, to make epics. The painter, the true painter for whom we are looking, will be he who can snatch its epic quality from the life of today and can make us see and understand, with brush or with pencil, how great and poetic we are in our cravats and our patent-leather boots. Next year let us hope that the true seekers may grant us the extra-ordinary delight of celebrating the advent of the *new*.[4]

But the following year was no better, and again Baudelaire bemoans the absence of any really contemporary art, concerned with modern themes and characters in the way that Balzac's novels are. This time he devotes several pages – the final section of the review of 'The salon of 1846' – to the theme of 'the heroism of modern life'. Modern life here begins to acquire some identifiable features: the uniform drabness of the colours of people's dress, the modern phenomenon of the 'dandy' who reacts against this, the 'private subjects' which Baudelaire extols as far more 'heroic' than the public and official subjects of painting:

The pageant of fashionable life and the thousands of floating existences – criminals and kept women – which drift about in the underworld of a great city; the *Gazette des Tribunaux* and the *Moniteur* all prove to us that we have only to open our eyes to recognize our heroism. . . . The life of our city is rich in poetic and marvellous subjects.[5]

These subjects are itemized in more detail in 'The painter of modern life' of 1859–60. By this time, Baudelaire has found a painter he considers equal to the task of depicting the modern: Constantin Guys, the subject of the essay. Guys' watercolours and drawings are generally considered to be talented but superficial works, of little importance in the history of art – though judgements like these do, of course, beg all sorts of questions about critical assessment. Berman dismisses Guys' 'slick renderings of the "beautiful people" and their world' and wonders that Baudelaire should think so highly of an art which 'resembles nothing so much as Bonwit's or Bloomingdale's ads'. Nevertheless, the essay is interesting for its expansion of the notion of 'modernity'. Guys, the 'painter of modern life', goes out into the crowd and records the myriad impressions of day and night.

He goes and watches the river of life flow past him in all its splendour and majesty. . . . He gazes upon the landscapes of the great city – landscapes of stone, caressed by the mist or buffeted by the sun. He delights in fine carriages and proud horses, the dazzling smartness of the grooms, the expertness of the footman, the sinuous gait of the women, the beauty of the children.... If a fashion or the cut of a garment has been slightly modified, if bows and curls have been supplanted by cockades, if *bavolets* have been enlarged and *chignons* have dropped a fraction towards the nape of the neck, if waists have been raised and skirts have become fuller, be very sure that his eagle eye will already have spotted it from however great a distance.[6]

This is the passage Berman dismisses as 'advertising copy'. But if it is an inventory of the superficial and the merely fashionable, then that is the point – the modern consciousness consists in the parade of impressions, the particular beauty appropriate to the modern age. And, more important, it is in this essay that Baudelaire suggests the formal features of the modern mind, which grasps 'the ephemeral, the fugitive, the contingent'. The dandy appears again, to be compared and also contrasted with Guys, similar in their concern for appearance and for personal originality, divided by the blasé and insensitive attitude of the former which Guys (according to Baudelaire) abhors. Guys is the *flâneur*, in his element in the crowd – at the centre of the world and at the same time hidden from the world.

The *flâneur* – the stroller – is a central figure in Benjamin's essays on Baudelaire and nineteenth-century Paris. The streets and arcades of the city are the home of the *flâneur*, who, in Benjamin's phrase, 'goes botanizing on the asphalt'.[7] The anonymity of the crowd provides an asylum for the person on the margins of society; here Benjamin includes both Baudelaire himself as a *flâneur*, and the victims and murderers of Poe's detective stories (which Baudelaire translated into French). For Benjamin, however, the city of the *flâneur* is historically more limited than for Baudelaire. Neither London nor Berlin offers precisely the conditions of involvement/non-involvement in which the Parisian *flâneur* flourishes; nor does the Paris of a slightly later period, when a 'network of controls' has made escape into anonymity impossible. (Baudelaire, and Berman, on the contrary argue that the Paris increasingly opened up by Haussmann's boulevards, which broke down the social and geographical divisions between the classes, is even more the site of the modern gaze, the ambit of the *flâneur*).

The *flâneur* is the modern hero; his experience, like that of Guys, is that of a freedom to move about in the city, observing and being observed, but never interacting with others. A related figure in the literature of modernity is the *stranger*. One of Baudelaire's prose poems, *Paris Spleen*, is entitled *L'étranger*. It is a short dialogue, in which an 'enigmatic man' is asked what or whom he loves – his father, mother, sister, brother?

his friends, his country, beauty, gold? To all of these he answers in the negative, affirming that he simply loves the passing clouds. For Simmel, the stranger is not a man without attachments and involvements, however. He is characterized by a particular kind of 'inorganic' membership of the group, not having been a member from its beginning, but having settled down in a new place. He is 'the person who comes today and stays tomorrow'; in this he differs from both the *flâneur* and Baudelaire's *étranger*, neither of whom will settle down or even make contact with those around him. But Simmel's stranger is always a 'potential wanderer': 'Although he has not moved on, he has not quite overcome the freedom of coming and going.'[8] These heroes of modernity thus share the possibility and the prospect of lone travel, of voluntary uprooting, of anonymous arrival at a new place. They are, of course, all men.

It is no accident, and no fault of a careless patriarchal use of language, that Richard Sennett's book on modernity is called *The Fall of Public* **Man**. The 'public' person of the eighteenth century and earlier, whose demise is charted, and who passed the time in coffee-houses, paraded in the streets and at the theatre, and addressed strangers freely in public places, was clearly male. (Although Sennett says that it was quite proper to address strange women in the parks or the street, as long as men did not thereby assume that a reply meant they might call on the woman at home, there is no suggestion that *women* might address strangers.) In the nineteenth-century city, no longer the arena of that public life, the *flâneur* makes his appearance – to be watched, but not addressed. Men and women may have shared the privatization of personality, the careful anonymity and withdrawal in public life; but the line drawn increasingly sharply between the public and private was also one which confined women to the private, while men retained the freedom to move in the crowd or to frequent cafés and pubs. The men's clubs replaced the coffee-houses of earlier years.

None of the authors I have discussed is unaware of the different experience of women in the modern city. Sennett, for example, recognizes that '(the) right to escape to public privacy was unequally enjoyed by the sexes', since even by the late nineteenth century, women could not go alone to a café in Paris or a restaurant in London. As he says: ' "The lonely crowd" was a realm of privatized freedom, and the male, whether simply out of domination or greater need, was more likely to escape in it.' He notes, too, that in the earlier period of 'public life' women had to take a good deal more care about the 'signs' of their dress, which would be scrutinized for an indication of their social rank; in the nineteenth century, the scrutiny would be in order to differentiate 'respectable' from 'loose' women. Simmel, whose essayistic sociology I have used very selectively, also paid much attention elsewhere to the condition of women. He wrote essays on the position of women, the psychology of women, female culture, and the women's movement and social democracy. He was one of the first to permit women in his private seminars, long before they were admitted as full students at the University of Berlin. Berman, too, considers women, acknowledging somewhat belatedly (on page 322 of his book) that they have a totally different experience of the city from that of men. He suggests that Jane Jacobs's *The Death and Life of Great American Cities* gives a 'fully articulated woman's view of the city'. Published in 1961, Jacobs's book describes her own daily life in the city – a life of neighbours, shopkeepers, and young children, as well as work. The importance of the book, says Berman, is that it reveals that 'women had something to tell us about the city and the life we shared, and that we had impoverished our own lives as well as theirs by not listening to them till now'.

The problem is, though, that it is also the literature of modernity which has been impoverished by ignoring the lives of women. The dandy, the *flâneur*, the hero, the stranger – all figures invoked to epitomize the experience of modern life – are invariably male figures. In 1831, when George Sand wanted to experience Paris life and to learn about the ideas and arts of her time, she dressed as a boy, to give herself the freedom she knew women could not share:

> So I had made for myself a *redingote-guérite* in heavy gray cloth, pants and vest to match. With a gray hat and large woollen cravat, I was a perfect first-year student. I can't express the pleasure my boots gave me: I would gladly have slept with them, as my brother did in his young age, when he got his first pair. With those little iron-shod heels, I was solid on the pavement. I flew from one end of Paris to the other. It seemed to me that I could go round the world. And then, my clothes feared nothing. I ran out in every kind of weather, I came home at every sort of hour, I sat in the pit at the theatre. No one paid attention to me, and no one guessed at my disguise. . . . No one knew me, no one looked at me, no one found fault with me; I was an atom lost in that immense crowd.[9]

The disguise made the life of the *flâneur* available to her; as she knew very well, she could not adopt the non-existent role of a *flâneuse*. Women could not stroll alone in the city.

[· · ·]

What explains the invisibility of women in the literature of modernity? The explanation is threefold, and lies in (1) the nature of sociological investigation, (2) the consequently partial conception of 'modernity', and (3) the reality of women's place in society. Much of this has been discussed in the recent work of feminist sociologists and historians, but it is worth rehearsing here in the specific context of the problem of modernity.

The rise and development of sociology in the nineteenth century was closely related to the growth and increasing separation of 'public' and 'private' spheres of activity in Western industrial societies. The condition for this was the separation of work from home, with the development of factories and offices. By the mid-nineteenth century, this had made possible the move to the suburbs in some major cities (for example, the industrial cities of England, like Manchester and Birmingham). Although women had never been engaged on equal terms (financial, legal, or otherwise) with men, this physical separation put an end to their close and important involvement in what had often been a family concern – whether in trade, production, or even professional work. Their gradual confinement to the domestic world of the home and the suburb was strongly reinforced by an ideology of separate spheres. At the same time, a new public world was in process of formation, of business organizations, political and financial establishments, and social and cultural institutions. These were almost invariably male institutions, though women might occasionally be granted some sort of honorary membership or allowed minimal participation as guests on particular occasions. In the second half of the century the rise of the professions excluded women from other expanding areas of activity, some of which they had traditionally been engaged in (like medicine), some of which had already excluded them (like the law and academic occupations), and some of which were new (the education of artists, for example). The two major implications for sociology as a new discipline were, first, that it was dominated by men, and second, that it was primarily concerned with the 'public' spheres of work, politics, and the marketplace. Indeed, women appear in the classic texts of sociology only in so far as they relate to men, in the family, or in minor roles in the public sphere. As David Morgan has said about Weber's *The Protestant Ethic and the Spirit of Capitalism*: 'It cannot have escaped many people's attention, at least in recent years, that women are very much hidden from this particular history; the lead parts – Franklin, Luther, Calvin, Baxter and Wesley – are all played by men and women only appear on the stage fleetingly in the guise of German factory workers with rather traditional orientations to work.'[10]

[...]

The particular experience of 'modernity' was, for the most part, equated with experience *in* the public arena. The accelerated growth of the city, the shock of the proximity of the very rich and the destitute poor (documented by Engels – and in some cities avoided and alleviated by the creation of suburbs), and the novelty of the fleeting and impersonal contacts in public life, provided the concern and the fascination for the authors of 'the modern', sociologists and other social commentators who documented their observations in academic essays, literary prose, or poetry. To some extent, of course, these transformations of social life affected everyone, regardless of sex and class, though they did so differently for different groups. But the literature of modernity ignores the private sphere, and to that extent is silent on the subject of women's primary domain. This silence is not only detrimental to any understanding of the lives of the female sex; it obscures a crucial part of the lives of men, too, by abstracting one part of their experience and failing to explore the interrelation of public and private spheres. For men inhabited both of these.

[· · ·]

The real situation of women in the second half of the nineteenth century was more complex than one of straightforward confinement to the home. It varied from one social class to another, and even from one geographical region to another, depending on the local industry, the degree of industrialization, and numerous other factors. And, although the solitary and independent life of the *flâneur* was not open to women, women clearly *were* active and visible in other ways in the public arena.

[· · ·]

Thus the establishment of the department store in the 1850s and 1860s provided an important new arena for the legitimate public appearance of middle-class women. However, although consumerism is a central aspect of modernity, and moreover mediated the public/private division, the peculiar characteristics of 'the modern' which I have been considering – the fleeting, anonymous encounter and the purposeless strolling – do not apply to shopping, or to women's activities either as public signs of their husband's wealth or as consumers.

We are beginning to find out more about the lives of women who were limited to the domestic existence of the suburbs; about women who went into domestic service in large numbers; and about the lives of working-class women. The advent of the modern era affected all these women, transforming their experience of home and work. The recovery of women's experience is part of the project of retrieving what has been hidden, and attempting to fill the gaps in the classic accounts. The feminist revision of sociology and social history means the gradual opening up of areas of social life and experience which to date have been obscured by the partial perspective and particular bias of mainstream sociology.

It is not at all clear what a feminist sociology of modernity would look like. There is no question of inventing the *flâneuse*: the essential point is that such a character was rendered impossible by the sexual divisions of the nineteenth century. Nor is it appropriate to reject totally the existing literature on modernity, for the experiences it describes certainly defined a good deal of the lives of men, and were also (but far less centrally) a part of the experience of women. What is missing in this literature is any account of life outside the public realm, of the experience of 'the modern' in its private manifestations, and also of the very different nature of the experience of those women who *did* appear in the public arena: a poem written by 'la femme passante' about her encounter with Baudelaire, perhaps.

Notes and references

1 Charles Baudelaire, 'The painter of modern life', in *The Painter of Modern Life and Other Essays*, tr. and ed. Jonathon Mayne (1863; Phaidon Press, Oxford, 1964), p. 13.
2 Marshall Berman, *All That is Solid Melts into Air: The Experience of Modernity* (Verso, London, 1983), p. 15.
3 George Simmel, 'The metropolis and mental life', in *The Sociology of George Simmel*, ed. Kurt H. Wolff (Free Press, New York, 1950), pp. 409–10.
4 Charles Baudelaire, 'The salon of 1845', in *Art in Paris 1845–1862*, (Phaidon Press, Oxford, 1965), pp. 31–2.
5 Charles Baudelaire, 'The salon of 1846', in *Art in Paris 1845–1862*, pp. 118–19.
6 Baudelaire, 'The painter of modern life', p. 11.
7 Walter Benjamin, *'Charles Baudelaire': A Lyric Poet in the Era of High Capitalism* (New Left Books, London, 1973), p. 36.
8 George Simmel, 'The stranger', in *The Sociology of George Simmel*, ed. Kurt H. Wolff (Free Press, New York, 1950), p. 402.
9 Berman, *All That is Solid Melts into Air*, p. 323.
10 David Morgan, 'Men, masculinity and the process of sociological enquiry', in *Doing Feminist Research*, ed. Helen Roberts (Routledge, London, 1981), p. 93.

20

The Myth of Marilyn Monroe

Graham McCann

Hortense Powdermaker, in her 'anthropological investigation' of *Hollywood*, observed:

> From a business point of view, there are many advantages in the star system. The star has tangible features which can be advertised and marketed – a face, a body, a pair of legs, a voice, a certain kind of personality, real or synthetic – and can be typed as the wicked villain, the honest hero, the fatal siren, the sweet young girl, the neurotic woman. The system provides a formula easy to understand and has made the production of movies seem more like just another business. The use of this formula may serve also to protect executives from talent and having to pay too much attention to such intangibles as the quality of a story or of acting. Here is a standardised product which they can understand, which can be advertised and sold, and which not only they, but also banks and exhibitors, regard as insurance for large profits.[1]

The economic importance of the stars is of aesthetic consequence in such matters as the positioning of spectacle in the presentation of the star, and the construction of narratives which display the star's image. Nonetheless, economics is certainly not the sole determinant of the phenomenon of stardom.

'Only the public can make a star,' said Marilyn Monroe, 'it's the studios who try to make a system out of it.' Such a system was encouraged early in cinema history. D.W. Griffith popularized the use of the close-up as a form of punctuation, a visual variant heightening the dramatic impact of certain moments in certain scenes. There was, however, a more powerful function implicit in the close-up. By moving in closer, Griffith was able to capture a subtler play of emotions on the actor's face, in the eyes. He was trying, he said, to 'photograph thought'. This activity was unprecedented in the history of any art – a breakthrough to (the illusion of) intimacy. Looming over the movie audience came magnified and magnificent images, intricate sections from a larger scene, studied with erotic narrowness and nearness. The close-up enabled the effect of isolating the actor in the sequence, separating the actor from the rest of the ensemble for close individual scrutiny by the audience.

As these images reappeared each week, the individual films began to be perceived (albeit unconsciously) not as discrete creations but as incidents in a more compelling drama – the drama of the star's life and career, the shaping and reshaping of the image that we carry in our minds. Struck by the succession of individual images, the audience starts to see stars. Movie producers began to notice the growing interest in the players who worked for them as reflected in the mail coming to the studios, and they saw the potential value in publicizing them. Actors' names became trademarks for the image: a 'close-up' was affected to produce a sense of propinquity to 'Chaplin', 'Valentino' and 'Fairbanks', eventually reaching an apotheosis with 'Marilyn'. Within four years of this acknowledgement, salaries for leading players rose from $5–15 per week to $250–2,500 per week. Suddenly, salaries were news in themselves, as was the manner in which they were spent, the company the stars kept, the style in which they passed their days. When stars began to make news with their illnesses, with their absence from work, their cultural prominence was assured: 'Marilyn off sick', 'Where is Marilyn?'

The relationship of stars to modernity attracted the attention of social theorists. Herbert Marcuse sees the 'cultural predecessors' of stars in the 'disruptive-characters [such] as the artist, the prostitute, the adultress, the great criminal and the outcast, the warrior, the rebel-poet, the devil, the fool', but the tradition has been 'essentially transformed'. 'The vamp, the national hero, the beatnik, the neurotic housewife, the gangster, the star, the charismatic tycoon perform a function very different. . . . They are no longer images of another way of life but rather freaks or types of the same life, serving as an affirmation rather than negation of the established order.'[2] The example of Marilyn Monroe represents the greatest challenge to this viewpoint. Monroe's image was given special attention by her image-makers because she was, for a time, the most marketable star in the world; Monroe herself came to resent the manipulation, and was extraordinarily adept at sometimes subverting her public persona.

The Marcusean approach does not confront the actual content of star images. Examination of these images reveals complexity, contradiction, and difference. 'Audience response' to the projected image is not passive but an active practice, an interpretive process. The close-up, we have seen, reveals the 'unmediated' personality of the individual performer, and this belief in 'capturing' the unique qualities of the performer is probably central to the star phenomenon. As Cavell observes, this reception is considerably affected by the play of our associative capacities, by our tendency to carry a mnemonic catalogue of previous appearances by particular performers – some correct, some blurred by poor memory, some transformed by fantasy and some a case of mistaken identity.

According to Sam Goldwyn, 'God makes the stars. It's up to the producers to find them.'[3] The modern image does not seek a context; it carries a kind of context within itself, sufficient for its own nourishment, and may work against being placed in history. Monroe's image on a T-shirt or on a postcard seems to animate anonymous raw material. The star's image is apprehended instantly, as a result of the amalgam of old roles, old gossip, old glosses, old publicity photos: such a figure is a walking context, a tradition being transmitted, the face as fashion. In the 1920s, the media had discovered techniques whereby almost any-one could be wrested out of any context and turned into images for the 'silver screen', *Time* and *Life* covers, and the daily tabloids. For no previous era is it possible to make a history out of images; for no subsequent era is it possible to avoid doing so. Countering the festering rumours of illicit sex and drugs in the movie community, Hollywood appointed Will Hayes, the Postmaster General, as head of a new Motion Picture Producer's Association (MPPA), given power to censor on-screen material and to act as moral guardian of the stars' off-screen behaviour. Screen lovers, in their twin beds, had to sleep with bathrobes within a forearm's reach. Kisses could only last five seconds, and lovers must kiss with their mouths closed. By 1930, with power concentrated in the big movie studios, any offender would soon be outside looking in, as Hollywood gave journalists gossip in return for vast discretion when Hollywood required it. The visual and the verbal conversed.

The introduction of 'talking-pictures' radically shortened the psychological distance between stars and their audience. The gods suddenly spoke back to the faithful; the sacred screen image became 'profane'. During the period stretching from the early 1930s to the early 1950s, a massive effort was made by press agencies to re-educate the movie-going public. A new fiction of 'ordinariness' was fostered, a fiction wherein erstwhile 'extraordinary' people were now presented as entirely like the audience in basic values and harmless vices. Publicity pictures featured the stars hard at work in the studios. Male stars were shown spending leisure time in Hemingway country – at the ranch, hunting, shooting and fishing. (Ronald Reagan appeared to retain this image when, as President of the United States, he wished to be seen 'on

vacation'.) Female stars, it seemed, had sufficient spare time to be devoted mothers and endlessly helpful wives. Movie stars were thus portrayed as 'regular guys'. People who possessed more, but nonetheless
more of the same. American middle-class normality was, it seemed,
worth hanging on to when one's salary started rising.

During the Second World War, an informal bargain was struck between the US government and the film industry. The government received virtually free, highly professional, assistance in publicizing almost
anything it decreed as useful in prosecuting the war. In return, the film
industry received favours that ranged from stock footage to delays in
the induction of stars who had films to finish. The war gave the entertainment industry the opportunity to extend the long process of 'demystifying' and 'democratizing' stardom: Clark Gable soon to appear in a
bomber near you, Errol Flynn sharing a drink with the guys in the
canteen.

The traditional task of American historians has been the attempt to
authenticate the indigenous mythology by providing it with local material
sources: hence Frederick Turner's 'frontier', David Potter's 'material
abundance', and Erik Erikson's 'psychological expansiveness'. The film
industry's version of this traditional mythology rested on two factors.
First, Hollywood's power to produce a steady flow of variations provided
the myth with the repetitive elaborations it needed to become convincing.
Second, the audience's sense of American exceptionalism encouraged
acceptance of a mythology whose fundamental premise was optimistic.
To a large extent, American space, economic abundance, and geographic
isolation – and the fictions embroidered around these features – had
been unavailable to the modern European imagination. We may describe
this mythology by observing that, like the invisible style, it concealed
the necessity for choice. The consensus contained an underlying premise
which dictated the conversion of all political, sociological, and economic
dilemmas into personal melodramas – melodramas revolving around
the regular, recognizable stars.

The movie-going public did not uncritically assimilate the post-war
notion of the Hollywood celebrity as a down-to-earth citizen. The gossip columnists remained powerful opinion prompters: Hedda Hopper,
Louella Parsons, Sheilah Graham amongst the Hollywood pack, and
Walter Winchell based in New York. These celebrity scribblers supplied
a dim, double vision of stardom, a shadowy sense that it was not always
as bright and clean and carefree as the picture stories in the fun magazines
insisted. A large percentage of the stars still messed up their marriages,
made up their biographies, indulged in scandalous affairs, sexual experiments, and alcoholism. So long as the tales from the dark side of

the woods did not get out of hand, the underlying 'wickedness' was accepted as an essential element in attracting and holding everyone's attention. *Hollywood Confidential* was an apt title: 'Confession' became an important mode of communication between the public and the private, and the known and the unknown. Epithets such as 'naughty', 'flirty', and 'roguish' took on an endearing quality. Errol Flynn survived a statutory rape charge and was accepted as a 'lovable rogue'. Studios 'protected' their star properties with long-term contracts. If one lived within one's image and did nothing to disappoint the behavioural expectations that image induced in the public, it was possible to have the proverbial 'swell time'. If, on the other hand, one rebelled against type, against formula, the studios could leave one high but dry, with few friends and fast-diminishing fortune.

Previously, success in American industry had been a unitary quality. The reward had been wealth, fame, and power. Those who succeeded received money, but fame went to the performers and power to the producers. The bosses, who felt they were the real risk-takers, looked on as their employees enjoyed the public acclaim and affection. The performers, who regarded this adulation as testimony to their importance, found that they lacked sufficient power to plan their futures. Rudolph Valentino had lamented, just before his death, 'A man should control his life. Mine is controlling me. I don't like it.' This tension reached a new intensity when Monroe became a star.

Andrew Tudor, considering this star–audience relationship, outlines four aspects that may contribute to the connection. 'Emotional affinity' is very common, occurring when the audience feels a loose attachment to a particular protagonist or performer. 'Self-identification' arises when involvement reaches a point at which the spectator 'fuses perspectives' with the star. 'Imitation' denotes a condition wherein the star is seen as acting as some sort of model for the audience. 'Projection' is an extreme version of this condition, wherein the star-struck live their lives according to their knowledge of their favoured star. Although Tudor's taxonomy is helpful in explaining what audiences may do with the star images they are offered, it does not tell us why the offered images take the form that they do. Why *Monroe*?

Alberoni argues that 'The star system . . . never creates the star, but it proposes the candidate for "election", and helps to retain the favour of the "electors".'[4] Long before 'Superman came to the Supermarket', stars campaigned for their own office. The role and performance of a star in a movie were taken as revealing the personality of the celebrity (which then was corroborated by the stories in the magazines and on the newsreels). What was seldom seen and seldom stated by Hollywood or the stars was that this 'personality' was itself a careful construction and expressed only through the flow of films, stories, publicity and gossip. On odd occasions, the spectator might actually confront a star and say, 'Who do *you* think you are?' Fame homogenizes life, and creative impoverishment becomes a constant threat as the person comes to see her or his 'personality'. Cary Grant (Archie Leach), Tony Curtis (Bernie Schwartz), Doris Day (Doris von Kappelhoff), Marilyn Monroe (Norma Jeane Baker): the stars literally made their names, their names made their fortunes, and their fortunes made their fate – there was no going back. Class distinctions were replaced by cash distinctions in an America where the famous are encouraged to turn almost anything into capital. Technology abhors a secret, and the stars make self-interest legendary in the culture of confession. Each star is a reminder of the conspicuous waste of talent where, exploited and exhausted by the voracious media, careers are seen to be made and then fade.

Marilyn Monroe began her career when Hollywood was resorting to an almost Keynesian policy of spending its way out of trouble, with lavish musicals and glossy comedies. Her career ended with the studios near to bankruptcy. Monroe's image has to be situated in the pattern of ideas about morality and sexuality that characterized the 1950s in America and can here be indicated by such instances as the flow of Freudian ideas in the post-war West (registered particularly in the Hollywood melodrama), the Kinsey report (1953), Betty Friedan's *The Feminine Mystique*, rebel stars such as Marlon Brando, James Dean and Elvis Presley, the relaxation of cinema censorship in the face of competition from television, and so forth. These instances must themselves be placed in relation to the other levels of social formation, such as actual social and sexual relations and relative economic situations of women and men. Marilyn Monroe's composition of sexuality and innocence is part of that pattern, but one can also see her distinctive attraction for her audience as being the apparent condensation of all that within her. Thus, Monroe seemed to 'be' the very tensions that inflected the ideological life of 1950s America.

Monroe was never a symbol of a sexual stereotype in the simplistic sense referred to by Sichtermann; the very point about Monroe was the tension, her extraordinariness. Sexuality, as Foucault has stressed, is itself indicative of the process by which power relations are arranged and enforced. The questions we ask about 'sexuality', the fact that we deem it significant, reveal a more wide-ranging tissue of presuppositions. As Foucault's work shows, the construction of sexuality in discourse represents a further development of the movement in society towards the positioning of the body as an object of surveillance and control.

Considerations on gender identity and sexual difference combine a range of notions centring on biological sex, social gender, sexual identification and sexual object choice. The assimilation of these in constructs of gender identity is an established process whose effect has been to establish a heterogeneous and determinate set of biological, physical, social, psychological and psychic constructs as a unitary, fixed and unproblematic attribute of human subjectivity. In ideology, gender identity lies at the heart of human subjectivity. Gender is what crucially defines us; we are encouraged to perceive ourselves in terms of our sexuality, which is thus interpreted as the core of the self. Yet what is sexual in one context may not be so in another: an experience becomes sexual by the application of socially learned meanings.

The conventional image of Monroe is founded upon the kinds of male fantasies noted by Klaus Theweleit. His study singles out two man-made archetypes: the 'White Woman' serves man's needs and withdraws into the home; the 'Red Woman' disturbs the man's composure, unsettling his 'masculine' image of self-control and moral strength. It is not simply that these feelings disturb the sense of masculine identity, but that the denial of these tender and erotic feelings establishes the very sense of male identity. Masculinity has to be constantly reconstituted in the continuous denial of vulnerability and 'feminine qualities'. As long as the sense of masculinity is built upon the systematic denial of 'feminine' qualities, men are left in a continuous and painful struggle with themselves, in constant anxiety and fear of the revelations of their natures. They believe they can control these fears within themselves, the fantasies about themselves, but they do so by projecting them on to women. Thus, as men learn to deny their emotionality, need and dependence, these parts of themselves do not go away, but rather find disguised forms within which to assert themselves. Sex, when admitted, is seen as a commodity, freeing it from concern with commitment, vulnerability, and caring in personal relations.

The man's description of woman vacillates between intense interest and cool indifference, aggressiveness and veneration. He yearns to possess her, yet when he does feel he can possess her he treats her with contempt. The 1950s movie moguls demanded the stereotype of a blonde, the dream (so they said) of returning soldiers and of *Men Only*, something Michelangelo might have carved out of candy. The idealized movie 'Marilyn' was seen as sensuous, lovable and passionate, but, at the same time, scrupulously chaste. Monroe described those men who criticized her 'lewd' love affairs as 'White-masking' themselves: purifying themselves by projecting their 'Red' fantasies on to her. Wilde suggested that 'Men always want to be a woman's first love.' It is said that Monroe's former husband Joe DiMaggio began to resent her when she appeared so 'available': as is so often the case with men, he seemed to distrust what he could possess, and worship what eluded him (after their divorce he became her devoted admirer again). The mixture of desire and fear in the male fantasy Red Woman is certainly evident in Norman Mailer's *Marilyn*, where he describes her as 'a queen of a castrator'.

Blondeness is the ultimate sign of whiteness: the blonde woman is offered as the prized possession of the white man, the most desired of women, the most 'feminine' of women. In *Bus Stop* (1956), the man, looking for 'an angel', sees the Monroe character and exclaims: 'Look at her gleaming there so pale and white!' In *Niagara* (1952), Monroe made a rare appearance as a Red Woman, a woman who acts: she ends up killed by a man for her infidelity. In *Gentlemen Prefer Blondes* (1953), we find the now 'natural' image of 'White Marilyn', a woman who is usually acted upon: she ends up worshipped by men. The Red and White archetypes are most clearly captured in the 'blowing dress' scene used in *The Seven Year Itch* (1955): the Monroe figure is standing over a subway grating, away from any other human being, swaying with pleasure as the cool breeze blows about her legs, sending her skirt waving around her waist, her white dress on display for our gaze. In 1984, the same pose is found in *The Woman in Red*: Kelly Le Brock takes Monroe's place, her eyes open and staring at you, her red dress blowing above her waist to reveal her red panties, her dark hair stroking her bare shoulders. The White Marilyn is purely for inspection, not for touching, meant for no man but Everyman; the Red Kelly is obtainable, down from the pedestal into your arms. Monroe's image was marketed as playful and elegant and everyone's Marilyn, thus alienating no one. She was like the movies: we can all see her, *there*, but no one can keep her.

[···]

The star's image is a complex totality, containing a chronological dimension. In order to grasp the temporality of this image we can refer to the notion of a *textured polysemy*. A star image is polysemic – it signifies several meanings and effects. This polysemy is textured: the several elements of signification may be mutually reinforcing (e.g. John Wayne as 'the all-American guy', the independent adventurer), or these elements may cause friction (as with Monroe's later image, characterized by her efforts to negotiate the difference between these elements). Images incorporate a temporal dimension: a change of roles may affect and inflect the image, as will a change in the person. Watching a star involves the use of hermeneutics: no 'reading' can be done purely in 'close-up', for each instance is impinged on by past instances and past interpretations. The star's personality in a movie is built up, negotiated by moviemakers and audience, across the whole movie. The audience arrives to watch a well-known star, armed with certain preconceptions about the performer derived from knowledge of past appearances, generic conventions, advertising campaigns, and critical reviews. It may be that the signals a star 'gives off' are sometimes not deliberate and yet constitute a major part of the star's image. Monroe's parted lips give the signal 'yielding sexuality', but the quivering upper lip (in fact attempting to hide her high gum line) may also be read as giving the signal 'vulnerability'.

Marilyn Monroe came to exude an aura that affected audiences on an unprecedented scale. She was not the first struggling starlet to strive to symbolize something other or more than sex. The significant difference was that a melodrama, much larger, richer, yet apparently more intimate than anything she ever appeared in on the screen, could be constructed in real life around this ambition. The mass media were powerful enough to transmit any image around the world; the medium of the movies was anxious enough to exploit any image that could see off the challenge of television; Monroe, when she began, was keen to escape from a wretched childhood and forge a brighter future. Eventually, the story would carry sub-themes of social and cultural criticism more potent then anything in the history of the star system, and it was assigned a firmly tragic denouement which has assured it a resonance that, if anything, seems to increase with the passage of time.

Notes and references

1 H. Powdermaker, *Hollywood: The Dream Factory* (Little, Brown, Boston, Mass.), pp. 228–9.
2 H. Marcuse, *One Dimensional Man* (Routledge, London, 1964), p. 60.
3 R. Griffith, *The Movie Stars* (Doubleday, New York, 1970), p. 25.
4 F. Alberoni, 'L'élite irresponsable', *Ikon*, 12–40 (1) (1962), p. 93.

PART III

Reading Popular Culture

PART III OPENS with three discussions of music, 'highbrow' and more popular. In Reading 21 Malcolm Bowie analyses aspects of Viennese high culture in relation to the works of Freud. The Freudian unconscious, Bowie suggests, might cast light upon some aspects of early twentieth-century music. He concentrates particularly upon the music of Mahler. Freud and Mahler actually met in 1910, when Mahler contacted Freud to try to get help for some domestic problems he was experiencing. Mahler's childhood had been traumatic and difficult. He recalled vividly a time in his childhood when he rushed out of the house during a furious scene between his mother and father, to be greeted by the sounds of a street organ playing a popular Viennese tune. From that time onwards, Mahler recounted, tragedy and comedy were inseparably linked in his mind – and this linkage appears in the moods of his music.

What is interesting about the meeting between Freud and Mahler, Bowie says, is the direct parallel between the experience of Mahler and that of Freud; Freud's psychoanalytic theory mixes high tragedy and elevated principles together with apparent trivialities of unconscious memory. In Mahler's music this 'contradiction' takes the form of the juxtaposition of popular themes with 'serious music', brutish impulses with spiritual striving. In Freud's thinking, and in the content of his writing, there is also this 'unforeseeable grinding of one structural order against another'.

John Shepherd (Reading 22) discusses the relation between pop music and jazz. Pop music is often said to operate with much the same elements as soap operas or romantic stories – clichéd phrases familiar to the audience that listens to them. Jazz, on the other hand, stands in more tensionful relation to musical convention. Black forms of jazz, Shepherd suggests, express the divisions between black and white as well as the relative distance between black and white cultures. The more blacks came into direct face-to-face contact with whites in the United States, the more tension became directly built in to musical tonality and rhythm. Yet to use music to confront the oppression to which they were subject, black musicians had in some part to appropriate elements of white music, making their own music 'dirtier'. The attempt to produce 'cool' jazz marked a way of accommodating the necessary mixture of alienation and appropriation.

Although white music has been directly influenced by these trends, whites have never had the experience of being wholly outside the social order in the way in which blacks have. White rock music and other forms of pop mimic the non-conventionality of black jazz, but thereby also tend to reconventionalize it, drawing rock into the general framework of pop music.

In Reading 23 Simon Frith discusses the fate of rock in current times. In a manner compatible with Shepherd's view, Frith argues that the rock era was something of a 'diversion' in twentieth-century popular music rather than a full revolution. It was an attempt to preserve the originality of the performer and the performance in a context in which technological advances were rendering such originality obsolete. The ease with which rock music has become incorporated into a commodified universe confirms its separation from the jazz and black musical forms which were its inspiration. Rock songs today have become advertising jingles. Yet processes of commodification always throw up counter-reactions. The demise of rock is sometimes described in terms of fragmentation, and thus assimilated to postmodernism; but there may be upsurges of protest and disaffection which take musical form and which throw into confusion, even if only temporarily, the orthodox frameworks of popular music.

In Reading 24 Lizbeth Goodman discusses the nature of feminist comic theatre. Theatre to some extent bridges the divisions between high and low culture, although in other respects it also serves to accentuate them. Like photography, 'middle brow' theatre preserves a strong element of the conventional and familiar: the same plays are put on and seen again and again. Feminist theatre seeks to puncture the complacencies of high brow and 'middle brow' theatre alike. The conventionality of 'middle brow' entertainment usually includes an acceptance of existing formulae of gender. The same is not always true of more elite forms of theatrical representation; its misogyny is expressed in different ways. Feminist theatre seeks to disturb convention in the nature of its theatrical forms as well as in its content. It attempts to subvert convention through the use of distinct costumes, set, props, experimentation with language and plot. Feminist comic theatre is related to, and to some degree borrows from, stand-up comedy, but in ways that seek to place in question that most conventional of comic forms.

The operettas of Gilbert and Sullivan are as good an example as one could get of 'middlebrow' taste – or seem so today. David Cannadine's analysis (Reading 25) of Gilbert and Sullivan offers a useful illustration of Bourdieu's theory of fields of cultural production. For how the works of Gilbert and Sullivan have been seen, interpreted by their performers and responded to, has varied over the years. These changes have been partly a matter of the internal 'dialogue' of performance, but also express wider systems of power in the society at large. In their own time, Cannadine says, Gilbert and Sullivan were theatrical revolutionaries. They aimed their work at those sectors of the nineteenth-century theatre that were ephemeral and oriented towards escapism. The quality of Gilbert's scores, however, was much higher than the usual musical plays that appeared on the London stage. His dialogue recalled sophisticated theatre of previous eras, but did so in such ways as to create new theatrical tastes. Following a period of prosperity the operas of Gilbert and Sullivan themselves fell from favour. The process of their revival was again one of creating new conventions and seeking new audiences; eventually they became institutionalized as themselves 'traditional'.

It is worth noting that the period at which Gilbert and Sullivan fell from grace was more or less the time at which modernism in art and literature got under way. In Reading 26 Mary Ann Caws traces some key elements of modernism in the art of Kandinsky. Modernism is often thought to involve 'seeing through' the veil of appearances to some deeper structures or forms. Kandinsky, however describes it as an opposite process: 'non-recognition'. Monet's *Picture of a Haystack* was not recognizable as a haystack. Kandinsky found this non-recognition painful. Yet at the same time the picture took hold of him and refused to fade from his memory, even in its details. Kandinsky perceived that the subject of the painting was actually the painting itself; for him this was something akin to a conversion experience and he determined to pursue its implications. What replaces the object is not the painting as such, but rather a constructed dialogue of freedom and necessity, involving the internal tension of colours. We might doubt how far the distinction between modernism and postmodernism is useful to analyse such cultural transitions; for we seem to find here, not just in Kandinsky's art but in his own intellectual reflections, the central trait of the 'postmodernist' universe.

In Reading 27, Michael Moriarty considers some parallel themes from the point of view of theatre, concentrating upon the writings of Roland Barthes. Barthes wrote more extensively on the theatre than is usually imagined. As Moriarty points out, Barthes' views on the theatre have received far less attention than most of his other writings on cultural production. Barthes gave most attention to the theatre in the earlier part of his career. Theatre, he argued, can in principle be more subversive than either literature or avant-garde art. An avant-garde novel, for example, can shake the pre-given assumptions of the reader, but has to do so by creating an alien world. Theatre, Barthes says, can react against the order of things at the same time as it makes that order comprehensible to us. Beginning with critical reflections drawn from Brecht, Barthes moved on to sketch the outlines of a semiotic theory of theatre. Theatre he sees as what he calls a 'cybernetic machine'; it gives forth multiple messages coming from the rhythms of speech, action and the various paraphernalia of the stage. Theatre is characterized by a 'density of signs' through which the semiotician should chart a way. Brecht's theatre makes us conscious of the variety of semiotic elements which we usually take in a more or less automatic way.

Fashions in taste are a basic element of Bourdieu's fields of culture. In Reading 28 Joanne Finkelstein looks at taste where it has an interesting double meaning – in the consumption of food. Commodified taste, as Haug would say, lives through fashion; it is the fashionable that acts as a dynamic for the constant malleability of needs. Fashion also, as Haug also says, detaches form from content, for what makes something fashionable has nothing to do with its actual substance but is governed only by its being 'of the moment'. Fashion today includes not only clothing but most forms of everyday commodity displayed in advertisements and available in the stores. It can be defined as the 'ever-shifting and continuous renewal of the new'. Here again it is not difficult to discern its origins in modernism. Fashion, Finkelstein suggests, allows the individual a sense of control in circumstances in which movements of change otherwise seem random and overpowering. Fashion is in a sense an attempt to control time, to arrest the process of active decay. Yet according to Finkelstein fashionability is also 'an opting out', a withdrawal from any obligation to seek to shape the future in a responsible way.

Fashions in food tastes are strongly influenced by practices of 'eating out'. The fashionability of a restaurant depends upon an assertion of its own individuality or exclusivity – in relation not just to the food that it offers, but to its décor, location, style of service and even perhaps its name. Once more we see that the fashion depends upon movements in wider chains of signifiers or cultural meanings. These are partly temporal; the 'fashionable place to eat' has to separate itself from that which is 'no longer in fashion', but also has to relate itself to fashionability in many other external items with which it shares associations of meaning: clothes, music, styles of behaviour and so forth.

Taste is also the subject of the discussion by Jean-François Lyotard (Reading 29). Art becomes a matter of taste once it has dropped all connection with religion or other directly moral imperatives. In place of morality comes the 'sublime'. Romantic art, even into the twentieth century, maintained connections with constraints of representation. Such art, one might say, in its emphasis upon emotion still carried the residue of some sort of moral character. Cézanne was not concerned to discover a 'painting style' but sought to answer the question: 'What is a painting?' The avant-garde saw itself as much more than mere fashion. But one might wonder if in the end the avant-garde was anything other than fashion presented in the guise of revolution. For 'being ahead' only counts as anything profound if it somehow allows the attainment of a deeper truth.

The avant-garde dissolves once the pretence of achieving deeper truth is abandoned. For Lyotard the abandonment of truth claims discloses the necessary separation of signifier from signified. Art which is governed only by innovation obeys the movements of the commodity and specifically the art market. As Lyotard puts it, 'one flatters the "taste" of a public that can have no taste'. Yet innovation can preserve a sense of the sublime in so far as it still has a sense of the ineffable – of that which is not reached and destroyed by the empty category of the commodity.

In the final selection (Reading 30) Zygmunt Bauman continues the theme of truth and doubt in relation to modernity and postmodernity. He distinguishes two kinds of doubt. There is doubt which derives from lack of evidence to support an agreed theory or narrative; and there is doubt which arises from the fact that a given narrative might be only one story among many others which could be told about a certain range of events. Doubt in the first sense is 'modern', Bauman says, while doubt in the second sense is 'postmodern'.

Two highly popular films, *The Exorcist* and *The Omen*, he says, are parables of these two forms of doubt. In *The Exorcist* the investigating priest, Father Damien Carras, only looks to non-scientific methods when the methods of science fail him. He is presented first of all as a modern, concerned to expunge tradition and dogma. Carras comes to recognize that science itself can become dogmatic if it fails to remember that its distinctiveness actually derives from scepticism. The methodical doubt that drives science hence can be turned against science itself – and also can be used to contemplate the possibility that spirits and demons do have some sort of reality. *The Exorcist* shows that the first kind of doubt cannot resist slippage into the second.

The Omen has a more radical message. Science itself, it suggests, might be a cover for dark and hostile influences. The forces of the Devil stand behind the turmoil and destructiveness so evident in many parts of the world. Such an interpretation makes as much sense of these phenomena as the 'official' line offered within modernity. For every observed pattern of events there is more than one explanation; which is chosen is ultimately a political matter. The point is not that we should replace scientific narratives with others held with greater conviction. That way lies a dangerous fundamentalism. As modernity shades over into postmodernity we have to learn to live with multiple narratives: we must learn to live, Bauman concludes, with ambivalence.

21

A Message from Kakania: Freud, Music, Criticism

Malcolm Bowie

Freud's theory of the human mind contained a moral fable for the fallen times in which it first appeared. For psychoanalysis, the mind was a scene of interminable conflict. It was a realm of competing drives, incompatible systems, irreconcilable agencies or dispositions, adjacent territories between which no reliable channels of communication could exist. Freud tirelessly re-imagined this discord and redramatized its consequences for civilization. Sometimes his descriptions have a light quotidian touch. 'The ego is not master in its own house,'[1] he wrote, espousing with some relish the voice of a paterfamilias who has begun to hear murmurings from below stairs. But at other times the voice is epic and self-heroizing: from its Virgilian epigraph onwards, *The Interpretation of Dreams* is the autobiography of one who has dared to enter Hell and subject his intellectual and moral authority to a series of truly infernal indignities. The evidence of dreams and of neurotic disorders made it necessary to grant the unconscious a mode of action, a logic and an entelechy of its own and these threatened to disrupt even the most straightforward-seeming cognitive operations. For the mind, pictured in this way, not only desires more than one thing at a time, not only drives the individual in separate directions at once: it is the realm of the incommensurable, a mechanism installed within the human creature for the production of endless dissonances and discrepancies. Freud's multi-systemic 'psychical apparatus' was to some extent the psychological model that Viennese high culture needed in order to understand its own predilection for irony, but there is a sense of extremity about the first main phase of Freud's theorizing, and especially about the books on dreams, slips and jokes that he wrote between 1899 and 1905, that belongs not just to Vienna but to Kakania, Musil's hyper-ironical dream Austria. If the conscious mind had ambitions to be *kaiserlich und königlich* in its handling of experience, the unconscious exerted upon it a continuous downward suction – towards the low-life world of the human drives, the genital, excremental and homicidal urges that high-toned 'mind' nonetheless also harboured. The very first dream to be discussed psychoanalytically in *The Interpretation of Dreams* – the celebrated dream of 'Irma's injection' – dramatizes the clash between high professional calling and abject unconscious desire and is an allegorical anticipation of much that is to follow later in the work. In this dream, one of Freud's real-life female patients presents bizarre organic symptoms, which are discussed, diagnosed and treated by a group of four medical men, including Freud himself. Their behaviour brings together incompetence, spurious theorizing and demented clinical practice. Simple contact with the clinical material turns the good sense and good intentions of the practitioners involved into a black comedy of self-promotion and obfuscation. It is scarcely surprising that this dream should reappear as a leitmotif later in Freud's book, for here was a potent image of the worst that could befall the public-spirited instigator of a new mental science.

This is not the place to re-examine in detail those features of psychoanalysis that are specific to the Viennese *fin-de-siècle*. What I shall do briefly, in the pages that follow, is look again at one kind of relationship – between Freud and the musicians who were his contemporaries – and suggest two distinct ways in which the Freudian idea of the unconscious may illuminate early twentieth-century art.

[···]

I shall begin with one of the very few moments of contact between music and psychoanalysis to have been recognized as 'official' and instructive by historians of both disciplines: the meeting between Freud and Mahler that took place in Leyden in August 1910. In such standard accounts of this meeting as those given by Ernest Jones and Donald Mitchell, the relationship between the two great men is self-evidently an asymmetrical one. Mahler had requested an interview with Freud for the purposes of discussing a marital difficulty, and Mahler was the only obvious beneficiary of the occasion: the informal psychoanalysis conducted during a four-hour perambulation through Leyden produced, we are told, positive therapeutic effects. Similarly, it is Mahler's work rather than Freud's that is immediately illuminated by the traumatic childhood memory that reappeared during their discussion. Jones summarizes the composer's new access of artistic self-knowledge in these terms:

In the course of the talk Mahler suddenly said that now he understood why his music had always been prevented from achieving the highest rank through the noblest passages, those inspired by the most profound emotions, being spoilt by the intrusion of some commonplace melody. His father, apparently a brutal person, treated his wife very badly, and when Mahler was a young boy there was a specially painful scene between them. It became quite unbearable to the boy, who rushed away from the house. At that moment, however, a hurdy-gurdy in the street was grinding out the popular Viennese air 'Ach, du lieber Augustin'. In Mahler's opinion the conjunction of high tragedy and light amusement was from then on inextricably fixed in his mind, and one mood inevitably brought the other with it.[2]

And Mitchell describes persuasively the various Mahlerian routes by which 'the vivid contrast between high tragedy and low farce, sublimated, disguised and transfigured though it often was, emerged as a leading artistic principle of his music, a principle almost always ironic in intent and execution.'[3]

Yet what is striking about the Freud–Mahler encounter, once Freud has been freed from the role of benevolent counsellor and sage, is the parallelism between the two participants, and the predicament they share. At one level, of course, Mahler tells Freud what he already knows, and confirms him in the leading psychoanalytic principle which holds that repressed memories of painful childhood experiences, if they are reactivated in the controlled conditions of the analytic dialogue, can relieve or remove neurotic symptoms. But Mahler is at the same time addressing a fellow victim of baseness and banality, one whose theoretical work no less than his case-histories is marked by a syncopated rhythm of 'high tragedy and low farce'. Freud's science has its own intrusive hurdy-gurdy music; his clinical practice involved 'grubbing about in human dirt'. The unconscious was at one and the same time the 'true psychical reality', the main source of certainty of the new psychology, and an agency that disturbed and contaminated its explanatory procedures; it provided psychology with its essential subject matter, yet was never fully circumscribable and available for inspection. 'Knowing' the unconscious was a matter of espousing a rhythm of appearance and disappearance in the quest for meaning, of accommodating oneself to an intermittence seemingly inherent in the structure of the human mind.

Let us examine a precise case of 'contamination' in Mahler's music: in the sixth symphony (1905), the cowbells which announce an interlude of pastoral rapture amid the trampling march-rhythms of the first movement. The 'low'–'high' antithesis serves, as we have just seen, a multitude of expressive purposes for the student of modern Viennese culture. It sets plebeian music against serious music, primitive libidinal impulse against the 'spiritual' striving of the artist, the brutish unconscious against the artful indirections of socialized desire. But in the case of Mahler's suddenly intruding cowbells the distinction works only by refusing to work. They are 'low' in that they are pieces of dairy-farming equipment, 'high' in that they suggest the uplands and uplift; they are gatecrashers in the modern orchestra, yet offer a privileged glimpse of bliss and resolution; the sound they make is inarticulate and monotone, yet it frames a partial reprise of the movement's tenderly soaring second subject. What is still shocking about Mahler's bells – even to a musical age that has heard far stranger special effects from the percussion section of the orchestra – is not their bovine lowness but their seeming irrelevance to the advancing symphonic argument. They interrupt. They interject another zone of experience – low in one way, high in another – which, for all the delicate allusions to the main thematic material of the movement that this pastoral episode contains, in acoustic terms refuses to blend and merge. They herald a premature bliss, a higher state that has not been attained in musical argument but dumped gratuitously upon a still emerging symphonic structure.

Faced with a disruptive blatancy of this kind, we could find ourselves tempted to speculate on the unconscious mental processes involved. Commentators have suggested that a fragment of word-play could have been at work: Mahler associated the second subject with his wife *Alma*, and in the intrusive interlude summons the reader to the green landscape of an *Alm* (Alpine pasture). But, although name-magic of this kind figures in the Mahler–Freud interview as reported by Jones, such connections cast only a feeble Freudian half-light upon the movement and understate by far its drama. The crucial connection with Freud lies in the suddenness and the unaccountability of the musical event. In the Mahler symphony, one structure intrudes upon another, seeming to come from another – obscure, irrelevant, disconnected – mental region. In due course, this hiatus is to be overcome and the emotional hesitation that accompanies it is to be further exploited and integrated within the four-movement span of the symphony, but early on the gap is unbridgeable. For Freud in one of his theoretical moods, the surest sign of the unconscious at work was to be found exactly in the unforeseeable grinding of one structural order against another. In the continuous fabric of experience, a sudden snag appeared The reasonable-seeming individual, equipped with comprehensible motives and creditable goals, gave evidence – in a symptom, a slip of the tongue, a word-association or a metaphor – of other desires that were not reasonable at all. He or she seemed suddenly to be speaking or behaving from an alien region.

And although that region could be expected in due course to reveal its continuities and regularities, its first emergence upon the scene was a scandal. One of Freud's extraordinary achievements as a writer was to preserve this sense of outrage in defiance of his own proficiency as a psychoanalytic explainer: rather than allow an all-purpose discourse of otherness and unknowability to inform his accounts of mind in action, he constantly rediscovered otherness in his own surprise, and wrote of it surprisingly. At the end of *The Interpretation of Dreams*, Freud reminds his reader that the ancients had already displayed in their superstitious respect for dreams an awareness of 'the uncontrolled and indestructible forces in the human mind', and that it was the task of the psychoanalyst to retain this awareness for scientific purposes. The proliferating catalogue of instantaneous unconscious effects that fills the pages of his early psychoanalytic works is his homage to this power, which he himself called 'daemonic'.

The discontinuity between musical worlds that Mahler introduces into the first movement of his sixth symphony speaks of a dangerous openness to fluctuating and multiform desire. Desire has rushed ahead of the opportunities for expression that the composer's chosen structure affords. Re-using a grammatical image of which Freud was particularly fond, we could say of the wish-fulfilment taking place in these bars that 'a thought expressed in the optative has been replaced by a representation in the present tense'. 'Oh, if only . . .' has been replaced by 'It is.' 'If only I could experience my mountain rapture *now*' has been answered by an irresponsible internal voice saying 'You can.' Yet although the Mahlerian wish that finds outlet here cannot be cancelled or withdrawn once it has made its disruptive entry, the musical language to which Mahler still adheres has of course its own controlling tonal conventions, and these keep a tight rein on the extravagance and precociousness of the desiring imagination. Things would be very different if the musical language itself were pressing towards a new openness and a new willingness to collude in the fulfilment of wishes.

Notes and references

1   S. Freud, *A Difficulty in the Path of Psycho-Analysis*, standard edn (Hogarth Press, London, 1917), vol. XVII, p. 143.
2   E. Jones, *Sigmund Freud: Life and Work* (Hogarth Press, London, 1958), vol. II, p. 89.
3   D. Mitchell, *Gustav Mahler: The Wunderhorn Years* (Faber, London, 1974), p. 74.

22

The Analysis of Popular Music

John Shepherd

It has been observed that 'popular music can be distinguished from real jazz [in terms of speed of tendency gratification]. For while "pop" music . . . makes use of a fairly large repertory of tones, it operates with such conventional clichés that gratification is almost immediate and uncertainty is minimized.'[1] What is meant by 'real jazz' has never been clarified, but the drawing of this kind of distinction raises questions concerning the social messages of Afro-American and Afro-American-influenced musics perceived as being in tension with the prevailing social–musical order. The discussion of these questions will be split into two, considering black forms of music first, and then white forms.

It would appear that the more helpless black people have been to counter the framework with which they were in tension, the less close and constraining is the framework in musical terms. Thus, in the early Delta blues, which grew up in the Mississippi valley among black people who were thoroughly subjugated and kept separate from white people, the musical framework drawn from functional tonality was not always obviously apparent. This does not mean that the framework was not present. Nor does it mean that the framework did not *contain* the highly inflectional elements which were very much to the fore in the Delta blues. It means that the framework was geographically and therefore culturally distant, and that there was consequently little possibility of, or point in, engaging it.

The Texas blues, on the other hand, grew up among black people who were more integrated with whites and less severely subjugated, and the framework was more apparent. It can be argued that the relative closeness of the framework was symptomatic of a situation in which black people were in a closer relationship to whites; further, that being in a *relatively* stronger position to take on the framework, black people faced the framework in a more immediately antagonistic manner; finally, that in order to overthrow the framework, black people must ultimately, in their music, take on some of the global and intellectually abstract qualities of that framework.

This line of thought may include more recent black forms such as rhythm-and-blues and avant-garde jazz. With the move of blacks to urban areas, their relative increase in political power and their increasingly overt aggressiveness towards white culture, the framework drawn from functional tonality became closer and more oppressive. Blacks were face to face with whites and the inflectional elements of rhythm-and-blues came face to face with the framework. Indeed, the word 'rhythm' in the rather generalized label of 'rhythm-and-blues' does little more than signify the increasing tightness of the framework. Tension becomes electric, not only in a political and social sense, but also musically.

At this point black people faced a dilemma, socially, culturally and musically. In order to contest the framework, it was necessary to take on some of its elements. That is why those blacks who could see little point in contesting the predominant social system, and who were resigned to living within it, had a music that was 'dirtier', 'less structured' and more symptomatic of an emotionally rich relationship to the here and now. But as black people gained a stronger sense of an ability to contest their dispossessed situation, and a stronger sense of the possibility of gaining more power, their music became less 'dirty', more 'cool' and 'laid back', and teleological. However, to eliminate all that was inflectional and 'dirty' would have been to espouse entirely the values of white society and ensure the destruction of black culture.

In order to provide a musical *alternative* as powerful as prevailing social realities and ideologies, it becomes necessary to develop musical languages capable of mediating the world in as global and extended a fashion as functional tonality, but without the centrally distanced control and alienation articulated through functional tonal music. It is perhaps for this reason that black rhythm-and-blues did not develop significantly as a musical *language* beyond the music of B. B. King. However, there is one form of black music where it is possible to argue for a development beyond the stage of confrontation with the framework derived from functional tonality. Black jazz developed an affinity with 'classical' forms of music during its 'cool' period. The reaction to this was 'hard bop' which then gave rise to black avant-garde jazz. It would be difficult to claim that a sense of framework is *totally* absent from the music of performers such as Cecil Taylor and Archie Shepp, but it is very weak.

Without a more detailed analysis it is difficult to make the case incontrovertibly. However, it can be argued that (a) it is first necessary for radical black (and, indeed, black-inspired) forms of music to develop a sense of the explicit in order to contest prevailing social–musical realities and ideologies; (b) in order to avoid being totally assimilated into the prevailing power structure, it is then necessary to infuse a strong sense of the explicit with an equally strong sense of the inflectional, so that extended formal principles grow out of the intuitional, the inflectional, the personal, immediate and spontaneous instead of these qualities being contained within pre-existing formal principles. Such music need not be anarchic in the sense of developing untrammelled non-redundancy. Formal principles grow out of musical characteristics inherent in the inflectional and become an extension of them.

The situation of white Afro-American-influenced music is different in the sense that although many white people have suffered considerable material and intellectual (and, to some extent, emotional) dispossession, they have never been outside the social system in the same way as black people. White people have never had a cultural and musical reality situated (in one way or another) solidly outside the social structures of industrial capitalism in terms of which to formulate disaffection towards that social structure. The social location of different forms of white Afro-American-influenced music has been at the margin of the structure rather than outside it. This is as true of 1920s white jazz as of the various forms of rock music that have grown up since the Second World War. The Second World War gave rise to substantial social upheaval which led a new, young generation to see the world in a different light from its parents. The marginal status of young people that has been a symptom of industrial capitalist societies received an additional emphasis from the increased youth spending power resulting from a capitalist system operating in full gear. For American, mostly working-class young people, the new cultural markets were filled musically by Elvis Presley, and for British, mostly middle-class young people, by the Beatles. Both Elvis Presley and the Beatles drew on the one hand from the music of their parent culture (country and western for Presley, and, it can be argued, music of the mainstream white ballad tradition for the Beatles) and, on the other, from a form of black music that would give sufficient expression to the marginal status of the cultures for whom they were performing (black rhythm-and-blues in both cases – mediated, for early British rock, to a significant extent through early rock 'n' roll).

Only once since the Second World War has there emerged a white culture whose degree of material, intellectual and, indeed, emotional dispossession remotely approached that of some black cultures. British punk grew up in the late 1970s among young working-class people (and 'avant-garde', middle-class youth) at a time when the country faced serious economic problems, and was entering a period of significant political realignment. Coming from a parent culture which, since the late 1930s, had experienced at least some reasonable expectations in life, these young people faced rampant unemployment and lacked the necessary skills to avoid the fate of an apparently pointless existence. Since, unlike the blacks of early, southern rural America, young British working-class whites of the late 1970s *did* come from a parent culture that had experienced reasonable expectations, their reaction was one, not of resignation and of spiritual survival based on an already established and vibrant culture, but of hostility and aggression towards a social structure that had deprived them of their very basis for being in the world. Although punk drew to a limited extent on black British reggae, this was hardly a culture in which white working-class young people could take wholehearted refuge. Experiencing a nothingness imposed by a greater social structure, punk culture had little alternative, as Hebdige (1979) has pointed out, but to take the established symbols of the greater social structure and, schizophrenic-like, throw them back in its face in a manner incomprehensible to those living securely within that structure. The symbols of capitalist society were used as a means of spiritual defence against the cultural annihilation threatened by that same society. The meaning of punk culture did not go beyond shock, raw aggression and sheer survival.

It is not difficult to draw structural homologies between the three kinds of white subculture referred to above – 1950s American working class, 1960s British middle class, 1970s punk – and their musics, although, once again, without more detailed analysis it is not possible to do more than establish the main lines of argument.

In *Profane Culture* Willis argues that rock 'n' roll 'has opened up "new" possibilities because it has avoided being trapped by the received conventions concerning rhythm, tonality and melody'.[2] While it is possible to agree with Willis that the continuous pulse of much early rock music articulates a temporal flow of consciousness, an emphasis on the ever-unfolding immediacy of the here and now essentially denied through the spatialized time of functional tonality, and that earlier rock music 'was not caught up in the end of the possibilities of harmony'[3] or, for that matter, in the harmonic teleology of extended emotional structures, it is not possible to agree that the rhythms of early rock music 'escaped from the determinations of the classic bar structure' to 'subvert the bar form'[4] or that 'the normal rules of progression, and forms of cadence, are replaced in rock 'n' roll by a kind of anarchy. . .'.[5] It would be fairer to say that while early rock's *more even* pulse (compared with some jazz and blues, as well as functional tonal music) and its 'simple' chord structures allow for a strong emphasis on the temporal flow of the subjective here and now, they at the same time constitute a largely neutral and apolitical reproduction of the musical framework derived from functional tonality. There is, to be sure, a 'timelessness' in early rock music, but it is the 'timelessness' (so-called: representing the abnegation simply of a spatialized sense of time, which itself squeezes out the true flow of temporality) of a social–musical framework that is taken for granted and largely unquestioned. This essential tension is caught in Willis's description of the time sense of one of the subcultures to espouse early rock music, the bikeboys.

> In one way, and concentrating on its oppositional aspects, the whole motorbike culture was an attempt to stop or subvert bourgeois, industrial, capitalist notions of time – the basic experiential discipline its members faced *in the work they still took so seriously*. The culture did not attempt to impute causality or logical progression to things. It was about living and experiencing in a concrete, essentially timeless, world – certainly timeless in the sense of refusing to accept ordered, rational sequences.[6]

There is a sense in which this kind of tension is characteristic of much working-class culture, albeit in a milder form. Although working-class people are subjugated (as are most people in the Western world) to the mechanical time of the work-place, they tend to concentrate outside the work-place on the enjoyment of the here and now. The crucial and more obvious tension within rock music would seem to come between the musical framework (itself containing tension) and the strong personalities revealed through the vocal lines. The singing of Presley and Buddy Holly reveals a marked innuendo of virile, individualistic masculine sexuality eminently successful in flouting the propriety of middle-class sensibilities. Early rock music subscribes to the traditional reality ('false consciousness') of working-class culture with the one exception of taking the rugged individuality of capitalist ideology and overblowing it to the point where it concentrates solely on the sheer hedonistic joy of being alive. This is what makes teddy boy, bikeboy and greaser sub-cultures marginal as against their parent culture.

[···]

In conclusion we may say that music as a socially constructed symbolic medium speaks immediately, concretely and globally to the experiential world of different individuals. There is in other words little or no disjunction between people and music. Within a particular cultural context, both are in intense dialectical relationship with the same social structure. It is possible to understand, therefore, how functionally tonal music speaks to the experience of those charged with manipulating, in an emotionally distanced, explicit, abstract and teleological fashion, the social structure within which most people live; how early rock 'n' roll speaks to the experience of those lodged securely enough within their own parent culture and thus the overall social structure that expression of marginal status is located in an optimistic exaggeration of a feature important to the ideology of the overall social structure; how punk rock speaks to the experience of those whose only salvation from extreme alienation comes from the social structure which caused the alienation in the first place; finally, how progressive rock speaks to the experience of those who dropped out (to differing extents) from white middle-class reality in order to attempt a more humane understanding and reordering of that reality. What is common to the social–musical reality of these kinds of rock music is an emphasis on the experiential richness of the here and now, on the inherent potential of people to exist fully in the world, which is essentially denied by the social–musical reality of functional tonal music.

Notes and references

1   L.B. Meyer, 'Some remarks on value and greatness in music', *Journal of Aesthetics and Art Criticism*, XVII (1959), pp. 486–500, esp. p. 494.
2   P. Willis, *Profane Culture* (Routledge, London, 1978), p. 76.
3   Ibid., pp. 76–7.
4   Ibid., p. 76.
5   Ibid., p. 77.
6   Ibid., p. 78.

23

Music for Pleasure

Simon Frith

I am now quite sure that the rock era is over. People will go on playing and enjoying rock music, of course (though the label is increasingly vague), but the music business is no longer organized around rock, around the selling of records of a particular sort of musical event to young people. The rock era – born around 1956 with Elvis Presley, peaking around 1967 with *Sgt Pepper*, drying around 1976 with the Sex Pistols – turned out to be a by-way in the development of twentieth-century popular music, rather than, as we thought at the time, any kind of mass-cultural revolution. Rock was a last romantic attempt to preserve ways of music-making – performer as artist, performance as 'community' – that had been made obsolete by technology and capital. The energy and excitement of the music indicated, in the end, the desperation of the attempt. Given what has happened, the despair was justified. Nowadays, rock anthems are used to sell banks and cars. As I write, *Rolling Stone* magazine is celebrating its twentieth anniversary as though it had always meant to be what it has now become – a slick vehicle for delivering the middle-class, middle-aged leisure market to the USA's most conservative corporate advertisers.

There are two ways to read this situation. Either what is being packaged now is no longer rock (*Rolling Stone* ceased to be a rock magazine years ago; 'I Feel Free' died as a rock song the moment it became a Renault jingle). Or else rock's 'new' commercial function proves that it was actually no different from any other leisure product all along. The first argument (the fanzine line) means developing a myth of 'true' rock – and there are plenty of 'authentic' stars and 'no sell out' fans from Bruce Springsteen on down ready to believe in it. I do not, if only for aesthetic reasons – there is something *essentially* tedious these days about that 4:4 beat and the hoarse (mostly male) cries for freedom. On the other hand, to reabsorb rock into general pop history, to discount its belief that it is 'different', means listening afresh to other forms of mass-produced music – maybe they don't work in the way we thought, either.

In Britain, more clearly than in the States (where it was quickly reassimilated as suburban rock and roll), new thinking about music and mass culture was inspired by punk. Even at the time I was writing *The Sociology of Rock* in the late 1970s, there were the first signs of 'crisis' in the rock business – the demographic shift from teenager to young adults, the rise of the cassette and the cassette player, the abrupt end to a decade of remarkable growth in sales and profit figures. I still think that its account of the rock world was accurate, but *The Sociology of Rock* came out just as that world was unravelling. In my subsequent rewrite of the story, *Sound Effects*, all I could do was register the contradictions: the way in which rock naturalism was being called into question by punk's do-it-yourself make-up; the fact that far from being 'counter-cultural', rock articulated the *reconciliation* of rebelliousness and capital.

After *Sound Effects* my critical interests pulled two ways. As an academic researcher I wanted to do more systematic work on the history of pop, on the organization of the music industry before rock and roll, on the aesthetics of show business and Tin Pan Alley, on the everyday use of music as a casual commercial soundtrack. As a rock critic I wanted to pay closer attention to the surfaces of musical events, taking genre labels for granted while charting the mechanisms through which different sounds give different pleasures. For three years, from 1983 to 1986, I went to two or three concerts a week – and it was a sign of the collapsing categories that I was appointed the *Sunday Times*'s 'rock critic' (to complement Derek Jewell's 'pop' criticism) at the moment when I no longer found the distinction sensible (and, in the event, it was Derek who went on celebrating old rock acts in all their pomp and circumstance, I who was enthralled by the 'new pop' acts in all their glitzy hype).

If I was confident that I knew what was going on in the record business – I enjoyed the music more than ever – developments in the academy at this time did bemuse me. Just as rock lost its privileged place as any sort of counter-culture, 'cultural studies' emerged to restate its radical significance – on the syllabus. By 1983–4 the music industry may have been organized 'like punk never happened', but the cultural studies industry was still wallowing in its consequences – semiotic readings of style, postmodernist accounts of video, psychoanalytic interpretations of the voice. These gave pop scholars a theoretical weight which rock studies in the 1970s had never had. What disturbed me was the apparent assumption that it did not matter now how pop production and consumption were organized *materially*. Because the 'reality' of a sound or style or image was just another ideological effect, it was quite OK, it seemed, to write about records, stars and videos as if they did just, somehow, fall to earth.

It is true that writing about pop music was much more fun in the 1980s than it had been in the 1970s. The meaning of music was itself up for grabs and rock criticism no longer meant placing each new release in its tradition, describing its *provenance*, codifying sounds in terms of accustomed social codes. But what this meant for me was the reversal of the old terms of my academic/journalist confusion. In the 1970s I had thought of myself as using sociological research methods to expose rock fan mythology, while depending on my personal involvement in music as a constant reminder that rock's other sociological observers just *didn't understand*. In the 1980s, as a fan I was amazed by academic theorists' cavalier way with social facts, while as an academic I enjoyed upsetting readers' consumer common sense with wild subjective theory.

[···]

In trying to place rock in twentieth-century pop history I found myself intrigued less by the organization of the music business as such than by the impact on it of technological change and by its dependence on the media of mass dissemination. For example, new technology (and its use by broadcasters) lies behind the current reorganization of the music business around the marketing of compact discs and the servicing of satellite and cable TV companies. And what is hearteningly clear from technological history is that no one in the business ever knows in advance which people will use which devices for which purposes. Far from manipulating and moulding public demand, the electronic goods industry has always had to adapt *to* it, sometimes quite drastically.

In this process, market forces are not the only ones in play. Because the meaning of popular music this century is inseparable from its use by the other mass media – radio, cinema, TV, video – so their organization and regulation shape the possibilities of pop. For example, there is a familiar rock cliché (most recently voiced in *Rock of Ages*, the official *Rolling Stone* history of rock and roll) which says that, because of the heavy hand of the BBC, British youngsters were deprived of good rock music in the 1950s and had to be liberated by 'Top 40' formats on the pirate radio stations before their own rock culture could flourish. Or, as I would rather put it, it was because of the BBC's public service attitude to youth programming that there were specifically *British* pop sounds and attitudes in place to inflect the meaning of 1960s rock. Rather than simply imitating the style of American Top 40 radio, British youth club shows such as 'Saturday Club' promoted local enterprise. Skiffle is a case in point. They also gave groups such as the Beatles a chance to develop a relationship with their radio audience that was not just a sales pitch. The importance of public service broadcasting for the 'indie' British scene is apparent in the continuing role of the John Peel show.

One reason why American rock critics scoff at the BBC is because they assume an equation about the British class system: broadcasters = (patronizing) middle class; rock and roll = (threatening) young proles. This is to misread British pop history and to misunderstand British rock ideology. Class readings are confused in general about the ways in which musicians 'represent' their audience – imagination is read as delegation. The continuing influence of subcultural theory is apparent here, and it has resulted in two different sorts of analytic error.

First, it roots 'authentic' rock (or punk or rap or hip hop) in 'the streets' without examining the continuous cultural exchange there between different social fantasies, differently mobile dreams of 'making it'. In both Britain and the USA (if with rather different implications), rock and roll and its associated genres are these days primarily forms of suburban youth expression. The idea of musical 'authenticity' is certainly a suburban idea. As I will argue, to understand British rock culture, in particular, is to understand what it means to grow up in suburbia rather than in the inner city.

The second problem of subcultural sociology (and rock writing) in this context is that it validates the 'amateur' musician (who somehow gives voice and body to the collectivity) at the expense of the 'professional' (who plays to industrial rules). This is a misleading distinction – all pop musicians (or, at least, all pop musicians of any cultural significance) are professionals even though they have different ideologies of professionalism. But it accounts for a peculiarity of much academic pop study: analysis is focused on qualities which musicians cannot help (social background, historical position, gender, ethnicity) rather than on ones which they can (their technical ability, musical judgements, sense of their own creative control). In Britain, the importance of these academically neglected strands of rock life – suburban fantasy and creative professionalism – can be measured by the remarkable pop impact of the art school.

[· · ·]

The 'death' of rock in the 1980s is sometimes described in terms of its fragmentation. There are now just scattered 'taste markets', and the central rock institutions of the 1970s – the music press and certain TV and radio shows – can no longer put together a general audience. This is not simply a matter of statistics. The important point is that no single pop taste, no particular rock fragment, seems any weightier, any *truer* than any other. That is why *Smash Hits*, which values acts only in terms of their commercial success, now outsells the rest of the music press put together (and why *Q*, its grown-up offshoot, is succeeding on the basis of a similar critical assumption – that all musical goods are *equal in the marketplace*).

24

Comic Subversions: Comedy as Strategy in Feminist Theatre

Lizbeth Goodman

The Reading examines one variety of theatre: comic theatre. More specifically, it examines theatre made by women who take positions on feminism: feminist comic theatre.... Sarah Daniels's play *Masterpieces* (1984) – the first major and most performed play by a woman about pornography – is an example of radical feminist theatre which deals with cultural representation in direct ways: by addressing the pornography problem as it intersects with issues of gender and power. The play continues to be a 'consciousness raiser' for its audiences, and has been received with many angry – as well as positive – reviews from theatre critics and academics.

While Daniels's plays have had significant impact on feminist audiences, they have also reached many women and men who do not tend to take a feminist perspective on social issues, much less on a night out at the theatre. But Daniels contends that labelling her work as 'feminist theatre' is problematic due to the status of the term 'feminist', rather than to the status of her work. She refers to the changing social context in which a word like 'feminism' evolves, and says: 'Feminism is now, like a panty-girdle, a very embar[r]assing word. Once seen as liberating, it is now considered to be restrictive, passé, and undesirable to wear.' For all that, Daniels does not deny that her work is feminist, nor that she is a feminist playwright. But she contends that these labels do not reflect the primary aims of her work, and implies that labels such as 'feminist' (and garments such as panty-girdles) have different values for different people in different contexts.

In the quotation above, as in many of her plays, Daniels makes her most powerful statement about feminist politics not through a theoretical argument or polemical diatribe, but rather through an ironic statement.

The reference to the panty-girdle is an example of a playwright's use of humour as a form of communication appropriate to the theatre. Daniels's work is sometimes referred to as 'radical feminist theatre'. The label is appropriate in some respects, and not in others. But more importantly, there are many kinds of feminist theatre which cannot be conveniently categorized according to such labels as 'socialist-feminist theatre' or 'radical-feminist theatre'.

Some feminist theatre treats 'issues of comedy as issues of power', as Susan Carlson has argued in her article 'Comic collisions: convention, rage and order'. Carlson cites Caryl Churchill's socialist-feminist play *Cloud Nine* as an example of a piece which demonstrates the ability of comedy to disengage stereotype from traditional power structures within the text of the play. But other feminist theatre, rather than privileging personal politics and issues of cultural representation within playtexts, focuses instead on *context*. By privileging the audience's role in the performance, some feminist theatre adopts Barthes's literary critical notion of 'the death of the author'. But this idea is complicated in feminist performance, when authors are nearly always alive and have often made their political positions public knowledge.

[· · ·]

Feminist theatre is a genre in which women's comedy has been developed as a subversive strategy using costumes, sets and props, lighting and sound systems, experimentation with language, music and text. But what is most interesting about feminist comic theatre is context. Feminist theatre relies on a subversion of 'reality' and on the presence – imagined or real – of an audience. In defining feminist theatre, the distinction between feminist writing versus women's writing is relevant: all women's theatre is not feminist, and all feminist theatre is not necessarily 'good' theatre simply because it is feminist. Feminist theatre is defined by its politics (feminism) rather than by its form (theatre).

It is only recently that 'feminist theatre' has been recognized as a distinct form or genre. Since its emergence in the late 1960s and early 1970s, feminist theatre has changed its forms and styles considerably. The earliest 'feminist theatre' performances were the demonstrations against the Miss World and Miss America pageants held in 1970. The Women's Street Theatre Group was one of the first organized feminist theatre companies, and much of its work in the 1970s was agit prop theatre: designed to convey polemical feminist messages, or what Sue Ryding of Lip Service has called 'tub thumping feminism'. In all feminist theatre, however, feminist women have been involved in the making and interpreting of plays (whether in the 'role' of playwright, director, performer, or spectator). The image of the feminist has therefore been prioritized, and because theatre is a platform for public representation, the physical appearance and costume of 'the feminist' (assumed to be ugly and 'unfeminine': the stereotype of Doc Martens and denim jeans) has been publicly scrutinized.

[· · ·]

Contemporary feminist theatre takes many forms. It is written and produced by women of many different backgrounds and many different positions, and nearly always relies on the subversion of 'norms' or conventions which tend, as in stand-up comedy, to be male-defined.

Feminist comic theatre has particular relevance to a comparison of social and theatrical roles for women, for two reasons: it relies to a large extent on costume and cross-dressing, and it demands an enhanced audience response: not only attention and applause at the end, but laughter throughout. Feminist comic theatre is therefore more closely related, in some respects, to stand-up comedy and cabaret than it is to 'serious drama' of other kinds. In fact, many feminist theatre companies are also considered to be 'comedy acts': Spare Tyre and Lip Service are two such companies. Lip Service has developed from a stand-up act to a theatre company composed of two women: Maggie Fox and Sue Ryding.

Maggie Fox explains that she and Sue Ryding met in university, where they were both cast in rather stereotypical parts in traditional plays:

> *Fox*: You were characterized either into being a Juliet or a character actress, which basically meant that you were fat. If you were something in between, there was nothing for you to do. We discovered in this production that we had a lot of comic talent. . . .
>
> *Ryding*: Which is interesting in an Ibsen play . . .
>
> *Fox*: There wasn't a lot of comic potential in Ibsen, but we found it.

Their 'finding' of comedy in Ibsen was actually a finding of their dual voice and their shared dissatisfaction with the roles on offer in Ibsen and other 'canonized' drama. They formed a double act and began doing stand-up comedy. They soon found that they felt more comfortable working in comic theatre than they did doing stand-up; they preferred

'being in character' on a stage to 'being themselves' behind a micro-
phone. Yet in writing and performing comic theatre, Fox and Ryding
found that their early 'tub thumping' feminist approach to the presentation of women in theatre was limiting them to certain (positive,
female) kinds of characters, while they wanted to present a range of
female (and male) characters. They decided that in order to be feminist
and funny but also to have a diversity of characters in their work, they
would have to combine positive images of women with absurd images
of women and men. It is significant that they chose Margaret Thatcher
as the model for one of their most extreme characters. This is also
ironic, as it casts Thatcher – clad in her Marks and Spencer blue suits
– as the iconic antithesis of the feminist image.

Lip Service wrote *Margaret III, Parts II and III*, a play which they
attribute in their programme notes – tongue in cheek – to Shakespeare.
The title of the play is a take-off of Shakespeare's *Henry IV: Parts I and
II*, but the style is, in the words of the authors and characters, 'very
modern'. The play revolves around a large open book positioned, up-
right, at the centre of the stage. The performers – as they very carefully
and patiently explain, exaggerating their eye contact with the audience
in the manner of school teachers with an unruly class – are 'on stage'
when positioned in front of the book, and 'off stage' when their backs
are turned, when they are out of sight behind the book, or when they
are not paying attention. In this way, Lip Service mock both the style
of 'the old fashioned fuddy duddy way' of delineating stage space
'frequently used by the Royal Shakespeare Company', and also the 'very
modern' theatrical conventions of the postmodern theatres of newly
canonized playwrights like Beckett and Pinter. The benefits of this
approach, they explain, are twofold: the effect is refreshingly different,
and it also 'saves a fortune on scenery'.

The central characters of the Lip Service play are the evil Queen
Margaret (an obvious Thatcher parody) and her 'fool' Motley Sue. All
other characters (peasants, horses, moon and star, warring tribes etc.)
are played by Fox and Ryding as well. The invention of the character
of Queen Margaret was a reaction to the lack of significant powerful
female roles in the dramatic canon. In Maggie Fox's words: 'what we
try to present is a very complex picture of women, so with *Margaret III*
you've got this picture of a tyrant, and yet there is something attractive
about her, because she is so extraordinary and over the top – she has
the essence of Laurence Olivier about her – you can't pin her down'.

The play tells the story of the magnificent adventures of Queen
Margaret: 'The tale is told how Margaret bold became fair England's
Queen' by killing the eighty-nine relations standing between her and

succession. The motto is encapsulated in the opening song: 'Nothing succeeds like succession'. In depicting Margaret as a power-mad murderous monarch, Lip Service illustrate some of the complicated issues surrounding female leadership. Significantly, Queen Margaret's power is 'put on' with her costume. The putting on of costumes is a central and very visible act in this play, wherein the characters demonstrate the modern theatre's preoccupation with 'demystification' by performing all costume, set and scene changes in front of the audience, as part of the play.

The first time Maggie Fox the performer becomes Margaret the mad Queen and Sue Ryding becomes Motley Sue, they pick up the sacks containing their frocks and props, and explain – with exaggerated patience – the process of their transformation to the audience:

> *Actor M*: I'm just getting into my Margaret costume which is in here.
> *Actor S*: I'm just getting into my Motley Sue costume which is in here. Now this is what we in modern theatre call 'demystification'. That's
> *Both*: Demystification.
> *Actor S*: That is we do everything in front of you –
> *Actor M*: Everything?
> *Actor S*: Everything.
> *Actor M*: Everything!?
> [M GOES OFF, LOOKING SHOCKED AND WORRIED.]
> *Actor S*: So you know exactly what's going on, and you don't have any surprises.
> [ACTOR M APPEARS SUDDENLY WITH A WIG ON.]
> *Both*: Margaret III, Parts Two and Three.
> [THEY GET UP AND OPEN THE BOOK TO REVEAL A LARGE CROWN.]

In this scene, which precedes the action of the play, the idea of 'demystification' is both derided and celebrated. Maggie and Sue become 'real people' distinguishable from the multiple characters they play. They are also recognizable as self-conscious wearers of costumes. Thus the object of traditional acting – to 'become' or portray the character as 'believably' as possible – is subverted so that the performers themselves (Maggie and Sue) become the focus of attention. The scene serves another purpose as well: it 'demystifies' the character of Queen Margaret, who is shown early on to be uncomfortable with the idea that everything she does will be seen. Later in the play, the word 'demystification' is accompanied by clouds of very heavy mist from a smoke machine, which is carried on stage and placed in a prominent position, thereby demystifying the idea that theatrical smoke and thunder are the products of anything more 'mystical' than dry ice and amplifiers. Ironically, it is those spectators seated near the stage who are most affected by the smoke, and for whom it is consequently more difficult to see.

[···]

The Lip Service play discussed above is unique in its depiction of a world inhabited by women, wherein women simply dress as men when the presence of 'men' on stage is required. In a different way, lesbian theatre is unique in its definition of worlds in which men do not figure, or figure only as reference points, but not often as significant characters. Lesbian comic theatre is unique in its use of cross-dressing as a form of representational liberation for women, rather than a representational mimicry of men. In this and in other ways, lesbian comic theatre provides a rich source for comparison of the playing of roles in life and in the theatre.

Note

1 Lesbian theatres, theatres by women of colour and many other feminist theatres are discussed in Goodman's *Contemporary Feminist Theatres* (Routledge, London, 1993) and in 'British feminist theatre: a survey and a prospect', *New Theatre Quarterly*, IX (33) (1993), pp. 66–84.

25

Gilbert and Sullivan: The Making and Unmaking of a British 'Tradition'

David Cannadine

However venerated and venerable they have since become, the fact remains that in their own day Gilbert and Sullivan were theatrical innovators so deliberate and so successful that they might almost be called revolutionaries. But like all revolutionaries, their achievement was significantly determined by the world they were trying to change: in this case the unrespectable nineteenth-century stage, patronized primarily by members of the working classes, who sought fun, laughter, excitement and escape from the dreary monotony of their humdrum lives. Theatre owners were generally regarded as shady characters, and their living was decidedly precarious. Writers were ill-rewarded, and could only make ends meet by maintaining parallel careers as actors or as journalists. The stage was neither an honourable nor a disciplined profession, and actresses were regarded as being little better than prostitutes. Not surprisingly, the upper and middle classes, who had delighted in the eighteenth-century theatre of Garrick and Sheridan, had effectively withdrawn their patronage altogether. There were occasional attempts to raise the tone and standard, as when Squire Bancroft and his wife staged Thomas Robertson's comedies at their Prince of Wales's Theatre in the 1860s; but this was very much the exception which proved the rule.

For the most part, the works that were produced on the London stage were singularly lacking in distinction or refinement. Tragedy, comedy and satire had effectively disappeared by the early nineteenth century, and had been replaced by a variety of inferior genres. The most popular was melodrama, with its stories of murder, torture, haunted castles and wicked baronets, such as Douglas Jerrold's *Black Ey'd Susan* (1829), and Dion Boucicault's *The Corsican Brothers* (1851). Almost as appealing was burlesque: the deliberate travesty of classical plays and characters, as in the works of James Robinson Planche, which included *Olympic Revels* (1831) and *The Golden Fleece* (1845). Pantomime and extravaganza were also highly popular with their emphasis on magic, love and the supernatural. And there was ballad opera: a genre which began with John Gay's *The Beggar's Opera* (1728), but which was by this time much debased and now devoid of satiric edge or musical merit. To this uninspired *mélange* was added imported comic opera: Offenbach's works reached the London stage in the 1860s, and Strauss's *Die Fledermaus* was first performed in 1875. But the libretti were often poorly translated, the music was badly performed and the tone of the productions was vulgar, slapdash and risqué.

It was in this unsavoury theatrical world that W.S. Gilbert learned his craft, appropriately moving, in his early years, between the law, journalism and the stage. Although trained as a barrister, he soon turned to writing, and produced a series of satirical verses eventually published as the *Bab Ballads* (1869), which brought him to the attention of theatre managers. Inevitably, many of his early plays were in the prevailing style of burlesque, pantomime and extravaganza, and these were the forms which were later parodied and mimicked in the Savoy Operas. *Thespis* was actually performed at the Gaiety – a theatre renowned for burlesque – and in its Greek gods and acting troupe contained two essential elements of that genre. *The Sorcerer* was based on *Dulcamara,* Gilbert's earlier burlesque of Donizetti's *L'Elisir d'Amore.* Both *HMS Pinafore* and *The Pirates of Penzance* owed much to nautical melodrama, while *Iolanthe,* with its fairies and final transformation scene, clearly harked back to pantomime. And with *Ruddigore*, Gilbert once more returned to Gothic blood-and-thunder melodrama, complete with haunted house and wicked baronets. Throughout his libretti, Gilbert's delight in disguise and mistaken identity, in topsy-turvydom, and in the last minute restoration of order by essentially implausible means, showed his indebtedness to this mid-Victorian tradition, just as his ageing and unattractive women – Ruth, Kathisa, Lady Sophy – preserved memories of transvestite dame parts in earlier burlesque.

[· · ·]

But it was the content of the operas themselves which most powerfully signalled their departure from earlier theatrical tradition. For Gilbert's libretti were of vastly superior quality to anything that had recently been played on the London stage. His complex plots were carefully and economically crafted. He created a series of memorable, outsize characters: the Lord Chancellor in *Iolanthe,* Poo-Bah in *The*

Edwardes was staging at the Gaiety Theatre. And in the early years of
the new century, these were followed by the sensational successes of
Lehar's *The Merry Widow* (first seen in London in 1907), Frederic
Norton's *Chu Chin Chow* (1916) and Harold Fraser Simpson's *The Maid
of the Mountains* (1917). When Sullivan died in 1900, his reputation as
a serious composer entered a sudden and seemingly irretrievable decline.
Gilbert, who lived on until 1911, expected no better: 'Posterity', he once
remarked, 'will know as little of me as I shall know of posterity.'[3] Yet
however harshly posterity has dismissed their non-collaborative endeavours, their joint works soon bloomed and blossomed anew. As *The
Times* explained in 1948, unconsciously echoing Gilbert's remarks of
sixty years before, the Savoy Operas had 'become a national institution'.
But how, exactly, did this quite unexpected development occur?

Part of the answer undoubtedly lies in the zeal with which the D'Oyly
Carte family exploited their exclusive rights of professional performance
in Britain – rights which they retained until the 1950s. After Richard
D'Oyly Carte's death in 1901, his widow Helen took charge of the
company, and she was followed from 1911 to 1948 by her stepson, Rupert.
The first major Gilbert and Sullivan revival took place in London
between 1906 and 1908, the productions being superintended by W.S.
Gilbert himself. Between the wars, Rupert D'Oyly Carte sponsored
a succession of London seasons and provincial tours, and gramophone
recordings were made of many of the operas. And in the late 1920s and
early 1930s, the company returned to the United States once more. The
result was that while most works that had been staged during the 1880s,
1890s and 1900s disappeared without trace after their initial London
run, the support provided by the D'Oyly Carte Company ensured that
Gilbert and Sullivan survived. Moreover, the operas themselves were
produced 'precisely in their original form, without any alteration in
their words, or any attempt to bring them up to date', and when permission was given to amateur societies to perform them, it was on
the same exacting condition that Gilbert's stage directions must be slav-
ishly followed. As a result, the operas soon ceased to be topical, and by
firmly resisting any changes, became renowned instead for being
unapologetically and proudly 'traditional'.

But this deliberate and very successful cultivation of anachronism
also suggests a deeper reason for their recovery and survival. For many
aspects of British life which by the inter-war years were regarded and
revered as 'traditional' had in fact been invented only during the last
quarter of the nineteenth century: the splendid public spectacles of monarchy, the Royal Tournament, the Henry Wood Promenade Concerts,
the old school tie, the Wimbledon tennis championships, Test Match

cricket and Sherlock Holmes, to name but a few. And to some extent at least, the Gilbert and Sullivan operas themselves survived because they had been, and thereafter remained, an integral part of this remarkably enduring late Victorian world. Their pageantry, their stirring marches, their gorgeous costumes, and their robust loyalty to crown and nation made them an essential and appropriate adjunct to the recently apotheosized monarchy. Sullivan's music was regularly played on state occasions at Buckingham Palace. The revived procession of Knights of the Garter, held at Windsor Castle, was a real-life version of the peers' entrance and march from *Iolanthe*. And when Henry Channon noted that there was a 'Gilbert and Sullivan atmosphere' about Queen Elizabeth II's unprecedentedly lavish coronation, he was essentially describing one invented British tradition in terms of another.

Notes and references

1 L. Barly, *Gilbert and Sullivan and Their World* (London, 1973), p. 92.
2 A. Hyman, *Sullivan and his Satellites: A Survey of English Operetta, 1860–1914* (Chappell, London, 1978), p. 116.
3 H. Pearson, *Gilbert: His Life and Strife* (Greenwood Press, London, 1957), p. 128.

26

The Great Reception: Surrealism and Kandinsky's Inner Eye

Mary Ann Caws

It all began with what Kandinsky sees as *non-recognition* – his own, in relation to Monet's haystack. "And suddenly," he recounts (a beginning we recognize as the classical setting for a statement about conversion or deconversion, the timing of which has to be sharp, immediate),

> And suddenly for the first time, I saw a picture. That it was a haystack, the catalogue informed me. I didn't recognize it. I found this non-recognition painful and thought that the painter had no right to paint so indistinctly. I had a dull feeling that the object was lacking in this picture. And I noticed with surprise and confusion that the picture had not only gripped me, but impressed itself ineradicably upon my memory, always hovering quite unexpectedly before my eyes, down to the last detail. . . . And, albeit unconsciously, objects were discredited as an essential element within the picture.[1]

Whether it was indeed, in this conversion or deconversion case, the lighting, the angle, some mistake or other – an upside-down hanging, as one legend runs – the result has nothing mistaken or strangely lit about it. It leads to the great discovery of Kandinsky, whom the surrealist Breton will honor as "one of the first and one of the greatest revolutionaries of vision."

Now, in the description of that non-recognition experience in all its suddenness, I am reminded of John Ruskin's sudden great "unconversion" experience at Turin, while the sermon was taking place in the pulpit and all nature was taking place outside. Ruskin left an institution, to found a new belief; he never looked back, nor did Kandinsky, to what they conceived of as a narrower outlook.

In the case of the haystack, it took the text of the catalogue to identify the subject. A haystack, it said, belonging to Monet. But now the text came in for interrogation by Kandinsky, the seer turned reader for the occasion. And he was not persuaded, he said later, looking back, by the catalogue title – that is, the *verbal* haystack. "I had the feeling that here the subject of the picture was in a sense the painting itself, and I wondered if one couldn't go much further along the same route."[2] Kandinsky, we know, went further, whether it was along the same route or not.

But is this metapainting, the painting about the painting, really the subject Kandinsky would stick to? In the final reaches of the inner soul, that soul he explicitly and repeatedly referred to, that soul he sought in all things and in all shapes and in all symbols, is the subject really just the painting itself and the painting of that painting?

"It took," Kandinsky admits, "a very long time before I arrived at the correct answer to the question: What is to replace the object?" The answer he found to this question seems not to have been "The painting itself," but the way the painting fuses freedom and necessity, a resonance of inner certainty and outer discovery, a harmony of spiritual sound made of the ideal tension of contraries, the holding-in-painting of a high-tension "internal pulse". Kandinsky's colors, vibrant on the surface of what we see, infuse and inform the depths of what we read: "I love colors simultaneously in two different ways; with the eye (and other senses) and with the soul, i.e. for their content – one would be perfectly entitled to use the today prohibited word 'symbolic'!"[3] These tensions, tightly held, control the rhythm of his verbal and visual work, based not on the limiting choice of "either/or" but on the conclusive and decisive word "and," so that his paintings, rather than reducing, cumulate, enlarge, widen. "You must open your arms wider. Wider, wider," claims his poem about seeing.[4]

These are not lessons for painting only, but life lessons, like life models. "Art," Kandinsky says, "does not seem able to follow life. Or was it maybe life that was unable to follow art? I would like to answer 'yes' to this question. A very energetic 'Yes'."[5] Art is what the soul imagines according to its inner dictates, to use another of Kandinsky's expressions: "The artist 'hears' how something or other tells him: 'Hold it! Where? The line is too long. It has to be shortened, but only a little bit!'" Or: "Do you want the red to stand out more? Good! then add some green. Now they will 'clash' a little, take off a little."[6] One must know how to "listen" when the voice sounds: it is on this point that he feels different from the surrealists, distinguishing his inner dictation

from what the surrealists term "knocking on the window of the unconscious," the hearing of which he conceives of as an outer voice.

Of course, the surrealists, far from refusing any relation to romanticism,
found themselves, as Breton said, "the tail of romanticism, but how
prehensile a tail!" I think we should consider first, however, that surrealism in its specific artists, and surrealism in its writers, still more in
its literary aesthetic theory, do not always converge even to the extent
of other movements. The theory of surrealism as of Dada before it
(Dada being more congenial to Kandinsky and far more than just the
high-camp dress rehearsal for or the negative ancestor of surrealism)
has much more in common with Kandinsky's theories and practice.
Far from simply receiving the outside world, or just building alongside
it a surreal one, as one might think from Kandinsky's initial statements
about it, surrealism is absolute in its refusal of the ordinary and the
exterior: witness Breton's repeated insistence, for example, in his essays
for *Le Surréalisme et la peinture (Surrealism and Painting)*, on an "interior model," believing, along with Pierre Reverdy, that "Creation is a
movement from the interior to the exterior and not from the exterior
over the façade."[7]

Wit and passion helped Breton to formulate surrealism's rejection of
the external element or "furniture surrounding us":

> Non-Surrealist and, to our way of thinking, regressive, is any work turned
> toward the daily spectacle of beings and things, that is, participating
> immediately in the animal, vegetable, and mineral furniture which sur-
> rounds us even if the latter should be rendered optically unrecognizable
> by being "deformed." The Surrealist work banishes resolutely anything in
> the realm of *simple* perception. . . . If the jug remains enemy number one
> here, it is understood that the Surrealist means to put in the same sack
> the little ship, the bouquet of anemones, and the obliging lady who used
> to pose either dressed or naked.[8]

Surrealism, in rejecting the still-life arrangements of jugs and flowers
and café scenes, as in cubist works, together, "it is understood," with the
coastal scenes and live models of impressionism and traditional French
art, means to create a new and inner sense of being by the analogical
energies of the human mind. Wanting more than art has given before,
surrealism states its high conviction of the internal necessity of the linking of elements, sensed in the

> spontaneous, extra-lucid, insolent relationship which is established, under
> certain conditions, between one thing and another that common sense
> would never think of bringing together. . . . The primordial contacts have

been cut: these contacts, I say, that only the analogical impulse succeeds fleetingly in reestablishing. Whence the importance assumed, at distant intervals, by these brief and infrequent sparklings of the lost mirror.[9]

In the journal *Koncretion*, Kandinsky describes the vision of most importance to him: "this experience of the 'hidden soul' in all the things, seen either by the unaided eye or through microscope or binoculars is what I call the 'internal eye.' This eye penetrates the hard shell of the external 'form,' goes deep into the object, and lets us feel with all our senses its internal pulse."[10] That it is within this eye that Breton will feel, or sense, or wish to feel and sense, the warm reception he will ascribe to Kandinsky suggests that this particular eye is not just a neutral image to be overlooked, but determined, even overdetermined, by the context and by sight itself.

Contemporary critics, imbued with reception theory of all sorts, may find themselves particularly sensitive to this projection by a poet into the eye of an artist, to what it entails and how it might be read. For in its light there may seem more fruitful topics for discussion about Kandinsky's relationship to the surrealists than are offered by, for example, his attitude towards them in his letters or his public statements – such as his guarded references to their "romanticism" in their attitude toward the exterior world:

> It seems to me that the Surrealists give precedence to the "romantic," while abstract painters, on the contrary, give precedence to the "classical." They are, nonetheless, inextricably related, since in both one can see the two forms of expression: Classicism and Romanticism. . . .
>
> Finally, the difference between these two species is that the Surrealist uses nature in his work (albeit in a surnatural way) as if it were a "plus," whereas the abstract painter omits nature as if it were a "minus."[11]

That relationship is based upon the bringing-together of distants and contraries upon the working field of surrealism, freeing surrealism, as it also frees abstract art, in both theory and practice, from what Kandinsky calls the "tyranny of the practical-purposive" into the intense and liberating resonance of inner sound, inner order, and inner depth. The non-purposive, alogical play and work of art gives full rein to the forces and tensions dynamizing the inner space where oxymorons and bipolar opposites are held in creative harmony – in the point, as it holds in check multiple tensions in the smallest visible space. Kandinsky's famous celebration of the point and Breton's equally famous celebration of the "point sublime" can be taken as the double metaphor for the poetry of surrealism itself, alogical and transforming in its intense illumination.

"If," says Kandinsky, "by magic these tensions were suddenly to disappear or die, the living work would instantly die as well."[12] The goal of poetry, as of art, says Breton, is to work against "the false laws of conventional juxtaposition" and easy evidence, so as to multiply just those short-circuits provoked by the blinding flash of contraries chanced upon or created. The "red-hot 'stuffing' inside an icy-cold chalice"[13] for which Kandinsky longs finds its double in the baroque blaze of explosive surrealist metaphors: Breton confessing his hope that the crow will return instead of the dove, the fiery hair in the black night, the bones of sun seen through the hawthorn of the rain – "oh flame of water lead me to the sea of fire." Admittedly the images are those of a romantic temperament, in contradistinction to the starker vision of Kandinsky's 1935 article called "Toile vide" ("Empty canvas") for the *Cahiers d'art*: "understanding better how to go upward and downward at the same time – at the same time 'up' (toward the heights) and 'down' (toward the depths). This power no doubt always involves extension as a natural consequence, a solemn tranquillity. One grows on all sides."[14]

But this expansion he saw himself working towards, the "polyphony" he aimed at, does not write a different program from that of the surrealists, only a different technique, different materials. They both were seeking that "inner cohesion achieved by external divergence, unity by disintegration and destruction. In the midst of anxiety, tranquillity, in the midst of tranquillity, anxiety."[15] Stretched out, every empty canvas, says Kandinsky, each empty page, says Breton after Mallarmé, is potentially a field of shock: "In appearance: truly empty, keeping silent, indifferent. Almost doltish. In reality: filled with tensions, with a thousand low voices, full of expectation."[16] The surrealist *état d'attente* or state of expectancy, transferred to the canvas or to the page, was this projection of interior tensions to the exterior surface. Against that resonating ground, the sublime point of the surrealists, conceptual rather than perceptual, and Kandinsky's graphic point, his dash extended into line, are outlined as the figures of a new art, expectant and never yet complacent.

What they were really seeking, both these revolutionaries of the eye, was the conversion of dispassion to passion, of the practical to what is beyond practice. "The accustomed eye responds dispassionately to punctuation marks. . . . The accustomed eye slithers dispassionately over objects. The dulled ear accumulates words and transmits them mechanically to the consciousness."[17] To transform that dulled eye and ear to the "astounded eye and ear" is both the graphic point of the artistic revolution and the real point of the inner enterprise of which I see them both, unabashedly, as true heroes.

The overriding attitude Kandinsky so convincingly calls the "mutual supervision" between feeling and thought Breton sees as the awareness of a continuing artistic and poetic effort named after a scientific experiment. In these "communicating vessels," he sees container and contained held in a perpetual exchange whose intense and alogical mixture of possibility and impossibility is determined by an interior freedom and interior necessity the parallel of Kandinsky's. Breton calls the awareness of this combined freedom and necessity a "lyric behavior": rereading this in the light of what we are contemplating here and today, it might not seem so distant from Kandinsky's own spiritual in art. That behavior has as its primary characteristic the recognition of the analogical marvelous, making possible that "insolent relationship between things" that alone can reveal those "brief and infrequent sparklings of the lost mirror" to which I have already referred.

The contacts re-established, in their continuity and their sparkle, bear witness to the always instantaneous clash of opposites whose reverberations render the work dynamic. Kandinsky's speculations about the ways in which these tensions energize even the empty white canvas and reside in the inner soul, the enormous potential of contraries holding against each other without resolution to lend their energy to the created work, work in his images just as in the surrealist *creed of clash*. To this Kandinsky's oxymoronic titles bear sufficient witness, from *Stable Mobility*, and *Hard, but Soft*, up to *Delicate Tensions* of 1942.

The goal of the point uniting contraries, like that of the surrealist "communicating vessels" holding container and contained in a perpetual exchange whose mobility is determined by an interior freedom and interior necessity, is what Kandinsky calls "mutual supervision" of feeling and thought. Whether in the popular language of Dada, where the yes and the no meet on street corners like grasshoppers, or in the loftier language of Breton, from whose sublime point or poetic viewpoint death and life, past and future, real and imaginary, height and depth can be seen to communicate, the goal is not to remain on that street corner or to dwell in that point: as Breton points out to his daughter, to dwell in it would be to lose it. The goal is rather that exchange of vision and the view, seeing and the seen, whose very exaltation of tone motivates Breton's own projection of his welcome within Kandinsky's vision, and of what he terms the stars of his sky with Kandinsky's thought, until their happiness seemed to him mutual, their experience shared, and their vision common: "vos oeuvres qui sont faites de la poussière des temps où l'on a été ou l'on sera encore heureux" ("Your works made of the dust of times when we were, and so will be again, happy").

This is not just wishful thinking on Breton's part – the idea that, because he so loved the art of Kandinsky (not just the two watercolors he purchased but his way of being), Kandinsky would share his vision – but what we might call projective thinking, or projective vision, or better still, *enabling* vision. Breton, who was to turn progressively from politics and the politics of revolution to a lyric and almost mystic celebration of some inner mysteries of human possibility, was never to lose the tensions, delicate and less so, between the two poles of his theory, outer and inner, in that balance Kandinsky was to call inner harmony.

Always Kandinsky equated, implicitly or explicitly, poetry and this balance of tensions between outer and inner, as of all the other dynamics of psychological creation: "Every true painting," says Kandinsky, "partakes of poetry." And elsewhere he insists that the true critic "would . . . need the soul of a poet, for the poet must be able to feel objectively in order to embody what he has experienced subjectively": he must understand the "internal necessity" of creator and creation. Breton's advocacy of the surrealist *disponibilité* or availability, this openness to outer experience or inner dictates, enables the poet to remain in touch with the "inner harmony," to hear the fundamental "inner tone" Kandinsky had seen in Munich, in 1909, as characteristic of Eastern art:

> It is precisely this general "inner tone" that the West lacks . . . we have turned, for reasons obscure to us, away from the internal towards the external. And yet, perhaps we Westerners shall not, after all, have to wait too long before the same inner sound, so strongly silenced, re-awakens within us and, sounding forth from the innermost depths, involuntarily reveals its affinity with the East. . . .[18]

And Breton evokes, in an essay on Max Ernst, an "Orient of anger and of pearls" in a lyricism based on the tension of contraries, typical always of surrealism as its emotional height: "You who are the shining image of my dispossession, Orient, beautiful bird of prey and of innocence, I implore you from the depth of the kingdom of shadows! Inspire me, so that I may be he who has no more shadow."[19]

The inner tones that Breton and Kandinsky heard were not so different, nor were their views about art. Breton's high poetic language, imbued with memories of Proustian longing, made it possible for him to seize, repeatedly, the very tone of experience remembered which is so moving in Kandinsky's *Reminiscences*, especially in the passage which cannot fail to remind us of Proust and the steeples of his narrator's

childhood on which he first practiced writing. Kandinsky shows himself
here a poet, and not just of childhood, describing

> the red, stiff, silent ring of the Kremlin Walls, and above, towering over
> everything, like a shout of triumph, like a self-oblivious hallelujah, the
> long, white, graceful, serious line of the Bell Tower of Ivan the Great.
> And upon its tall, tense neck, stretched up toward heaven in eternal
> yearning, the golden head of the cupola, which among the golden and
> colored stars of the other cupolas, is Moscow's own.
>   To paint this hour, I thought, must be for an artist the most impossible,
> the greatest joy.[20]

That the artist became the one we know, in whose inner vision the
outer bell tower took on a new shape and a new reality, whether we call
it abstract or adopt his sense of the word 'concrete,' in no way lessens
either his initial experience of the bell tower or the poetry of his style.
That very poetry, later found in other guises, is what I think Breton was
reacting to so strongly in his admiration for Kandinsky. Not just the
colors, or the shapes, or the technique of what he painted, but what he
was able to see with his inner eye. The 'lyric behavior' about which the
surrealists cared always and deeply has not to do with one's manner of
living or doing politics or not doing them, or this or that, but, and most
genuinely, with how one sees and with what depth that is transcribed.

What is most striking about Kandinsky's writings on art may not be his
frequently stated concern about the inner necessity, the inner eye, and
the inner element, but rather his accurate and strangely precise meditations on specific issues. I am thinking here of the quite remarkable
passages on, for example, what happens to the color red by itself, with
its potential energy, or in combination with other colors, or painted
on a tree, or a dress, or a horse – those passages comparing the color
to music (if darkened, it is like the middle or lower registers of the cello;
if brightened, like the clear tones of the violin; if warmed by yellow, like
a church bell, a contralto voice, or a viola playing a largo; if cooled
down, like the cor anglais). His meditations are full of nuance about the
psychology of perception and association, as about punctuation: the
period or the point and its introversion, its concision, and its concentric
tension; the dash as the extension of the point, and how it comes to play
a role beyond that of the practical–purposive on a canvas; or the graphic
arabesque "often seeming deceptively like a world of total freedom, but
which conceals its servile subordination."
   If we are tempted to think that Kandinsky's later writings on art
became, with his conversion to the concrete, less poetic or any less rich

in surprises in perspective and odd slants of vision than in his reminiscences of Moscow, then we have only to read the conclusion of his essays called "Toile vide," published in Christian Zervos's *Cahiers d'art* in Paris, 1935, from which I have already quoted. The conclusion runs, "I look through my window. Several chimney stacks of lifeless factories rise silently. They are inflexible. All of a sudden, smoke rises from a single chimney. The wind catches it and it instantly changes color. The whole world has changed."[21] This passage too is about color, as in the writings on art just commented upon, but is more profoundly about seeing, as was his poem "Seeing" (quoted earlier) read in 1916 at the Cabaret Voltaire. It is also, more broadly, about the sensitivity to detail that can best be called poetic, in the wider sense: "The critic would need the soul of a poet. . . ."[22]

With that concentration on detail, with that special looking ("Seeing") of Kandinsky, whether with the inner or outer eye, Breton's own angle of vision of the same period was completely congenial. From the 1934 poem "Toujours pour la première fois" ("Always for the first time"):

> The elusive angle of a curtain
> A field of jasmine I found at dawn by a road near Grasse
> The diagonal slant of its girls picking[23]

"The whole world has changed," we remember Kandinsky saying. To thank him for the drypoint Kandinsky had sent for a volume of his poetry, at Breton's suggestion, René Char sent him a poem called simply "Migration" (1934). Its very beginning echoes the same feeling of change, of sudden angling, of displacement:

> Le poids du raisin modifie la position des feuilles
> La montagne avait un peu glissé.

> (The weight of the grape alters the leaves' position.
> The mountain had slipped a little.)[24]

By this displacement, all three poets and seers are placed nearer our own present perspective, surviving in part by that ability to detect a slippage in our grasp of things.

Now, Breton, of course, was not just a critic with the soul of a poet, but a poet with the eye of an art lover, understanding angles, caring about the slant of the object seen, and knowing about the reception of a view within the eye. How we read is really what is at issue here: not so much how Kandinsky read the art of surrealism, not so much what he borrowed or included from Miró, for example, as what of surrealist theory and vision, what of its real pulse and its real soul, past the hard kernel of its actual or supposed form, might indeed have merited that only projected reception in his inner if not his outer eye.

For, if surrealism found in itself a passion for the essential conjunction of inner necessity and outer chance, in relation to which encounter its expectancy was endless, and a passion for the unity between inner perception and its linking power, these are exactly the qualities Breton finds to praise in Kandinsky. His high lyric tone of celebration is equivalent to Kandinsky's loftiest prose, and makes me surmise it no accident that Kandinsky should have given him a piece called "Volant," or "Soaring." Breton's preface for Kandinsky's exhibit at Peggy Guggenheim's London gallery in 1938, as translated by Beckett, emphasizes the essential, the analogical, and that fusion we find also in Kandinsky's poem "Fused Chain," comparable in its longing for continuity to Breton's crystal chain discoverable by analogy: "I know of no painter more apt to distinguish the essential from the accidental of circumstance.... He has found a punctuation that fuses into one the firmament of stars, a page of music, and all the eggs of all the nests under heaven."[25]

The view surrealism took of itself and of its own risk-taking can be shown to parallel the view Kandinsky took of his art and of its ancestral figures. *Du côté de chez le Douanier*: the figure chosen by Kandinsky and whom I would choose here, among possible others, is that of the Douanier Rousseau, with his frontally posed forms and his will-to-flatness, effecting an extraordinary iconic isolation from conventionally pictured "reality" and simultaneously from other ways of seeing. He projects from within, which is exactly that quality Breton salutes in him, cherishing it as emblematic of his own endeavors.

Breton's celebration of the Douanier, through whom, he said, his own sinuous and freely chosen *non-party line* could be seen to pass, of this Rousseau whose work he saw as exchanging sparks with that of Jean-Jacques, and whose genius he saw as a force moving outward to expression from an interior strength, implies a defense of that in-to-out direction rather than a capitulation to or reception of the exterior emblems of any institutionalized grouping, including that of surrealism itself. It is this isolating social and artistic risk which is undervalued when Breton is limited to the all-too-easy identification with the more obvious products of visual surrealist art.

Breton is not without self-reflection, I think, in recalling "The jeers that greeted, but did not discourage the artistic effort of the Douanier Rousseau, who had vowed to develop his potential for instinctive expression independent of any school." Breton's own projected reception in Kandinsky's sight, which had so warmly received Rousseau, should be read in terms of self-recognition and self-definition, worked out through the reception of the other.

"Every true painting partakes of poetry," said Kandinsky, celebrating what he himself termed an *open eye*. It was just this sort of vision he was gifted with – not the eye of reflection but that of creation. It envisions continuities:

> I say that the eye is not *open* as long as it limits itself to the passive role of a mirror – even if the transparency of that mirror offers some interesting peculiarity: exceptionally limpid, or sparkling, or bubbling or faceted. . . . It was created for the purpose of throwing a line across, of laying down a conduit between things of the most heterogeneous appearance. This line, pliable in the extreme, should enable one to grasp in a minimum of time the relationships which link, with no continuity to explain them, innumerable physical and mental structures.[26]

With what I hope is an equally open eye, I have tried here to rediscover the inner links between two critics and visionaries, whose own continuity is not obvious, even in the fused syntagmatic space of artistic discourse that was, and is, Paris. Between these two seers, opposed in appearance and in character, the relationships could have only been understated on one side and unstated on the other. Meyer Schapiro points out that, in Kandinsky's case, "The most responsive spectator is . . . the individual who is similarly concerned with himself and who finds in such pictures not only the counterpart of his own tension, but a final discharge of obsessing feelings."[27] Breton's celebration of Kandinsky's eye and his projection of his own reception within it is more than a touching artwish. I have taken it as a clue not just to one of them, but to both.

Finally, to return to Kandinsky's statement about surrealism as turned toward the outer world: in the actual consciousness of reading-as-exchange of inner and outer, the present rebellion against fixed categories in their supposed stability as yesterday's too-facile limits see themselves deconstructed, might not the reader question whether the absolute opposition established here between the two poles of in and out is not already challenged by the pulsations painting and writing create? The surrealist faith – "What is possible," or, elsewhere, "what is imagined, tends to become the real" – has as much to do with inner dictates as did the dreams of Henri Rousseau, and his dictated painting. It is, in surrealism, the outer world which reveals the inner, some chance encounter showing us, as Breton so movingly puts it, "an answer to the question we did not know we had." But the chance is to be waited for, the surprise to be prepared, and the burden is not, finally, on the outside world but on us. What Kandinsky calls an "inner directive" or intuition is finally not so different from the directive discovered inside at the epiphanic moment when an exterior encounter – of an object, a person, a voice, a painting – becomes what I would call an *enabling object* or encounter, like Kandinsky's own encounter with the Monet haystack.

Now, with a certain poetic or critical license, I want to imagine a tale, or at least a comparison, on the following lines. What if, against the received opinion of the diametrical opposition between Kandinsky and the surrealists he was not always prone to laud, Breton's own gradual turning-inwards, after his disillusionment with political revolution – that turning-inwards for which he was and is frequently under attack from the more politicized surrealists and surrealist sympathizers of then and now – came to crystallization when he came under Kandinsky's spell at Jeanne Bucher's gallery in Paris in 1936? Writing to him after the exhibition, he projects a strong feeling of companionship:

> I haven't had the time to tell you what a strong spell the works I saw chez Madame Bucher cast over me. They are made of the essence of all the times we have been happy and will be happy again. Do you know, dear Kandinsky, that, to speak the language of astrologers, many of the stars of my heavens have met a warm welcome in your eye?

Earlier, as I suggested, he had been warmly impressed with Kandinsky, recommending him to René Char for a prefatory drypoint illustration for Char's celebrated *Le Marteau sans maître* (*The Hammer with no Master*, now doubly celebrated through the music of Pierre Boulez), those oddly powerful texts of dream and waking quite as inwardly directed as Kandinsky's own. *Seeing* (the title of Kandinsky's text read at the Cabaret Voltaire on one of those Dada evenings) is quite surely what surrealism was and is mostly about – seeing wider and deeper, and seeing into the profounder self we call soul. The distance between Kandinsky's art, whether he called it concrete or abstract, and that impressionist or romantic figuring he turned away from is one Breton and Char, in their different ways, traversed also: Breton, towards a passionate engagement with the innate possibilities of dream and inner revolution; Char, towards a conception of poetry which was to link the moral with the aesthetic, like the most modest and well-tilled land with the highest texts that land could nourish, with its inner gods.

We recollect the "fused chain" of Kandinsky's poem of that title. Breton's vision of a crystal chain in the necessary and inwardly seen connection of the universe and human sight, that chain "where not one link is missing," has nothing of the logical about it. "Art," says Breton in relation to Kandinsky's paintings, "has never been logical" but has rather been alogical. It is with that perception of alogicality – linked with inner and not outer necessity – that Breton was to celebrate, more than once, Kandinsky's vision, and to merge his own vision of a crystal chain: "His admirable eye, merging with his faint veil of glass to form perfect crystal, lights up with the sudden iridescent glitter of quartz. It is the eye of one of the first and one of the greatest revolutionaries of vision."[28] For, with that inner determination of all great artists, and all great revolutionaries of vision, Kandinsky and Breton both sought the "reciprocal permeation" of inner and outer, the "inner tone" and the "inner eye" informing that high-tension chain of exchange, the vibrations of inner objects whose sounds and colors only we perceive, stretched to their very innermost limits to create the pulse and the "interior pressure" of a possible art that life could follow, were it only to dare.

Kandinsky's poem "Seeing" begins by starting afresh: "That's where everything begins . . ."; [29] and concludes by a brief warning the critic with a poet's soul might see as directed to some deconversion from a simpler art, moving from non-recognition to recognition. "You can't go back," as he says in "Water."[30] That great Dadaist and early surrealist Tzara, for whom Kandinsky illustrated a book called, not unsignificantly, *La Main passe* (*The Hand Passes*), had spoken in 1917, in a "Note on Art," of how the making hand joins with sight at its most intense. No better rendering has been made of what links Kandinsky to the surrealist mode of seeing: "Art is at present the only construction complete unto itself, about which nothing more can be said, it is such richness, vitality, sense, wisdom. Understanding, seeing. Describing a flower: relative poetry more or less paper flower. Seeing."[31]

Notes and references

1   Wassily Kandinsky, *Complete Works on Art*, ed. Kenneth Lindsay and Peter Verbo (G.K. Hall, Boston, Mass., 1982), p. 363. Further references prefixed *CWA*.
2   *Encyclopaedia Britannica*, 11th edn (1956), vol. XX, pp. 377–9.
3   *CWA*, p. 738.
4   Wassily Kandinsky, *Klange/Sounds*, tr. Elizabeth R. Napier (Yale University Press, New Haven, Conn., 1981), p. 21. Further references prefixed *K*.
5   *CWA*, p. 801.
6   *CWA*, p. 799.
7   André Breton, *Le Surréalisme et la Peinture* (Gallimard, Paris, 1965), p. 4.
8   André Breton, *La Clé des Champs* (Editions du Sagittaire, Paris, 1953), p. 100.

9   Ibid., pp. 111–13.
10 *CWA*, p. 832.
11 *CWA*, p. 743.
12 *CWA*, p. 548.
13 *CWA*, p. 781.
14 *CWA*, p. 782.
15 *CWA*, p. 783.
16 *CWA*, p. 780.
17 *CWA*, p. 423.
18 *CWA*, p. 59.
19 André Breton, *Point du Jour* (Gallimard, Paris, 1934), p. 35.
20 *CWA*, p. 361.
21 *CWA*, p. 783.
22 *CWA*, p. 249.
23 André Breton, *Selected Poems of André Breton*, ed. and tr. Jean-Pierre
    Cauvin and Mary Ann Caws (University of Texas Press, Austin, Tex., 1983),
    p. 109.
24 René Char, *Poems*, tr. Mary Ann Caws and Jonathan Griffin (Princeton
    University Press, Princeton, N.J., 1976), p. 23.
25 Breton, *Le Surréalisme et la Peinture*, p. 286.
26 Ibid., p. 199.
27 Meyer Schapiro, *Modern Art: 19th and 20th Centuries* (Braziller, New York,
    1978), p. 199.
28 *CWA*, p. 938.
29 *K*, p. 21.
30 *K*, p. 65.
31 Tristan Tzara, *Approximate Man and Other Writings*, ed. and tr. Mary Ann
    Caws (Wayne State University Press, Detroit, Mich., 1973).

Barthes on Theatre

Michael Moriarty

Barthes's writings on the theatre are far more abundant than one might suppose from the scant amount of critical attention devoted to them. On the other hand, this lack of interest is easily comprehensible. It is not just that Barthes's discussion of theatre is in parts ephemeral. To talk about theatre is to talk about institutions: very 'impure' theory. Then again, the political commitment is intense and explicit, and Barthes's later adoption of a more nuanced (to say the least) ideological position seems to authorize neglect of writings imbued with his earlier convictions, except where, as with *Mythologies*, the theoretical innovations of a work keep it in the critical gaze. It is also true that Barthes himself lost interest in the theatre and in theatrical debates in the early 1960s, and that his theatre criticism is less original than other parts of his work. Yet, quite apart from the general point that it is always worth looking at what is going on when something is forgotten, the statement quoted at the head of this chapter suggests that to forget Barthes's connections with the theatre is to miss something important.

A keen theatre-goer in his teens, as a student, Barthes helped to found the Groupe de théâtre antique of the Sorbonne. He played Darius in a production of Aeschylus' *The Persians* of which there is a photograph in *Roland Barthes par Roland Barthes*. He prepared a Diplôme d'Etudes Supérieures on incantations and evocations in Greek tragedy and was regarded as sufficiently expert on Greek theatre to have been commissioned to write the entry on it for the *Histoire des spectacles* volume of the prestigious *Encyclopédie de la Pléiade*. During the 1950s he became associated with the journal *Théâtre populaire*, committed to breaking with the conventions and institutions of bourgeois theatre, and bringing progressive theatre to a broad public. Barthes's reviews and other articles for *Théâtre populaire* and other publications are numerous, wide-ranging, and unfailingly thought-provoking.

For Barthes in the 1950s theatre held a special position. It offered a hope of escaping from the impasse of literature so pessimistically diagnosed in *Le Degré zéro de l'écriture*: literature is a bourgeois phenomenon; to challenge its conventions is therefore subversive; but, equally, that subversion is purely ethical and aesthetic in character and is easily reabsorbed by the bourgeois order. The avant-garde has an unwitting inoculative function, like some of the messages analysed in *Mythologies*; it is bourgeois culture injecting itself with a little freedom, a little subjectivity, the better to resist external threat. The most the avant-garde novel (as exemplified by Robbe-Grillet) can do is to estrange the reader from the essentialist art of the bourgeois novel by subverting its own founding categories of character and plot. It cannot be both in accordance with its time and in advance of it.

Yet theatre can. It can express both the way things are, and the will-to-be of human beings. It can protest against the world, and yet reconcile us to it in the sense of making it comprehensible. At least some theatre can. In particular Brecht. Seventeen years after the Berliner Ensemble, directed by Brecht himself, visited Paris in 1954, Barthes was still writing of being bedazzled by the experience of seeing them, what he elsewhere calls 'une illumination subite . . . un incendie' (a sudden illumination . . . a blaze).[1]

In the 1955 article 'La Révolution brechtienne', originally an editorial in *Théâtre populaire*, Barthes summarizes the assumptions challenged by Brecht, assumptions so deeply rooted in the Western tradition that they seem merely natural: that theatre consists in the imitation of an action, with which, and in particular with the hero of which, the audience is led to identify, chiefly through the actor's identification with the character. These assumptions could be summed up in two words: psychology and analogy.

'Psychology' is the great enemy: the belief that theatre depicts individuals, states of mind so as to produce an emotional effect on the audience. In Greek drama, Barthes argues, the feelings of the characters are important only as expressions of social and political alignments. But since the classical period of French literature, 'psychology' means considering states of mind in isolation from, and as an evasion of, the political. And there is a more general critique of the notion of character as a fixed essence motivating individual acts. This essentialism, and Barthes's denunciation of it, applies both in literature and in life. It is the foundation of the discourse of law and punishment: the notion of character serves to elide social and cultural differences, permits lawyers and judges to tell convincing stories that can lead to the death of a human being. This critique is not, of course, peculiar to Barthes. 'Character', for psychoanalysis, is derivative rather than primary, the precipitate of psychological conflicts. For Marxism, individual character has no explanatory significance. Sartre criticizes the limitations of psychological explanations of the individual. In literature, 'character' as a value, severely circumscribed by the modernists (Proust, Joyce, Kafka), was eliminated root and branch by the *nouveaux romanciers* of the 1950s. For Artaud, the focus on individual character and emotional conflicts makes theatre incapable of raising questions about the existing social and moral, let alone the metaphysical, order.

Yet the primacy of psychology is inscribed in the theatrical institution. The theatre-goer pays for his seat, and expects value for money: an actor literally sweating to produce emotion. This quantitative aesthetic (part and parcel of the bourgeois world-view outlined in *Mythologies*) causes the text to be treated as an accumulation of discrete effects, marking the transaction between spectator and actors, rather than as an aesthetic whole. The public consumes Racine as a series of set-piece speeches (*tirades*), not the plays as dramatic wholes; the 'bourgeois art of detail' and the bourgeois myth of Racine have a disastrous effect on the actors' delivery. Racine is supposed to be 'psychological', so they labour to transmit psychological insights by dwelling on nuances of meaning; but he is also 'musical', hence a quite contradictory attempt at melodic diction. These struggles for effect obscure communication between the characters, and deform the verse-structure of the alexandrine, the true source of the music.

For an alternative to this theatrical ideology and practice it is hardly surprising that Barthes should have turned to Brecht. Brecht holds that the audience's involvement in the action should be partial, so that it is conscious of what is going on, not merely passively submitting to an experience; the actor should foster this consciousness by pointing to his role, not fusing himself with it; the spectator should not be led to identify completely with the hero, but remain sufficiently detached to be able to assess the causes of, and the remedies for, his suffering; the theatre should tell a story, not *(pace* Aristotle) imitate an action; and it should be a critical and intellectual, rather than a magical, experience; psychological conflicts should be replaced by historical conflicts.

This dramaturgy alone is in accordance with the major progressive themes of the age, which I shall restate without (postmodern) irony: our troubles are self-inflicted, therefore removable by human action; art can and should intervene in history, and should collaborate with the sciences to this end; its function is explanation, not only expression; it should help history on its way by showing how it works; staging techniques are in themselves ideological options; there are no eternal canons of art, but art must be constantly reinvented in keeping with the goal of liberating society.

The critique of empathy may be illustrated by two of Barthes's examples, one from cinema, the other from Brecht himself. At the end of *On the Waterfront*, after going through hell to free his fellow-workers from an oppressive labour union, Marlon Brando has to lead them back to work under the eye of a caricatural fat capitalist with a cigar. Since Brando is being visibly exploited by the capitalist, and the capitalist is visibly unpleasant, this looks like a left-wing representation. Nothing of the kind, says Barthes: Brando is the hero, and so the viewer is being invited to identify with his heroic gesture in leading the other workers back, to perceive it as a return to order. The boss may be unpleasant, but the system he represents thus comes across as an eternal Necessity, the submissive worker as a tragic, therefore impotent, hero. Brecht would have shown Brando's character as sympathetic, but also muddled about the real causes of his own and his fellows' oppression. Again, in *Mother Courage* what we are shown is not the sufferings of an eternal mother-figure, but an individual failing to come to grips with her historical situation – and suffering cruelly as a result. We participate in Mother Courage's blindness, at the same time as we are made aware of it. As Barthes elsewhere observes, to see someone else not seeing is the best way to see intensely what he or she does not see.

So far, Barthes has basically done little more than assimilate the major Brechtian positions to his own experience of theatre. But in an article of 1956 on 'the tasks of Brechtian criticism', he begins to speak of Brecht's theatre in explicitly semiological terms. In so doing he challenges the notion of theatrical representation as analogous, founded on likeness to what it represents. The goal of Brecht's dramaturgy is not, he says, to express, but to signify the real. It therefore institutes a certain distance in the relation between signifier and signified, lest that relation be perceived as natural. An example from Brecht: a Chinese actor has to represent 'terror'. He does not quake all over, simply hides his face in his hands, and when he looks up his face is dead white because of the white make-up on his hands. For the rest, he is calm. The physical state of terror and its sign are kept quite distinct. The relation between them is explicitly conventional, in that sense arbitrary. The actor's movements are not replicas of the real effects of the state he is depicting. This distancing is ideologically crucial. For to naturalize the sign, running it together with that which it refers, is characteristic of bourgeois culture, unable to tolerate signification as such, because signification, being cultural, reminds bourgeois culture that it too is cultural, an effect of history, not a manifestation of Nature. But the naturalization of art is also characteristic of Stalinism, with its judgement that bourgeois aesthetic conventions are less dangerous than the attempt to challenge them. Political commitment in art again appears, for Barthes, as a commitment to form, not to a revolutionary content which discards form as bourgeois. Although suspicious of the non-Brechtian theatrical avant-garde, Barthes thus welcomes its formal and technical innovations as means of detaching politically progressive theatre from conventions that simply harness it to the established order.

Like his treatment of realism in the novel, Barthes's discussions of the semiology of theatre raise the question whether it is being offered as a general semiological theory of representation or as a way of classifying and evaluating texts. Take Greek theatre. On one level, it can be viewed as a complex semiological system combining dance, music, and poetry. The actors wore masks (originally expressionless, impersonal); costumes were highly conventional, sets symbolic; the actors were few, and the chorus highly important; the dances performed by the chorus were coded, legible, not merely visually or emotionally striking. Yet apparently all this could coexist with a tremendous impression of presence: the spectators of Aeschylus' *Eumenides* fled in terror when the Furies appeared. The spectator is by turns required to decode a set of symbols and confronted with immediate reality: he encounters a super-reality, not signs instead of the world, but the world plus its signs. As Barthes points out, the realism of an art cannot be gauged independently of the mentality of its audience (its belief in the gods, for instance). Conventions of representation, too, must be taken into account: since the impact of Aeschylus' Furies seems to have been due to the break with tradition involved in their entering one by one, we may say that realism here is also an effect of the transgression of the conventions or codes.

Strong codes, strong transgressions: this is what, I think, Barthes means by 'dialectical realism'. Yet this turns out to be a historical phase (Aeschylus, maybe Sophocles). It is succeeded by an analogical realism (Euripides), in which increasingly the representation tends to *look like* reality, instead of signifying it in distanced form or apparently embodying it directly. Masks become expressive, the chorus's role declines, sets become complex; perhaps, also, the audience has simply become used to representation, less and less likely to confuse the figure on stage with the real thing, more and more prone, however, to require that the one should resemble the other. Euripidean theatre increasingly makes a value of (ominous word) interiority: staging techniques permit the manifestation of what is *inside*, the corpses in the palace, the gods in Olympus; just as the masks lose their impersonality and come to indicate a psychological essence behind them. Greek theatre is already undergoing *embourgeoisement*. Both comedy and tragedy cease to put questions to the world and to society, and fall back on the depiction of character: and, paradoxically, this aesthetic decline goes hand in hand with the etiolation of the theatre's religious dimension, an effect of ideological 'progress'.

The accuracy of this narrative is of less importance to us than its form. It is anti-teleological. Not just in that plainly, for Barthes, it registers a decline – as with 'white writing', we have a powerful new mode of representation that with time becomes defused and domesticated; not just in its assertion of the non-correspondence of aesthetic and ideological development; but also in that its logic reverses the logic we apply to our own history; as if modern bourgeois theatre were a falling-away from an original Brechtian purity. Despite the differences between them, the apparent naïvety of the early theatre and its spectators is more akin to Brechtian sophistication; the Greek theatre develops towards what modern theatre tries to escape from: analogical realism. For Barthes, the copy is always a negative value; he can desire only the sign, or alternatively the thing itself. This opposition between, on the one hand, two values themselves antithetical and, on the other, the mean that is supposed to reconcile them, or to combine what is valuable in each while excluding their negative qualities, this promotion of the extremes against the middle, is a constant in Barthes: 'une constante, c'est-à-dire un sens', he says himself in this essay, in another context. It sets him, of course, against a whole tradition of post-Aristotelian ethics and aesthetics, just as his interpretation of Greek theatre is premised on values diametrically opposed to those upheld by Aristotle, and reminiscent of those he finds in Brecht.

We find then that, as *Le Degré zéro de l'écriture* seemed to suggest in connection with the novel, there is no general attempt to reduce realism to an effect of signification. The Aeschylean theatre could incorporate, not, obviously, the reality of the Furies, but a mode of representing them that went beyond likeness to suggest direct presence. The spectator's distance from the spectacle was not reduced to the consistent safe minimum of the later theatre, but, suddenly, almost abolished. Likewise, the modernist novel could incorporate chunks of social discourse not kept at a safe distance by a dominant narratorial language, distanced only by their combination with other discourses, by the plurality of the text. To this extent, Barthes is prepared at this stage to accept, along with an art of pure signification, a realism of direct presentation; and this would throw light on the value he accords to photography. What he will not accept is analogical realism as an aesthetic value. In literature, indeed, it is not even a possibility: writing simply cannot copy reality (only signify or incorporate it, in the sense we have seen), and if it appears to do so, this is purely an effect of literary mechanisms such as mode of discourse and tense-structure. In theatre, obviously, some kind of likeness to reality can be directly conveyed. But that, for Barthes, is never very interesting.

Semiology, then, is invoked to gauge the ideological and/or aesthetic effect of various kinds of theatre. The language of this evaluation is frequently ethical, even hygienic. Brecht spoke of Chinese acting technique, with its alienation effects, as 'healthier' than its Western counterpart, and Barthes systematically prolongs this type of expression. There can be a pathology of the sign: theatre costumes are prone to various diseases. Alongside an honest, ludic, duplicity of the sign, as in wrestling, there is also a hypocritical duplicity. Mankiewicz's film of *Julius Caesar* almost attains a healthy comic effect by grafting Roman fringes onto American faces, but this is plainly unintended. The sign is systematically naturalized. The characters sweat, in token of an omnipresent moral dilemma, but their anguish is allowed literally to exude from them: there is no distancing of signifier from signified. The body is present purely as a carrier of the sign, but instead of frankly asserting itself as such (like the Chinese actor's body) it serves to disguise the sign as a physical emanation. The sign is thereby degraded; but so is the body. For the body is a theatrical value in its own right; theatre is among other things a festival of the human body.

The use of semiological concepts in the analysis of theatre and cinema thus reflects three of Barthes's major concerns of the 1950s: the responsibility of form (form as asserting political and ethical values); the critique of existing theatre, and the promotion of Brechtian theory and practice; beyond this, the general critique of bourgeois and petty-bourgeois culture and ideology. But there is yet no full-scale semiology of theatre. He sketches in the main outlines of such a semiology in 'Littérature et signification' (1963). Theatre is a 'cybernetic machine', emitting multiple simultaneous messages, from the set, the costumes, the lighting, the movements and speeches of the actors, which function, however, at different rhythms. Theatricality, then, is this density of signs, and the crucial problem for semiology is the relationship between them: between analogical visual codes and non-analogical codes, for instance, such as that of language.

But more particularly 'Littérature et signification' suggests a new relationship between value-judgement and semiological analysis. Attention shifts from the ideological signified transmitted by a set of formal signifiers and capable of being summarized separately to a *process* of signification. Barthes now denies that, for all its explicit political concerns, Brecht's theatre has a positive message. What his theatre shows is not, say, that capitalism is exploitative, but that the world requires to be deciphered, that it has no inner meaning for theatre to express. At the point where the Marxist message is about to take shape, solidify, Brecht halts the process of signification, so it ends in a question, not a solution. The solution is left to the spectator to work out. The suspension of meaning is also characteristic of avant-garde Absurdist theatre, which subverts ordinary language and theatrical convention; but in this case, the question being vaguer, the answer kept at a distance is less powerful than with Brecht, the tension between the insistence of the answer and its deferral less striking.

Whatever the worth of this analysis, the point here is to compare it with the earlier and apparently similar claim that Brecht does not deliver ready-made Marxist slogans but reinvents Marxism through the working-out of concrete situations. Barthes's goal is no longer to defend Brecht against the charge of propaganda, but to enlist him into the resistance to the signified in the name of the signifying process. What is at stake in this revaluation of Brecht and of the goal of semiology will emerge from later chapters.

Brecht's name appears in the title of two pieces by Barthes from the 1970s. The more celebrated, 'Diderot, Brecht, Eisenstein', I shall leave for another occasion. I deal with 'Brecht et le discours' now in order to point to Barthes's apparent need to go on working in company with Brecht, even though Brecht no longer means the same to him as twenty years earlier. Brecht is invoked to guarantee the value of various techniques and strategies adopted by Barthes in that interval. These will be more fully discussed elsewhere, and they appear in this chapter only in summary form.

First of all, Brecht is praised as one who pierces the layers of language that surround us like the atmosphere; the virtue of Brecht's theatre is to clarify the air, to make us suddenly conscious of the provenance and destination of the particular linguistic substances we normally inhale without realizing. Its characteristic effect is the jolt ('la secousse'). Thus, when Brecht brings the bourgeois Herr Puntila drunk on stage, the point is not, mimetically, to suggest that the typical bourgeois is a drunkard: rather, drunkenness disturbs Puntila's language just enough to reveal the nature of his relationship to his subordinates (and intellec-tually, not by arousing a moral protest: Puntila is actually nicer when drunk).

Brecht's valorization of discontinuity ('each scene for itself') is again taken up by Barthes. Generally, what Walter Benjamin calls the 'fits and starts' of epic theatre are seen as functioning to forestall the crystal-lization of empathetic response, and to produce the necessary space for the gestus to be read. Barthes takes Brecht to witness a rather different point: continuity is what produces the 'truth-effect' of false discourses. To break up a discourse can thus reveal the spuriousness of its truth-claims; equally, to break up one's own discourse preserves it from the contagion of falsity imparted to it by the continuity that would char-acterize it as Truth. Again, the aim is to avoid allowing definitive meaning to solidify. The interrogative non-conclusive nature of Brecht's theatre, praised in 'Littérature et signification', is here more specifically explained by its deliberately episodic and fragmentary structure: a structure that Barthes, for this very reason, himself adopts in the essay, as in most of his writings of the 1970s.

The issues raised by this reformulation of Barthes's debt to Brecht require fuller treatment. Moreover, theatre as such (with the exception of the Japanese puppet theatre) ceases to interest him after the early 1960s. Meanwhile, the point has been to show theatre as one of the key areas in which Barthes's twofold concern, to theorize and to judge the process of signification, finds expression, and to suggest that, of the writers who 'thought in Barthes's head', Brecht is not the least important.

Note

1   R. Barthes, 'Témoignage sur le théâtre', *Esprit*, May (1965), p. 834.

28

Fashion, Taste and Eating Out

Joanne Finkelstein

In contemporary Western society, continuous consumption and the pursuit of fashion are accepted as respectable preoccupations. When the pursuit of fashion is extended to include everyday commodities such as new food products vividly displayed in supermarkets and in media advertisements, new styles of eating such as grazing, the fashioning of local heroes from star sports players or media personalities, in short, when the ordinary entertainments of daily life are transposed into fashions, then we have a culture dominated by an ethic that sees value in the ever-shifting and continuous renewal of the new. Fashionability, not only of the kind attached to the purchase of exclusive items but also of the daily recasting of the ordinary into the extraordinary, has become a motif of modernity and a characterizing feature of modern social life which has influence on everyone's conduct irrespective of class and status.

Spending time and money on appearance, on entertainments and pastimes as if they were consumer items, and having discretionary power of consumption is taken, in modern society, as a sign of good fortune and an emblem of social prestige. Through conspicuous consumption and competitive display the individual can claim a particular self-image and social value. By interweaving fashionability with the individual's self-image and sense of social location, an implicit theory of human sociality is being stated which specifically grants to the individual who follows fashion a strong sense of delight in the changing nature of the world. Fashions allow him/her to sense a degree of self-control over the external realm and to feel as if s/he has some mastery over what have been traditionally regarded as the ineluctable movements of history. For the individual to be in fashion seems to provide him/her with a locus in history. This fusing of oneself with the times (with the temporal which is commonly thought the most unassailable and unassimilative of social facts in that one cannot turn the clock back or forward, or stop it), can seem as if one has escaped the inevitable ravages and domination of time. In other words, to be fashionable makes it seem possible to achieve a sense of timelessness because one has gained a semblance of control over the present and, with this purchase or leverage, one has enfeebled the inevitable march of time by making it of only fleeting importance.

Particular habits of dress, styles of gastronomy, household furnishings, shapes of cars and so on have been useful in establishing historical periods. For instance, the fashion of the male necktie emerging from the seventeenth-century cravat can be used to date a change in the status of men's appearance. At the end of the Regency period, and after the decline of Beau Brummell's influence, about the 1840s, the necktie's transformation into its modern guise can usefully mark the end of men as fashion slaves and the beginning of women in this role. Fashions, in this sense, identify specific periods and contexts. Fashion and time are intricately connected. The way that fashion is used in this study is to make the idea itself a historical indicator. That is, the currency of fashionability in the commerce of daily life is itself an indicator of a specific historical epoch, in this case, the age of modernity. Fashions need not be only conceived of as a periodizing artefact, fashionability itself can be characteristic of an era.

The view of fashion as a historical marker is useful and interesting; however, the way in which the concept is used in this study is not to concentrate on particular items of fashion unique to certain times and places; rather, the intention is to show how fashion itself has become a technique employed in the daily commerce of individuals to produce a specific moral and ethical character of social relations. Fashion has been described as the essence of modernity, as 'an ideal for which the restless human mind feels a constant, titillating hunger'.[1] The continuous manufacture of change which fashion produces, and the implication it carries of the plasticity of the social world, means that all mannerisms, practices and objects can be re-evaluated and transformed into a fashion. When any object or practice can be redefined as valuable and desirable, then there can be no claims to enduring, permanent standards of worth and no intrinsically superior criteria which guide the discourses of the everyday. In a society where no object has any inherent value and where any substance or device can become fashionable at any moment, the general social ethos is one of ethical promiscuity.

In a milieu where there is widespread interest in fashion, individuals become deeply enthralled in the present and are eager to live within the moment. They avoid any sustained interrogation of the meaning or social significance of those objects and practices which have come to be esteemed. The transitory nature of fashion makes it especially attractive to those individuals who are restless and have the most to gain from social change. From this position, the fashionable can be regarded as the most dangerous in society because they seek out change without requiring a reason or principle for it. In their view change is always the harbinger of progress and democracy. The argument presented here is that fashionability allows individuals who follow the imperatives of fashion to abandon the responsibility to make history and shape culture. In this chapter I explore the effect of fashionability on modern social relations through the example of the increasingly popular practice of dining out.

[⋯]

The fashionability of restaurant rests with its capacity to represent itself as an arbiter of an abstract commodity which means having the ability to assert its own fashionability either through its exclusivity, physical location, head waiter, tableware, wine cellar or some other element in the repertoire of dining out. Its fashionability may rest on the publicity and image propagated by the restaurateur; the restaurant may be fashionable because it has tapestry wall coverings that are known as 'works of art' and by choosing to dine there one is suggesting an association between the elegance of the restaurant's atmosphere and one's own aesthetic sensibilities, or the restaurant may be popular with a particular set with whom one wishes to identify, say, the Establishment, the Fringe, the Bohemian, or the Glitterati. There are, indeed, restaurants with names such as The Establishment, The Society, The Bohemian, Grazing and so on, which are thereby advertising that the diner will meet up with the group to which s/he aspires.

What makes a specific restaurant fashionable has less to do with actual features of the restaurant and more to do with fluctuations in cultural meanings and patterns of consumer interests. It is for this reason that fashion is an integral part of a study of modern manners. The fashionability of dining out follows the same principle which designates other items of the everyday, such as styles in clothing, music, sports, certain ideas and customs, as items of high consumer interest. Importantly, the association of fashionability with the restaurant has less to do with the nature of restaurants and more to do with the practice of fashion. The restaurant emerges as an example of how the cult of fashion can affect human sociality and how the meaning of fashion can have

significance in terms of human conduct and expressions of civility between individuals.

[···]

Fashions are mechanisms of social regulation not just because they
direct us to follow certain styles of conduct but because they influence
how we think about human conduct and social relations. For example,
with the practice of dining out we are simultaneously being instructed
in a variety of postures, tastes and interests which have relatively little
to do with eating. In the restaurant we observe the activities and tastes
of others, we observe fashions displayed in their physical appearances
as well as in the details of their tastes in comestibles, clothing accessories
and even topics of conversation. In a society where fashions are highly
valued, our daily study of the other and our imitation of them, in certain
activities, is a crucial social mechanism in the maintenance of the status
quo. What we see in him/her are the cues which alert us to what is
current and interesting. It may well be that the formidable attraction of
the restaurant is in its capacity to expose us to the other and to what
is being accorded value in the currents of the day. In the restaurant, we
see ourselves in direct relation to the other. We are with peers, who are
also strangers, to whom we are not introduced but who are inadvertently
providing both standards and information about our own behaviour and
appearance. The other is simultaneously the source of our self-estimate
as well as that which we envy, and so dining out becomes an activity
which introduces us to patterns of behaviour that include what we may
come to regard as personally desirable and interesting.

The fashionability of dining out has meant that the practice has become
more than a means for maintaining the body, it has become a source of
shared cultural beliefs. For example, foodstuffs have frequently acquired
social meanings that refer to properties beyond their nutritional qualities.
In certain times and places, the taste for game has been associated with
wealth and prestige because it was hunted by the landed gentry; oysters
have been regarded as aphrodisiacs; truffles have been seen as embodi-
ments of the mysteries of old Europe. Barthes has described food as 'a
system of communication', 'a body of images', 'an intimate part of the
protocol of social life'.[2] Similarly, the places in which one eats carry
various meanings; a restaurant has distinctions that a café, a tavern and
a picnic do not. The diner sees in both the restaurant and its foodstuffs
some broader social values; for example, a luxuriously appointed restaurant may evoke an aristocratic way of life long associated with the
pleasures of being served by an indentured class. Or an appetite for

nouvelle cuisine may be taken as a reflection of the diners' sophisticated and *au courant* view that food is not a banal and simple ingredient in the maintenance of life but rather a cultural event and form of aesthetic in which its arrangement and colouring should be appreciated as if they were works of art. In these ways, the practice of dining out in a restaurant can also be seen as a purveyor of cultural values and social images; it is where we can learn to act and feel in accord with the desires of the times.

When people start flocking to a small, inner city bar because they have learned that cocktails are in (again), they also come to see that the hours spent over a gaudily coloured beverage are amongst their most pleasurable; when the pasta restaurant becomes the favourite haunt of the cosmopolitan it has much to do with his/her acceptance of the idea that ethnic diversity is attractive. The different meanings and cultural values attached to the various forms of dining out indicate that tastes in foods and preferences in the style of dining out are not independent of other features of the social epoch.

Restaurants have been included in the orbit of fashions. In the modern era, restaurants have become part of the entertainment industries which have been so successful in producing a continuous and growing interest in conspicuous consumption. For the most part, the entertainment industries are a diversionary institution in modern society which manufacture partial interpretations of social reality by widely promoting a variety of illusions and desires. It is not that we are victims of a form of mass manipulation in the sense that we unwittingly take in, directly and without selectivity, the products of the entertainment industries. Indeed, most members of the general public are well aware that the entertainment industries are in the business of marketing large-scale illusions and fantasies to millions of people. However, these industries are not generally regarded as sinister in any way and they are infrequently described in everyday parlance as mechanisms of propaganda. Indeed, they are commonly valued for their creation of employment and their contribution to the economy of the society. Even if it is considered that the entertainment industries may exert an inordinate amount of influence over public knowledge, this is still not thought of as necessarily dangerous. If these industries do in some instances conceal the inequalities within a community by engrossing the majority of us in the pursuit of fantasies, or if they trivialize social reality by presenting simplistic analyses of human behaviour, or if they promote an ideology such as a belief in a meritocracy in a society that has clear class divisions and little social mobility, then it is still difficult to convince us that entertainment industries, including the restaurant trade, are promoting misleading views in order to inhibit the individual's ability to see how society works. It is equally difficult for us to acknowledge that if there are rapacious interests in existence in our society, then they are being deliberately concealed from us. Even with some acceptance of the idea that the entertainment industries may definitely influence public culture, they are persistently seen in panglossian terms as largely benign.

[⋯]

The importance of fashionability is that it makes consensus seem attractive and the alternatives of diversity and doubt seem a source of discomfort. Fashions provide a barrier of protection for the individual against which the unfashionable seems foreign. The sociological significance of this is that a separation between the individual and the group is established and legitimated. The individual comes to see him/herself as a separable entity and not necessarily responsible for, or a part of, the historical circumstances of the society. The assumptions of fashionability establish the appearance and performance of the individual as ciphers of status and social value; thus the fashion habitué who has pared down the reading of character to the outer garments and a choreography of the human body has succeeded in abbreviating human character to a concatenation of signs.

[⋯]

Fashions appeal to those who need the protection of the typical, customary and acceptable but, at the same time, following a fashion allows the individual to pursue activities that would be repugnant if practised alone. Fashions distinguish individuals and integrate them, they elevate the lowly by making them appear more than they are, and they reduce the exalted by making them appear part of the fashionable mainstream. Fashions can also regulate individuals by appearing to offer them choices of self-expression and they can single out the individual and, at the same time, satisfy the individual's desire for absorption into the mass. In following fashions, and the customs and trends in human commerce which they subsequently establish, individuals are relieved from a consideration and interrogation of the ethics of their own social activities. When the individual can affiliate with others who are conducting themselves in a similar manner, then s/he is able to relinquish the responsibility for thought about the meanings of his/her own activities. The presumption is that the majority is right, and so an attraction of being fashionable is that it weakens any suggestion or sign of conflict between individuals, and it disguises the suggestion that social relations may be organized about the unethical imperatives of conspicuous consumption and competitive display. In this way, manners and fashions are instrumental in shaping human interaction and in defining what passes for civility.

Fashion has an architectonic dimension; it can structure the physical world in a material way by defining what is pleasing, say, in the designs of houses, cars, restaurants and works of art, and it can shape the interior world of the individual by establishing thresholds of sentiments that classify what is repugnant and appealing in certain ideas, practices and desires. As such, fashions regulate public conduct as well as shaping private sensibilities, and fashionable pastimes such as dining out in restaurants are essential vehicles in this process.

Notes and references

1 Charles Baudelaire, *The Painter of Modern Life and Other Essays*, ed. and tr. J. Mayne (Phaidon Press, London, 1964), p. 32.
2 Roland Barthes, 'Towards a psychosociology of contemporary food consumption', in *European Diet from Pre-Industrial to Modern Times*, ed. E. Forster and R. Forster (Harper Torchbooks, New York, 1975), pp. 47–59.

29

The Sublime and the Avant-Garde

Jean-François Lyotard

With the advent of the aesthetics of the sublime, the stake of art in the nineteenth and twentieth centuries was to be the witness to the fact that there is indeterminacy. For painting, the paradox that Burke signalled in his observations on the power of words is that such testimony can only be achieved in a determined fashion. Support, frame, line, colour, space, the figure – were to remain, in romantic art, subject to the constraint of representation. But this contradiction of end and means had, as early as Manet and Cézanne, the effect of casting doubt on certain rules that had determined, since the quattrocento, the representation of the figure in space and the organization of colours and values. Reading Cézanne's correspondence, one understands that his *oeuvre* was not that of a talented painter finding his 'style', but that of an artist attempting to respond to the question: what is a painting? His work had at stake to inscribe on the supporting canvas only those 'colour-istic sensations', those 'little sensations' that of themselves, according to Cézanne's hypothesis, constitute the entire pictorial existence of objects, fruit, mountain, face, flower, without consideration of either history or 'subject', or line, or space, or even light. These elementary sensations are hidden in ordinary perception which remains under the hegemony of habitual or classical ways of looking. They are only accessible to the painter, and can therefore only be re-established by him, at the expense of an interior ascesis that rids perceptual and mental fields of prejudices inscribed even in vision itself. If the viewer does not submit to a complementary ascesis, the painting will remain senseless and impenetrable to him. The painter must not hesitate to run the risk of being taken to be a mere dauber. 'One paints for very few people', writes Cézanne. Recognition from the regulatory institutions of painting – Academy, salons, criticism, taste – is of little importance compared to the judgement made by the painter-researcher and his peers on the success obtained by the work of art in relation to what is really at stake: to make seen what makes one see, and not what is visible.

Maurice Merleau-Ponty elaborated on what he rightly called 'Cézanne's doubt' as though what was at stake for the painter was indeed to grasp and render perception at its birth – perception 'before' perception. I would say: colour in its occurrence, the wonder that 'it happens' ('it', something: colour), at least to the eye. There is some credulity on the part of the phenomenologist in this trust he places in the 'originary' value of Cézanne's 'little sensations'. The painter himself, who often complained of their inadequacy, wrote that they were 'abstractions', that 'they did not suffice for covering the canvas'. But why should it be necessary to cover the canvas? Is it forbidden to be abstract?

The doubt which gnaws at the avant-gardes did not stop with Cézanne's 'colouristic sensations' as though they were indubitable, and, for that matter, no more did it stop with the abstractions they heralded. The task of having to bear witness to the indeterminate carries away, one after another, the barriers set up by the writings of theorists and by the manifestos of the painters themselves. A formalist definition of the pictorial object, such as that proposed in 1961 by Clement Greenberg when confronted with American 'post-plastic' abstraction, was soon overturned by the current of Minimalism. Do we have to have stretchers so that the canvas is taut? No. What about colours? Malevitch's black square on white had already answered this question in 1915. Is an object necessary? Body art and happenings went about proving that it is not. A space, at least, a space in which to display, as Duchamp's 'fountain' still suggested? Daniel Buren's work testifies to the fact that even this is subject to doubt.

Whether or not they belong to the current that art history calls Minimalism or *arte povera*, the investigations of the avant-gardes question one by one the constituents one might have thought 'elementary' or at the 'origin' of the art of painting. They operate *ex minimis*. One would have to confront the demand for rigour that animates them with the principle sketched out by Adorno at the end of *Negative Dialectics*, and that controls the writing of his *Aesthetic Theory*: the thought that 'accompanies metaphysics in its fall', he said, can only proceed in terms of 'micrologies'.

Micrology is not just metaphysics in crumbs, any more than Newman's painting is Delacroix in scraps. Micrology inscribes the occurrence of a thought as the unthought that remains to be thought in the decline of 'great' philosophical thought. The avant-gardist attempt inscribes the occurrence of a sensory now as what cannot be presented and which remains to be presented in the decline of great representational painting. Like micrology, the avant-garde is not concerned with what happens to the 'subject', but with: 'Does it happen?', with privation. This is the sense in which it still belongs to the aesthetics of the sublime.

In asking questions of the *It happens* that the work of art is, avant-garde art abandons the role of identification that the work previously played in relation to the community of addressees. Even when conceived, as it was by Kant, as a *de jure* horizon or presumption rather than a *de facto* reality, a *sensus communis* (which, moreover, Kant refers to only when writing about beauty, not the sublime) does not manage to achieve stability when it comes to interrogative works of art. It barely coalesces, too late, when these works, deposited in museums, are considered part of the community heritage and are made available for its culture and pleasure. And even here, they must be objects, or they must tolerate objectification, for example through photography.

In this situation of isolation and misunderstanding, avant-garde art is vulnerable and subject to repression. It seems only to aggravate the identity crisis that communities went through during the long 'depression' that lasted from the 1930s until the end of 'reconstruction' in the mid-1950s. It is impossible here even to suggest how the Party-states born of fear faced with the 'Who are we?', and the anxiety of the void, tried to convert this fear or anxiety into hatred of the avant-gardes. Hildegarde Brenner's study of artistic policy under Nazism, or the films of Hans-Jürgen Syberberg, do not merely analyse these repressive manoeuvres. They also explain how neo-romantic, neo-classical and symbolic forms imposed by the cultural commissars and collaborationist artists – painters and musicians especially – had to block the negative dialectic of the *Is it happening?* by translating and betraying the question as a waiting for some fabulous subject or identity: 'Is the pure people coming?', 'Is the Führer coming?', 'Is Siegfried coming?' The aesthetics of the sublime, thus neutralized and converted into a politics of myth, was able to come and build its architectures of human 'formations' on the Zeppelin Feld in Nürnberg.

Thanks to the 'crisis of overcapitalization' that most of today's so-called highly developed societies are going through, another attack on the avant-gardes is coming to light. The threat exerted against the avant-garde search for the artwork event, against attempts to welcome the *now*, no longer requires Party-states to be effective. It proceeds 'directly' out of market economics. The correlation between this and the aesthetics of the sublime is ambiguous, even perverse. The latter, no doubt, has been and continues to be a reaction against the matter-of-fact positivism and the calculated realism that governs the former, as writers on art such as Stendhal, Baudelaire, Mallarmé, Apollinaire and Breton all emphasize.

Yet there is a kind of collusion between capital and the avant-garde. The force of scepticism and even of destruction that capitalism has brought into play, and that Marx never ceased analysing and identifying, in some way encourages among artists a mistrust of established rules and a willingness to experiment with means of expression, with styles, with ever-new materials. There is something of the sublime in capitalist economy. It is not academic, it is not physiocratic, it admits of no nature. It is, in a sense, an economy regulated by an Idea – infinite wealth or power. It does not manage to present any example from reality to verify this Idea. In making science subordinate to itself through technologies, especially those of language, it only succeeds, on the contrary, in making reality increasingly ungraspable, subject to doubt, unsteady.

The experience of the human subject – individual and collective – and the aura that surrounds this experience, are being dissolved into the calculation of profitability, the satisfaction of needs, self-affirmation through success. Even the virtually theological depth of the worker's condition, and of work, that marked the socialist and union movements for over a century, is becoming devalorized, as work becomes a control and manipulation of information. These observations are banal, but what merits attention is the disappearance of the temporal continuum through which the experience of generations used to be transmitted. The availability of information is becoming the only criterion of social importance. Now information is by definition a short-lived element. As soon as it is transmitted and shared, it ceases to be information, it becomes an environmental given, and 'all is said', we 'know'. It is put into the machine memory. The length of time it occupies is, so to speak, instantaneous. Between two pieces of information, 'nothing happens', by definition. A confusion thereby becomes possible, between what is of interest to information and the director, and what is the question of the avant-gardes, between what happens – the new – and the *Is it happening?*, the *now*.

It is understandable that the art-market, subject like all markets to the rule of the new, can exert a kind of seduction on artists. This attraction is not due to corruption alone. It exerts itself thanks to a confusion between innovation and the *Ereignis*, a confusion maintained by the temporality specific to contemporary capitalism. 'Strong' information, if one can call it that, exists in inverse proportion to the meaning that can be attributed to it in the code available to its receiver. It is like 'noise'. It is easy for the public and for artists, advised by intermediaries – the diffusers of cultural merchandise – to draw from this observation the principle that a work of art is avant-garde in direct proportion to the extent that it is stripped of meaning. Is it not then like an event?

It is still necessary that its absurdity does not discourage buyers, just as the innovation introduced into a commodity must allow itself to be approached, appreciated and purchased by the consumers. The secret of an artistic success, like that of a commercial success, resides in the balance between what is surprising and what is 'well known', between information and code. This is how innovation in art operates: one re-uses formulae confirmed by previous success, one throws them off-balance by combining them with other, in principle incompatible, formulae, by amalgamations, quotations, ornamentations, pastiche. One can go as far as kitsch or the grotesque. One flatters the 'taste' of a public that can have no taste, and the eclecticism of a sensibility enfeebled by the multiplication of available forms and objects. In this way one thinks that one is expressing the spirit of the times, whereas one is merely reflecting the spirit of the market. Sublimity is no longer in art, but in speculation on art.

The enigma of the *Is it happening?* is not dissolved for all this, nor is the task of painting, that there is something which is not determinable, the *There is* (*Il y a*) itself, out of date. The occurrence, the *Ereignis*, has nothing to do with the *petit frisson*, the cheap thrill, the profitable pathos, that accompanies an innovation. Hidden in the cynicism of innovation is certainly the despair that nothing further will happen. But innovating means to behave as though lots of things happened, and to make them happen. Through innovation, the will affirms its hegemony over time. It thus conforms to the metaphysics of capital, which is a technology of time. The innovation 'works'. The question mark of the *Is it happening?* stops. With the occurrence, the will is defeated. The avant-gardist task remains that of undoing the presumption of the mind with respect to time. The sublime feeling is the name of this privation.

30

The Exorcist and *The Omen*, or Modern and Postmodern Limits to Knowledge

Zygmunt Bauman

Pretences of knowledge can be doubted in two ways. One can point out that there are events for which the kind of knowledge there is (knowledge that has received endorsement from the sites that men of knowledge admit to be sound and credible) does not have a convincing, agreed narrative; events that cannot be made into a story that men of knowledge would recognize as their own. Or one can say that the narrative that knowledge does offer is not the only story that may be told of the events; not even the best story, or at least not the only one able to claim the right to be considered 'better tested'. The first kind of doubt is modern; the second is postmodern. To say this is not to speak of chronological succession. Both modes of doubt have been around as long as science itself. Their co-presence was one of the constitutive features of that modern culture which prodded modernity on its road to postmodernity.

The two doubts have been given widely popular (populist?) literary form in the two works of fantasy – both huge box-office successes in their novelistic as well as their cinematic renditions. They may well serve us as parables for the two doubts that silently yet unflaggingly sapped, and in the end toppled, modern self-confidence.

Father Damien Karras of William Peter Blatty's novel *The Exorcist* turned exorcist only *after* all his and his professional colleagues' psychiatric routines, based on the most formidable, impeccably scholarly and up-to-date therapeutic skills and scientific knowledge, came to nought. Karras was, one may say, a psychiatrist's psychiatrist. Bearer of the most enviable scientific credentials, an alumnus of the most prestigious professional schools, a universally respected practitioner with a long record of spectacular therapeutic successes, a theorist armed with a truly encyclopaedic knowledge of the best scientific psychiatry could offer, a recipient of the most prestigious distinctions the profession could bestow – he was the scientific authority incarnate. Calling him to act on Regan's case was the ultimate resort and last hope of psychiatric science and practice: all his illustrious co-professionals, one by one and all together, tried, did their best and failed; the most up-to-date therapeutic technology proved insufficient. Karras's own actions – much as his accounts of the actions – were kept strictly within the frame of the collectively guarded scientific idiom; they were carefully calculated to restate, reaffirm and reinforce everything the profession believed and wanted its public to believe. Karras was not a witch-doctor or natural healer, that agent of dark and barbaric forces resisting the modern science set to annihilate them; like his learned colleagues who turned to him for help, Karras was a bearer of modern intellect sworn to extinguish the last vestige of superstition.

Up to the last moment – with the ultimate mystery staring in his face – Karras doggedly asserts scientific reason's uncontested right to narrate the evidence, to compose the sole acceptable version of the story – and rebuffs the layperson's temptation to succumb to interpretations that science refused to tolerate. When hapless Regan's mother turns to Karras in utter despair (her 'freckled, clasped fingers twitched in her lap') – 'I just don't know. . . . What do *you* think, Father?' – Karras's answer is professionalism itself: 'Compulsive behaviour produced by guilt, perhaps, put together with split personality.'

> 'Father, I have *had* all that garbage! Now how can you say that after all you've just seen!'
>
> 'If you've seen as many patients in psychiatric wards as I have, you can say it very easily,' he assured her. . . .
>
> 'Then explain all those rappings and things.'. . .
>
> 'Psychokinesis.'
>
> 'What?' . . .
>
> 'It's not that uncommon, and usually happens around an emotionally disturbed adolescent. Apparently, extreme inner tension of the mind can sometimes trigger some unknown energy that seems to move objects around at a distance. There's nothing supernatural about it. Like Regan's abnormal strength. Again, in pathology it's common. Call it mind over matter, if you will.'

'I call it weird.'. . .
'The best explanation for any phenomenon,' Karras overrode her, 'is always the simplest one available that accommodates all the facts.'. . .

And so on. Karras would not concede an inch: phenomena are explicable, explanations are available, an energy's being unknown (as yet, of course) is not for that reason inexplicable. One that spent much time in wards where things are seen that a layperson would never set her eyes on, knows that. (You should trust the expert; he *saw* things you would never see.) And – as the final argument, the ultimate reassurance – this is *common* (statistically frequent; it happens to others). And it has its name: a respectable scientific name, like 'emotionally disturbed adolescent' or 'psychokinesis'.

The layperson, particularly one who like Regan's mother has been repeatedly disappointed by learned advice and driven into despair by its practical impotence, may refuse to draw comfort from what now seem empty promises of reason. Indeed, Regan's mother 'was staring in unblinking incredulity. "Father, that's so far out of sight that I think it's almost easier to believe in the *devil*!". . . . For long, troubled seconds, the priest was still. Then he answered softly, "Well, there's little in this world that I know for a fact." ' Regan's mother suggests another doctrine, another orthodoxy, another explanatory key; Karras responds with *humility*. Prudent modesty, sagacious self-limitation of the scientist, scepticism in the face of the-yet-unknown is his last line of defence against the only real danger: an alternative to science, a legitimate knowledge that does not draw its legitimation from scientific authority. When he finally decides to step into the Unknown (a step made perhaps easier by the fact that, unlike his fellow scientists, but like his patient Regan, he has himself a split personality – he is, after all, a devoted priest much as he is a learned psychiatrist), Karras makes sure that the prerogatives of science are not infringed: 'If I go to the Chancery Office, or wherever it is I have to go, to get their permission to perform an exorcism, the first thing I'd have to have is a pretty substantial indication that your daughter's condition isn't a purely psychiatric problem.'

David Seltzer's *The Omen* conveys a different message altogether. It speaks out the unspeakable: perhaps science's prerogatives are themselves a sham – nothing but a convenient hideout for the *devil*? Is 'the common', by the very fact of being common, reassuringly explicable? Are the explanations that science together with scientifically censored and endorsed common sense have to offer, really the 'simplest ones available'? Does not the lauded 'simplicity' stand merely for the satisfaction of scientific authority? Do not things, uncommon and common alike, lend themselves to other, alternative, heteronomous descriptions? And if they do, how to choose between the stories? And how are the choices made in practice by those who make them for us?

The Omen contains one series of events, but two narratives. One is the common and the ordinary, and therefore raising no brow: the kind of story told over and over again by the experts and their journalist popularizers, and thus becoming indistinguishable from the world it tells about. The other is a kind of story which the luckless hero of the book, the brilliant and erudite intellectual Thorn, could only suppose – *fear* – to be 'his imagination', and (as any other well-informed and civilized person certainly would) see as a good reason 'to see a psychiatrist'. One is the well-known story, repeated *ad nauseam* by the chorus of politicians, journalists and social scientists, of human and state interests, political platforms, not-wholly-eradicated irrational sentiments. The other?

> The coven was made up mostly of working class people, but a few were professional, highly placed men. On the outside they all led respectable lives – this their most valuable weapon against those who worshipped God. It was their mission to create fear and turmoil, to turn men against each other until the time of the Unholy One had come; a small group called Task Forces would forage out to create chaos wherever possible. The coven in Rome took credit for much of the turmoil in Ireland, using random sabotage to polarize Catholic from Protestant and fan the fires of religious war. . . .
>
> [In 1968] Tassone was dispatched by Spiletto to South-East Asia, there organizing a small band of mercenaries in Communist-held Cambodia to cross into and disrupt the cease-fire in South Vietnam. The North blamed it on the South, the South on the North, and within days of Tassone's entrance, the hard-won peace of this land was shattered. . . .
>
> Knowing of his knowledge of the country, Spiletto sent Tassone to assist the revolution that eventually brought Idi Amin, the insane African Despot, to power. . . .

And so on. Of the second story, 'only *they* knew'. 'No one else had ever had a clue.' Once told, their story would make as much sense – no more and no less – of terrorism, senseless killings, hostilities without a cause, civil wars, mass murders, crazy despots, as all the stories that officially guaranteed their rationality. The problem, however, was that this other, apocryphal story has been never told; not in public, that is. Those who saw things told by this story as they happened, all perished; the only surviving witness, Thorn himself, was – naturally – confined to a lunatic asylum. The world found it easier (and more reassuring) to

assume that Thorn's unshared beliefs were symptoms of mental distur-
bance than to accept the possibility that the world's own truth might
have been just one of the many, that to every interpretation, however
massively hailed, there might be an alternative. Murder, imprisonment,
the verdict of insanity were the worldly truths' last lines of defence.
Perhaps the only lines of *effective* defence.

Most of us would easily agree that the explanations Seltzer puts in
the mind and on the lips of Thorn are ridiculous or outrageously insane.
All the more striking is the point he tries to hammer home – that
without recourse to force and suppression, the dominant truth cannot
protect itself by the weapons of logic, canons of induction, rules of fact-
collecting and all the other devices that, as it claims, suffice to guarantee
its superior quality and hence its privileged standing. (Note that it is
only Thorn's *story* that sounds unquestionably insane; the supposition
that we would not be so sure of its insanity were not the supporting
evidence suppressed, does not.) For every sequence of events, there
is more than one interpretation that would pass muster. The choice,
ultimately, is a political matter. . . .

And so there are two doubts. The first kind of doubt does not undermine the authority of science. On the contrary, transforming the ideal
of truth into the 'imaginary target' of knowledge-producing pursuits,
into the horizon of the territory now being travelled through (a horizon
always receding and forever elusive, and hence always beyond the reach
of practical test) – this doubt effectively *protects* the authority of science
from discreditation. In fact, it renders knowledge as such (at the cost of
virtually each and any of its specimens) immune to questioning. It sees
to it that no hostages are ever given to fate, and that in the game of
knowledge the worthiness of the game is never at stake. It guarantees
the immortality of knowledge as a truth-gaining enterprise by rendering
it independent of the vicissitudes of each specific truth it spawns. It
allows the enterprise to go on unabated while being demonstratively
abortive: it transforms its very abortiveness into the mainspring – the
motive and the legitimation – of its continuing vigour.

Ostensibly, this doubt puts in question the finality of any successive
incarnation of the truth ideal. More surreptitiously, yet more importantly,
it belittles the significance of any specific case of ignorance. It tempor-
alizes ignorance – and so it disarms the uncertainty and ambiguity that
ignorance brings in its wake. Instead of paralysing action, ignorance
prompts more effort and boosts the zeal and determination of actors.
Ignorance is a not yet conquered territory; its very presence is a challenge, and the clinching argument of any pep talk summoning support
for the next attack in the interminable, yet always confident of the

ultimate victory, offensive of reason. It allows science to declare credibly its determination to work itself out of a job, while constantly staving off the moment when it could be asked to act on its promise: there is always a job to be done, and fighting ignorance is such a job. The first kind of doubt, therefore, harnesses ignorance to the chariot of science. In advance, ignorance is defined as another feather in science's cap. Its resistance is significant solely for the fact that it is about to be broken. Its danger is somewhat less terrifying as it is bound to be chased away – soon. The uncertainty and ambivalence ignorance nurtures is but an occasion to another display of the potency of reason, and so it breeds, ultimately, reassurance.

The second kind of doubt is anything but innocuous. It hits where it hurts most: it undermines the trust that whatever is being said by science at a given time is the best one can say at that time. It questions the holy of holies – the creed of the superiority of scientific knowledge over any other knowledge. By the same token, it challenges science's right to validate and invalidate, legitimize and delegitimize – to draw the line between knowledge and ignorance, transparency and obscurity, logic and incongruity. Obliquely, it makes thinkable the most heretical of heresies: that instead of being a gallant knight bent on cutting off, one by one, the many heads of the dragon of superstition, science is one story among many, invoking one frail pre-judgement among many.

The second kind of doubt never for a single moment ceased to haunt modern mentality. From the start it was firmly entrenched in the inner recesses of modernity; fear of the 'unfoundedness' of certainty was, arguably, the most formidable among modernity's many inner demons. Many times over it put the modern project on the defensive. Even when, for a time, forced into the limbo of the subconscious, it went on poisoning the joy of victorious offensives. Unlike the first kind of doubt, found resonant and useful and therefore rapturously displayed in public, the second kind was treated with unqualified and unremitting hostility: it was marked for total and irrevocable destruction. It stood for everything the transparent and harmonious world that science was to build had to be purified of: unreason, madness, obscurity, undecidability.

Like all doubts, this one was creative as well: it strained human imaginative power to the utmost, giving birth to contraptions so varied as, for instance, Descartes's *cogito,* Husserl's *transcendental reduction,* Popper's principle of *refutation,* Weber's *rational constructs,* or the ever more ingenious research methods that – like the Swiftian wheel at the Academy of Lagado – were hoped to allow any able-bodied man to thresh out the healthy grain of truth from the chaff of error. From Descartes's *malin génie* and up to Husserl's heroic act of *epoché,* the war against uncertainty and ambiguity of evidence went on unabated – the most vivid testimony, if one was needed, to the ubiquitous and perseverant presence of the doubt.

It was the presence of the second kind of doubt – and its presence *as a doubt*, as a belief able to weaken the resolve needed for the success of the project – that was the distinctive mark of modern mentality. It is the disappearance of that doubt *as a doubt* (that is, the retention of the belief, yet the defusion of its past corrosive impact) that marks most vividly the passage of modernity into its postmodern stage. Modernity reaches that new stage (so sharply distinct that one is ever so often tempted to allocate it to an entirely separate era, to describe it in a typically modern style as a negation, pure and simple, of modernity) when it is able to face up to the fact that science, for all one knows and can know, is one story among many. 'To face up' means to accept that certainty is not to be, and yet persevere in the pursuit of knowledge born of the determination to smother and weed out contingency.

It was the treatment of the first kind of doubt as a temporary nuisance, as an irritant with a limited life-expectancy, sooner or later to be dead and buried, that was another distinctive mark of modern mentality. It was an axiom of that mentality that if there were one thousand potential items of knowledge as yet undisclosed, discovering one of them would leave but nine hundred and ninety-nine in the pool., The abandoning of that axiom marks the passage of modernity into its postmodern stage. Modernity reaches that new stage when it is able to face up to the fact that the growth of knowledge expands the field of ignorance, that with each step towards the horizon new unknown lands appear, and that, to put it most generally, acquisition of knowledge cannot express itself in any other form but awareness of more ignorance. 'To face up' to this fact means to know that the journey has no clear destination – and yet persevere in the travel.

There is one more mark of the passage of modernity to its postmodern stage: the two previously separate doubts losing their distinctiveness, becoming semantically indistinguishable, blending into one. The two limits of knowledge appear to be artefacts of modern diffractive vision; their alleged separateness, a projection of the now abandoned design. In place of two limits and two doubts, there is an unworried awareness that there are many stories that need to be told over and over again, each time losing something and adding something to the past versions. There is also a new determination: to guard the conditions in which all stories can be told, and retold, and again told differently. It is in their plurality, and not in the 'survival of the fittest' (that is, the extinction of the less fit), that the hope now resides. Richard Rorty gave this new

– postmodern – project an epigrammatic precision: 'if we take care of political freedom, truth and goodness will take care of themselves'.[1] All too often taking care of truth and goodness resulted in the loss of political freedom. Not much truth and goodness has been gained either.

Unlike science and political ideology, freedom promises no certainty and no guarantee of anything. It causes therefore a lot of mental pain. In practice, it means constant exposure to ambivalence: that is, to a situation with no decidable solution, with no foolproof choice, no unreflective knowledge of 'how to go on'. As Hans Magnus Enzensberger recently remarked, 'you can't have a nice democracy. . . . Democracy is something which can get very much on your nerves – you are constantly battered by the most obnoxious things. It is like Freudian analysis. All the dirt comes out in democracy.'[2] The real problem of the postmodern stage is not to allow things to 'get on one's nerves' while hoping that they will not get on one's back. Lacking modernity's iron fist, postmodernity needs nerves of steel.

Notes and references

1   R. Rorty, *Contingency, Irony and Solidarity* (Cambridge University Press, Cambridge, 1989), p. 80.
2   Hans Magnus Enzensberger, 'Back in the USSR', *New Statesman and Society*, 10 November 1989, p. 29.

Index